Applied Language Learning: New Tools and Applications

Applied Language Learning: New Tools and Applications

Contributors

Nagwa A. Soliman et al.

www.aurisreference.com

Applied Language Learning: New Tools and Applications

Contributors: Nagwa A. Soliman et al.

Published by Auris Reference Limited
www.aurisreference.com

United Kingdom

Copyright 2016

The information in this book has been obtained from highly regarded resources. The copyrights for individual articles remain with the authors, as indicated. All chapters are distributed under the terms of the Creative Commons Attribution License, which permit unrestricted use, distribution, and reproduction in any medium, provided the original author and source are credited.

Notice

Contributors, whose names have been given on the book cover, are not associated with the Publisher. The editors and the Publisher have attempted to trace the copyright holders of all material reproduced in this publication and apologise to copyright holders if permission has not been obtained. If any copyright holder has not been acknowledged, please write to us so we may rectify.

Reasonable efforts have been made to publish reliable data. The views articulated in the chapters are those of the individual contributors, and not necessarily those of the editors or the Publisher. Editors and/or the Publisher are not responsible for the accuracy of the information in the published chapters or consequences from their use. The Publisher accepts no responsibility for any damage or grievance to individual(s) or property arising out of the use of any material(s), instruction(s), methods or thoughts in the book.

Applied Language Learning: New Tools and Applications

ISBN: 978-1-78154-723-6

British Library Cataloguing in Publication Data
A CIP record for this book is available from the British Library

Printed in the United Kingdom

Contents

List of Abbreviations .... *vii*
List of Contributors .... *ix*
Preface .... *xi*

Chapter 1   **Using E-Learning to Develop EFL Students' Language Skills and Activate Their Independent Learning** 1
Nagwa A. Soliman

Chapter 2   **Addressing Foreign Language Learning Anxiety with Facebook** 11
Serge Gabarre, Cécile Gabarre, Rosseni Din, Parilah Shah, Aidah Abdul Karim

Chapter 3   **A Review of Models in Experimental Studies of Implicit Language Learning** 29
Si Liu, Huangmei Liu

Chapter 4   **Why Asynchronous Computer-Mediated Communication (ACMC) Is a Powerful Tool for Language Learning** 47
Mark Brooke

Chapter 5   **Ubiquitous Learning Analytics in the Real-World Language Learning** 61
Kousuke Mouri and Hiroaki Ogata

Chapter 6   **Online E-Learning Application for Practicing Foreign Language Skills with Native Speakers** 89
Ilya V. Osipov, Alex A. Volinsky, Evgeny Nikulchev and Anna Y. Prasikova

Chapter 7   **The Effects of an Online Student Question-Generation Strategy on Elementary School Student English Learning** 99
Fu-Yun Yu, Yu-Ling Chang and Hui-Ling Wu

Chapter 8   **Learning 2.0: Collaborative Technologies Reshaping Learning Pathways** 123
Popovici Veronica

Chapter 9	**Collaborative Language Learning in Teletandem: A Resource for Pre-Service Teacher Education** **145**	

Ana Cristina Biondo Salomão

Chapter 10	**English Language and Literacy Learning: Research to Practice** **169**	
Chapter 11	**Designing For Language Learning: Agency and Languaging in Hybrid Environments** **197**	

Françoise Blin and Juha Jalkanen

Chapter 12	**Content Domain and Language Competence in Computer-Mediated Conversation For Learning** **225**	

Paola Leone

Chapter 13	**Interlanguage Speech Recognition By Computer: Implications For Sla and Computational Machines** **253**	

Larry Selinker and Rita Mascia

Citations **285**

Index **287**

List of Abbreviations

AGL	Artificial grammar learning
CEFR	Common European Framework of Reference for Languages
CHAT	Cultural historical activity theory
CMC	Computer-mediated communication
CS	Communication strategies
CSUL	Computer Supported Ubiquitous Learning
DBR	Design-based research
EFL	English Foreign language
ELLP	English language learning progressions
ELLs	English language learners
ESL	English as a second language
FAQ	Frequently asked questions
GIS	Geographic information system
IEPs	Intensive English programs
LCTLs	Less commonly taught languages
LULs	Lesser-used languages
MALL	Mobile assisted language learning
MSLQ	Motivated Strategies for Learning Questionnaire
OUNL	Open university of the netherlands
PDAs	Personal Digital Assistants
PLE	Personal learning environments
RSD	Repetitive strain disorder
SL	Sequence learning
SLA	Second language acquisition
SNS	Social networking sites
SRC	Speech recognition by computer
TL	Target language
ULA	Ubiquitous Learning Analytics
ULG	Ubiquitous Learning Graph
ULL	Ubiquitous Learning Log
VLE	Virtual Learning Environment
ZPD	Zone of proximal development

List of Contributors

Nagwa A. Soliman
English Department, the British University in Egypt, Cairo, Egypt

Serge Gabarre
Department of Foreign Languages, Universiti Putra Malaysia, Serdang, Malaysia
Faculty of Education, Universiti Kebangsaan Malaysia, Bangi, Malaysia

Cécile Gabarre
Department of Foreign Languages, Universiti Putra Malaysia, Serdang, Malaysia
Faculty of Education, Universiti Kebangsaan Malaysia, Bangi, Malaysia

Rosseni Din
Faculty of Education, Universiti Kebangsaan Malaysia, Bangi, Malaysia

Parilah Shah
Faculty of Education, Universiti Kebangsaan Malaysia, Bangi, Malaysia

Aidah Abdul Karim
Faculty of Education, Universiti Kebangsaan Malaysia, Bangi, Malaysia

Si Liu
School of Foreign Languages and Literatures, Lanzhou University, Lanzhou, China

Huangmei Liu
School of Foreign Languages and Literatures, Lanzhou University, Lanzhou, China

Mark Brooke
Department of Linguistics and Modern Languages, Hong Kong Institute of Education, Hong Kong, China

Kousuke Mouri
Faculty of Arts and Science and the Graduate School of Information Science and Electrical Engineering, University of Kyushu, Fukuoka, Japan

Hiroaki Ogata
Faculty of Arts and Science and the Graduate School of Information Science and Electrical Engineering, University of Kyushu, Fukuoka, Japan

Ilya V. Osipov
Department of Mechanical Engineering, University of South Florida

Alex A. Volinsky
Department of Mechanical Engineering, University of South Florida

Evgeny Nikulchev
Department of Mechanical Engineering, University of South Florida

Anna Y. Prasikova
Department of Mechanical Engineering, University of South Florida

Fu-Yun Yu
Institute of Education, National Cheng Kung University

Yu-Ling Chang
Institute of Education, National Cheng Kung University

Hui-Ling Wu
Institute of Education, National Cheng Kung University

Preface

Sometimes called applied linguistics, the field of Applied Language Learning is devoted to the study of particular domains of language learning and use, such as foreign language learning and teaching, bi- and multilingualism, translation and interpretation, communication in professional contexts, or intercultural communication. Applied Language Learning New Tools and Applications is to provide a forum for the exchange of ideas and information on instructional methods and techniques. First chapter presents the advantages of the E-learning Moodle and its role in enhancing "English Foreign language" (EFL) students' language skills and independent learning. Second chapter addresses foreign language learning anxiety with Facebook. Third chapter analyzes experimental research on implicit learning using linguistic stimuli, and proposes five key procedures of a framework for empirical studies of implicit learning. Fourth chapter focuses on the experimental models on implicit learning. Fifth chapter proposes an innovative visualization system that integrates network visualization technologies with Time-Map based on Ubiquitous Learning Analytics (ULA). Sixth chapter describes an online e-learning web-based application for practicing foreign language skills with native speakers. Educational materials are a part of the application, along with the live audio–video feed between the participants. Seventh chapter examines the effects of student question-generation (SQG) and traditional drill-and-practice strategies on English performance. Eighth chapter focuses on the influence of such tools in the educational field as an emerging worldwide trend, endeavouring an objective depiction of pros and cons when considering the integration of social media within current conservative teaching and learning patterns. Ninth chapter presents some of the results of a qualitative research project about the influences of the pedagogic strategies used by a mediator (graduate student in applied linguistics) in the supervision process of a Teletandem partner on her pedagogical practice. Tenth chapter emphasizes on English language and literacy learning. Eleventh chapter focuses on designing for language learning. Eleventh chapter presents three educational design models and approaches, namely learning design, designed based research and activity theoretical designs, which are being used to assist course designers and teachers with the design of technology - rich learning environments and activities. Twelfth chapter addresses the issue of interactional dominance in Teletandem conversations, in which two speakers communicate via video calls and chat and alternatively use their L2, the latter being the native language of the interlocutor. In last chapter, we explore the potential of one new class of technology in facilitating second language acquisition research: speech recognition by computer.

Chapter 1

USING E-LEARNING TO DEVELOP EFL STUDENTS' LANGUAGE SKILLS AND ACTIVATE THEIR INDEPENDENT LEARNING

Nagwa A. Soliman

English Department, The British University in Egypt, Cairo, Egypt

ABSTRACT

The report presents the advantages of the E-learning Moodle and its role in enhancing "English Foreign language" (EFL) students' language skills and independent learning. An already running and established virtual learning environment, namely the E-learning Moodle software, is being used successfully in the British University in Egypt. The different activities and resources that are provided by E-learning have been described with an analysis of how they can be used to develop EFL students' language proficiency and independent learning.

INTRODUCTION

Increasing EFL students' language skills and independent learning are issues of paramount concern because the contact hours in traditional face to face classes are not enough to help students develop their language skills. The E-Learning Moodle is an interactive tool that could be used to address this issue, as it could activate and increase EFL students' language skills as they are exposed to the language outside the classroom and work independently on improving their language skills. The E-Learning Moodle is used in the British University of Egypt and it is used in teaching English for Academic Purposes. This paper will show how to use the E-Learning Moodle to improve students' language skills and activate their independent learning. It will start with the definition of E-Learning and its different types, and then it will discuss advantages and disadvantages of E-Learning, and next it will give a recommendation and finally, draw a conclusion.

DEFINITION OF E-LEARNING

E-Learning was defined by many researchers. Waterhouse (2003) defined it as a medium of computer technology that could be utilized to develop the application of learning and teaching. Moreover, The European Commission (2001) defines e-learning as "the use of new multimedia technologies and the internet to improve the quality of learning by facilitating access to resources and services as well as remote exchanges and collaboration". Using a narrower concept, Rosenberg (2001) stated that e-learning permits data saving, sharing and updating while Horton (2006)believes that e-learning allows the building up of "learning experiences of information and computer technology". It is important to note that all definitions agree to the fact that e-learning involves using computer technology to facilitate and enhance learning. E-Learning in this paper refers to the E-Learning Moodle that is used by institutions to enhance teaching and learning and to motivate students' independent learning.

TYPES OF E-LEARNING

The literature acknowledges five types of e-learning. The five categories are e-learning that is learner-led, instructor-led, embedded, facilitated, and telementored (Horton & Horton, 2003; Ilie & Pavel, 2006; Kokkosis, Charitopoulos, Prekas, & Athanasopoulou, 2006; Gulbahar, 2009). While Learner-led e-learning provides course material to students (Horton, 2006 as cited in Esgi, 2013), facilitated e-learning allows student discussion via Forums and Chats that are related to an assignment (Ilie & Pavel, 2006). As for embedded e-learning, it is when teachers embed videos and web pages to enhance students' learning. The latter is different from instructorled e-learning which consists of instructors' presentations via real-time webcast technology which could include audio and video conferences, speaking, screen sharing and whiteboard applications. Students' direct participation here is via audio, video or instant messages (Ruiz J.G.; Mintzer M.J.; Leipzig 2006 as cited in Esgi, 2013). Last but not least is the telementored e-learning which involves a combination of distance learning and the use of technology. For example, students are given printed material, and then instructors provide them with extra guidance and information about this material via video conferences, instant messages and internet phones (Gulbahar, 2009). E-Learning in this paper refers to the E-Learning Moodle. The word MOODLE "was originally an acronym for Modular Object-Oriented Dynamic Learning Environment" (Nedeva & Dimova, 2010). It includes a mixture of learner-led, facilitated and embedded types of E-Learning as will be explained below in the components of the E-learning Moodle.

THE COMPONENTS OF THE E-LEARNING MOODLE AND THEIR EFFECT ON LANGUAGE PROFICIENCY AND INDEPENDENT LEARNING

The E-learning Moodle has two main components, namely activities and resources. The activities include assignment, chat, choice, Database, External Tool, Forum, Glossary, Hotpot, lesson, Quiz, SCORM Package, Survey, Wiki, and Workshop. The following is a brief explanation of each activity and resource component according to the British University of Egypt's (BUE) E-Learning Moodle:

E-Learning Activities

The following E-learning activities could be used to enhance students' language proficiency and independent learning as will be explained at the end of each activity.

Chat: The chat activity module enables participants to have text-based, real-time synchronous discussions. These discussions develop students' fluency and are a springboard for exchanging ideas and experiences. Thus, students' independent learning develops as they are engaged in acquiring information from others without the help or intrusion of instructors.

Choice: The choice activity module enables a teacher to ask a single question and offer a selection of possible responses. It is useful when teachers want to stimulate students' thinking via a poll or would like to test their understanding. This again allows them to use the language and to be exposed to their peers' views through votes. Independent learning here is acquired through students' accessing these polls and being able to analyse their results outside class whenever it is convenient and at their own pace.

Database: The database activity module enables participants to create, maintain and search a collection of entries (i.e. records). The structure of the entries is defined by the teacher as a number of fields. Field types include checkbox, radio buttons, dropdown menu, text area, URL, picture and uploaded file. Students could gain information via different means that could tailor for different learning styles. By reading text their vocabulary and grammar improves and while listening to audio material their pronunciation develops. The database material could be accessed at any time according to the students' preferences which encourages independent learning.

External Tool: The external tool activity module enables students to interact with learning resources and activities on other web sites. For example, an external tool could provide access to a new activity type or learning materials from a publisher. This interaction has a positive effect on students' language skills as it makes them read the available resources independently.

Forum: The forum activity module enables participants to have asynchronous discussions i.e. discussions that take place over an extended period of time. The Forum effect is similar to the Chat in its allowing students to share and exchange their ideas and experiences independently, with or without their instructor's participation. Moreover, E-learning Forums and Chats develop students' personal identity (Bing Wu, 2012) as they become familiar with their own identity and the personality of others.

Glossary: The glossary activity module enables participants to create and maintain a list of definitions, like a dictionary, or to collect and organise resources or information. Students can compile new vocabulary which could be shared with others; this could eventually lead to building up the students' vocabulary. They could brainstorm ideas for a project or class essay and become exposed to their classmates' ideas which stimulate interest in the topic that is discussed. This glossary could encourage students to work independently on enlarging it with all the new vocabulary and definitions that they learn throughout and after their university stage.

Hotpot: The HotPot activity allows teachers to distribute interactive learning materials to their students via Moodle and view reports on the students' responses and results. The e e-learning exercise may be a static web page or an interactive web page which offers students text, audio and visual prompts and records their responses. This motivates independent learning as students get to attempt the exercises and get instant feedback. The prompts push them to use the language as they read, watch and listen. Teachers could ask students to write after going through the text, audio and visual prompts. Thus they practise the four language skills which improve their proficiency and simultaneously, motivates their independent learning.

Lesson: The lesson activity enables a teacher to deliver content and/or practice activities in interesting and flexible ways, such as, multiple choice, matching and short answer questions. The activity could be done by students independently and it will test their understanding of the content. Depending on the students' choice of answer and how the teacher develops the lesson, students may progress to the next page, be taken back to a previous page or be redirected down a different path entirely and this solidifies independent learning.

Quiz: The quiz activity enables a teacher to create quizzes comprising questions of various types, including multiple choice, matching, short-answer and numerical. The teacher can allow the quiz to be attempted multiple times, with the questions shuffled or randomly selected from the question bank. A time limit may be set and the students could access the quiz independently and learn from their mistakes if the teacher provides them with answers.

SCORM Package: A SCORM Package is a collection of files and content is usually displayed over several pages, with navigation between the pages. There are various options for displaying content in a pop-up window, with a table of contents and navigation buttons. Furthermore, content could be uploaded as a zip file and added to a course. A SCORM Package may be used for presenting multimedia content and animations as well as an assessment tool. This could be accessed by students at any time and they will be able to watch, read and listen to the content material which will improve their language skills and encourage them to work independently.

Survey: The survey activity module provides a number of verified survey instruments and these survey tools are pre-populated with questions.

Workshop: The workshop activity module enables the collection, review and peer assessment of students' work. Students can submit any digital content (files), such as word-processed documents or spreadsheets and can also type text directly into a field using the text editor. Students are given the opportunity to assess one or more of their peers' submissions. Submissions and reviewers may be anonymous if required. This helps them learn independently from their peers' errors and their submission of digital content improves their writing skills.

Wiki: The wiki activity module enables participants to add and edit a collection of web pages. A wiki can be collaborative, with everyone being able to edit it, or individual, where everyone has their own wiki which only they can edit. Participating in a wiki encourages students to read other students' writing and motivates them to write independently.

E-Learning Resources

The following E-learning resources could be used by students' independently at their own pace to enhance their language proficiency as they access information in different forms which tailors to their different learning styles thus becoming independently immersed in the language.

Book: The book module enables a teacher to create a multi-page resource in a book-like format, with chapters and subchapters. Books can contain media files as well as text.

File: The file module enables a teacher to provide a file as a course resource. It could be used to share presentations given in a class or to share a mini website or draft files of certain software programs as Photoshop.

Folder: The folder module enables a teacher to display a number of related files inside a single folder, reducing scrolling on the course page.

IMS content package: An IMS content package is a collection of files and there are various options for displaying content in a pop-up window, with a navigation menu or buttons. An IMS content package may be used for presenting multimedia content and animations and content could be uploaded as a zip file.

Label: The label module enables text and multimedia to be inserted into the course page in between links to other resources and activities. It could be used to split up a long list of activities with a subheading or an image, to display an embedded sound file or video directly on the course page and to add a short description to a course section.

Page: The page enables a teacher to create a web page resource using the text editor. A page can display text, images, sound, video, web links and embedded code, such as Google maps. The page could be used to present the terms and conditions of a course or a summary of the course syllabus and to embed several videos or sound files together with some explanatory text.

URL: The URL module enables a teacher to provide a web link as a course resource. Anything that is freely available online, such as documents or images, can be linked to the students.

AN ANALYSIS OF THE E-LEARNING MOODLE

The Advantages of the E-Learning Moodle

- It is an interactive and appealing mode of instruction and learning.
- It motivates students and increases their global awareness (Meloni, 1998).
- It encourages learners to work independently as each student can work on different tasks with the "integrated learning environment" (Wu et al., 2012). In other words, it addresses differentiation and it allows students to work according to their own pace. Advanced learners could thus be able to work faster and finish more activities than novice learners (Nedeva & Dimova, 2010). This makes students keep their personal schedules as they work at their own place and according to their own preferences.
- It improves students' language skills as they practice reading, listening, speaking and writing via the different E-learning resources and tasks.
- It increases human sustainability as students acquire skills, attitudes and attributes that benefit themselves and others and lasts in the long-term future (Irwin, D., 2012).

- It appeals to students' different learning styles as they can choose from a variety of activities and resources. It allows students who are introverts the chance to interact virtually through Forums and Chats which improves their communicative competency.
- It increases students' study time of English over the week (Fryer et al., 2014) which improves their overall language proficiency.

The Disadvantages of the E-Learning Moodle

- The absence of face-to-face teaching and body language could lead to its becoming a "solitary activity" because E-learning social interactions are mainly virtual and different from face-to-face classroom interaction.
- The lack of an actual teacher's one-to-one face-to-face feedback may be difficult for some students who might not be comfortable with virtual feedback.
- Some students may not be able to use it if they do not have Internet access.
- It leads to a decrease of social relations between students (Mohammedi et al., 2010).
- Novice learners may be unable to participate if they lack human support (Nielson, 2011).

RECOMMENDATIONS

Despite the above mentioned drawbacks the recommendation of the author is to use E-learning together with face-to-face learning, as the former is supported by the latter. The E-Learning Moodle is being used at the British University in Egypt to supplement all Modules that are taught in face-to-face classes. It has proved successful, as students reach the intended learning objectives by this blended type of learning in which the concept conveys the idea of "blend" and refers to different situations in which technology is used to complement classroom activities (Dziuban et al., 2004).Heinze and Procter (2004) define it as "learning that is facilitated by the effective combination of different modes of delivery, models of teaching and styles of learning, and founded on transparent communication amongst all parties involved with a course". Thus, it is via E and b-learning that teaching and learning could be enhanced and developed, as students work in and outside the class which makes modules "more participated, interactive and student-centered" (Garrison & Vaughan, 2008). Working outside class encourages students to study independently using the E-learning interactive activities and thus spend more time engaged and immersed in the English language which improves their language proficiency.

CONCLUSION

E-learning is an essential tool that should be used to supplement the EFL face-to-face class. It includes various activities and resources that if used by the students and monitored by the teacher could enhance the students' language proficiency and independent learning. As the world progresses, we need to utilize technology and to synchronize ourselves with it. The wide variety of activities and resources on the E-learning Moodle needs to be activated in the English language Modules to increase the time that students interact with the language and motivate them to work independently and thus eventually they become life-long learners.

REFERENCES

1. Wu, B., Xu, W., & Ge, J. (2012). Experience Effect in E-Learning Research. SciVerse Science Direct. Procedia, 24, 2067- 2074. www.sciencedirect.com
2. Dziuban, C. D., Hartman, J. L., & Moskal, P. D. (2004). Blended Learning. Internet, 7, 1-44.
3. Esgi, N. (2013). Comparison of Effects of E-Learning Types Designed. International Journal of Academic Research, 5, 443- 450. http://dx.doi.org/10.7813/2075-4124.2013/5-5/B.69
4. European Commission (2001). The E-Learning Action Plan: Designing Tomorrow's Education (p. 20), Brussels.
5. Garrison, D. R., & Vaughan, N. D. (2008). Blended Learning in Higher Education: Framework, Principles, and Guidelines. Booksgooglecom, 1, 272.
6. Gulbahar, Y. (2009). E-Learning. Turkey: Pegem Academy Publishing.
7. Heinze, A., & Procter, C. T. (2004). Reflections on the Use of Blended Learning. Education in a Changing Environment. Salford: University of Salford.
8. Horton, W. (2006). E-Learning by Design. Hoboken, NJ: Wiley Publishing, Inc.
9. Horton, W. and Horton, K. (2003). E-Learning Tools and Technologies. Hoboken, NJ: Wiley Publishing, Inc.
10. Ilie, S. M., & Pavel, C. (2006). E-Learning Techniques to Study Dynamics of Mechanism. Research Reflections and Innovations in Integrating ICT in Education.http://era.teipir.gr/era1/b.4.teleeducation_session/abstracts/b.4.8.doc

11. Irwin, S. D. (2012). Using E-Learning for Student Sustainability Literacy: Framework and Review. IJSHE.
12. Kokkosis, A., Charitopoulos, A., Prekas, C., & Athanasopoulou, L. (2006). E-Learning Present and Future in Greece. http://era.teipir.gr/era1/b.4.tele-education_session/full_papers /b.4.8.doc
13. Meloni, C. (1998). The Internet in the Classroom: A Valuable Tool and Resource for ESL/EFL Teachers. ESL Magazine. http://www.eslmag.com/Article.htm
14. Nielson, K. B. (2011). Self-Study with Language Learning Software in the Workplace. Language Learning & Technology, 15.
15. Rosenberg, M. J. (2001). E-Learning: Strategies for Delivering Knowledge in the Digital Age. New York: McGraw-Hill.http://findarticles.com/p/articles/mi_7587/is_200910/ai_n42041564/?tag=content;col1
16. Nedeva, V. and Dimova, E. (2010). Some Advantages of E-Learning in English Language. Trakia Journal of Sciences, 8.
17. Waterhouse, S. (2003). The Power of E-Learning the Past, the Present, and the Future.http://ritim.cba.uri.edu/wp2003/pdf_format/Wiley-Encycl-Internet-Diffusion-v12.pd

Chapter 2

ADDRESSING FOREIGN LANGUAGE LEARNING ANXIETY WITH FACEBOOK

Serge Gabarre[1,2], Cécile Gabarre[1,2], Rosseni Din[2], Parilah Shah[2], Aidah Abdul Karim[2]

[1]Department of Foreign Languages, Universiti Putra Malaysia, Serdang, Malaysia
[2]Faculty of Education, Universiti Kebangsaan Malaysia, Bangi, Malaysia

ABSTRACT

Learning a foreign language can be a daunting task which challenges students in several ways. Although students more readily identify anxiety as linked to speaking, all other language skills have been linked to Krashen's affective filters. The present study sought to address these filters, with an emphasis on anxiety, by incorporating Facebook on mobile phones in the language classroom. A grounded action research method was adopted for the implementation as it enabled the researchers to alter their intervention, and provided a means to systematically analyze the data. A Facebook page and group were introduced to one single cohort of students in their French as a foreign language class. During three semesters, data were collected through online observations and interviews. A three-level coding scheme adhering to Strauss and Corbin's grounded theory enabled the construction of models describing the implementation. Findings revealed that students positively evaluated the incorporation of Facebook in their language course. An assessment of reports linked to anxiety indicated a positive change over the course of the study. Besides reduced levels of anxiety, the use of Facebook was associated with increased self-confidence and motivation. The benefit of learning with friends in an online environment was connected to adaptive strategies leading to improved learning experiences. These findings are discussed in light of the use of a social networking site in a social constructivist perspective.

INTRODUCTION

Learning a foreign language is not an easy task. Language students are often challenged with the assimilation of a new lexicon, a different phonologic system, unfamiliar syntax, and communication precepts. As described by Oxford (1999), daunting aspects of foreign language learning are often assimilated with anxiety. For new foreign language learners, speaking is frequently the hardest hurdle in their apprenticeship, however the other skills are not exempt from issues of affect (Cheng, Horwitz, & Schallert, 1999). The combination of the three factors of motivation, anxiety, and self-confidence form the Affective Filter hypothesis described by Krashen (2009) as well as by Dulay and Burt (1977). These three factors have a positive impact on acquisition as learners with higher motivation and strong self-confidence have the tendency to perform better in a foreign language. Similarly, lower levels of anxiety have a positive impact on language acquisition. The current study focuses on the anxiety affective filter in the context of language learning and language acquisition. Language acquisition is understood through Krashen's acquisition-learning distinction.

Through an action research intervention, the present study aimed to improve as much as possible on the aquisition situation by addressing issues of affect. Krashen posited that the Affective Filter prevents students from being in an optimal attitude for the input to "reach the part of the brain responsible for language acquisition" (2009, p. 31). Consequently, reducing anxiety and increasing motivation and self-confidence limit the Affective Filter which prevents a sufficient level of input from contributing to acquisition. In the present study, the intervention is relevant to affect in four ways. First, using tools and a familiar environment which the students viewed as motivating stimulated them to interact, access and share learning material. Consequently, a reduction of the Affective Filter was able to boost distribution. Second, the development of an online community of practice where students readily communicate in the target language lowered anxiety and increased self-confidence, thus lowering the Affective Filter. Third, empowering the students with some level of control over the distribution process was able to positively impact affect, particularly self-confidence. Fourth, as Krashen (2009) has defended, a reduction in the Affective Filter provided an increased level of input and thus facilitated acquisition of the foreign language.

Studies on social networking sites have demonstrated the potential that such networks hold to positively reduce the affective filters. Overall, the literature reveals a strong tendency towards positive experiences with social networking sites (SNS) in education. This is related to social acceptance in university and learning outcomes as noted by Yu, Tian, Vogel, and Kwok (2010). Furthermore, Kabilan, Ahmad, and Abidin (2010) clearly demonstrated the potential of a popular SNS to promote language learning. For these reasons, it was believed that incorporating an SNS in the foreign language could positively impact the learning process. It was furthermore assumed that this incorporation could be strengthened with the use of a mobile technology.

Mobile learning is a dynamic research field as attested by the numerous review articles on the topic(Ally, 2007; Cochrane, 2010; Godwin-Jones, 2011; Hung & Zhang, 2012; Keskin & Metcalf, 2011;Wang & Shen, 2012). These articles revealed that a majority of experiments demonstrated an accrued effectiveness over traditional methods of learning. This effectiveness impacted the level of learning (Başoğlu & Akdemir, 2010; Hwang & Chen, 2011), anxiety (Gabarre & Gabarre, 2010), motivation (Daher, 2010; Nah, 2011), satisfaction, perceived usefulness, and perceived ease-of-use(Chang & Hsu, 2011). For these reasons, the effectiveness of m-Learning should no longer be the main focus of research, as this has already been well established. On the other hand, a strong lack of knowledge on the processes that occur outside the classroom remained, and warranted further investigation. The present study addressed this lack of knowledge by focusing on the use of Facebook in a mobile environment.

METHODOLOGY

The action research method was selected for this study as it provided the opportunity to conduct an intervention in the authors' classroom. Action research provided a cyclical approach where results of the action plan were continuously evaluated. This evaluation was systematized by the adoption of grounded theory during the data analysis phases. The combination of action research and grounded theory, known as grounded action research, has demonstrated positive results in several previous studies (Baskerville & Pries-Heje, 1999; Olson, 2008; Simmons & Gregory, 2003).

Sample

In accordance with qualitative research sampling techniques (Silverman, 2000), a purposive sampling approach was used whereby one entire cohort of French language students was invited to participate in the present study. As such, 17 second-year students enrolled in a Bachelor of French as a foreign language in a Malaysia public university were recruited to participate in group interviews. All ethical requirements set by the university's research management center were adhered to. As parts of such requirements, pseudonyms were attributed to each student in order to protect their identity. Data collected during the group interviews were analyzed and a theoretical sampling selection reduced the number of respondents to three students. A snowballing technique was subsequently used which resulted in increasing the number of respondents to ten. This sample of ten students participated in five cycles of semi-guided individual interviews over the course of the study. The sample was constituted of seven females (three Malays and four Malaysian Chinese) and two males (one Malay and one Malaysian Chinese). Their ages ranged from 20 to 21 years.

Action Plan

The action plan was designed along two axes. First, lecture notes were converted to a mobile-friendly format and posted in the Facebook group where students could readily download them. Second, adhering to guidelines set by Ellis (2000), a task based learning approach was used throughout the study where students were assigned four types of activities. These activities consisted of 1) posting videos of roleplays which they had shot with their mobile phones, 2) posting textual feedback in order to guide their peers to improve their productions, 3) posting short text in response to articles posted on Facebook, and 4) posting comments on French news portal in response to articles posted on the Web. This action plan which incorporated language learning with Facebook on mobile phones is designated as mobile assisted social networking language learning, hereafter abbreviated with the MAS2L acronym.

Data Collection

In the present study, two types of sources were used for the data collection. First, online observations of the exchanges which occurred on the social networking site and on the Web were recorded in an observation grid. This observation grid was designed to record the type of exchange, the language used, the name of the person who initiated the exchange, the type of reply, and the name of the person who replied. A sample of a completed observation grid is available in Appendix A. Second, interviews were conducted to gather rich data pertaining to the students' experience with the action plan. One cycle of group interview was initially conducted with the entire cohort. Subsequently, five cycles of individual interviews were conducted to obtain more specific feedback from the students. This feedback was crucial to revise and improve the action plan as advised by Kemmis and McTaggard (1982).

Data Analysis

The initial step of the data analysis consisted in the transcription of the recorded interviews. ForEvers (2011), the transcription process enables the researcher to forge an initial impression on the data, which facilitates the open-coding process. This was methodically carried out on the same day as interviews were conducted. In systematic grounded theory as defined by Strauss and Corbin (1990), open coding refers to the first level coding which occurs as the researcher conducts a line by line assessment of the data. Themes were applied to relevant words or phrases. These themes were then evaluated for similarities with the constant comparative method, and merged to reduce the number of codes to a more manageable number of categories. In the present study, a computer assisted qualitative data analysis software was employed to ease the management of the numerous codes and categories. Based on reviews of several such software (García-Horta & Guerra-Ramos, 2009), the ATLAS. ti software was selected for its ability to handle vast quantity of data, and for its ease of use. Using this software, a category in relation to the objective of the study was selected as the central category, and then the data were explored in order to discover relationships among the remaining categories. This process where relationships are identified is referred to as axial coding. For this second-level coding, Strauss and Corbin propose five relational links which form the axial coding paradigm. These are the causal condition, the context, the intervening condition, the action/interactional strategies, and the consequence (Strauss & Corbin, 1990: p. 96). In the present study, this second-level coding resulted in axial coding models which described relevant aspects surrounding themes such as anxiety, foreign language learning, and learning with Facebook. Selective coding, the third level of coding in grounded theory, was employed to obtain an overview of the implementation. With third-level coding scheme, the theme of foreign language learning anxiety with Facebook was articulated. Selective coding follows the same coding paradigm as axial coding, but incorporates relationships between axial coding models instead of categories.

Validity and Reliability

In order to ensure that the results of the present study were trustworthy as understood by Lincoln and Guba (1985), three techniques were used. These were 1) member reflections where the respondents were asked to verify that the analysis of the data corresponded with their own experience, 2) triangulation within the same method to ensure that data were consistent, and 3) the use of reflexive memos as an audit trail which provided a traceable account of the proceedings of the study. These three techniques are consistent with those employed in qualitative studies. Member reflection follows the precepts set by Tracy (2010), triangulation adheres to guidelines described by Silverman (2000), and reflexive memos form an integral part of grounded theory as elaborated by Strauss and Corbin (1990).

FINDINGS AND DISCUSSION

The analysis of the data yielded positive findings which highlighted how the use of Facebook on mobile phones addressed issues of affect, and more specifically issues of anxiety. Over the course of the study, students shared their experiences which revealed the strategies they put in place to cope with such issues. Learning with their friends in a networked online environment provided advantages which do not readily occur in the traditional classroom. The following paragraphs illustrate these findings at each of the three level of coding. Verbatim excerpts of interview transcriptions are included to better demonstrate the students' perspectives. Pseudonyms are used throughout the text in order to keep the identity of the students anonymous.

Open Coding

The open coding process was conducted throughout the study as data were collected. After the interview data were transcribed and the observation grids completed, all textual information was reviewed to identify relevant themes. By applying the open coding process, the theme of anxiety was clearly identified in the data. A decrease in anxiety was noted by Annaelle, a student who explained that she initially felt lost when she was confronted to material which she did not understand. However, when faced with practical activities, Annaelle realised that she was capable of carrying them out successfully. As a result, Annaelle was able to understand what she initially could not grasp, and thus felt less anxious. However, issues of anxiety were still reported. Sarah explained that she felt particularly anxious when her oral proficiency was evaluated. The two dimensions of this theme are presented in the following quotes.

Yes, of course, because usually, to be honest, I don't know how to, when you are... when you are show us the PowerPoint, in the beginning I will: "What is this? What is this?" And then, if have the activity, it's help me to... to understand what is actually, the lecturer wants us to learn, the applic, applic, the application... (Annaelle C5:8:127).

I don't know, maybe for Test 2, because Test 2 is more oral things that we actually get nervous when we have to do oral things (Sarah C5:4:217).

Shyness was another such theme which was identified through open coding. Students remarked that they felt less shy to communicate in class. Although the time at which this change occurred was identified as the introduction of the MAS2L platform, students did not spontaneously attribute this change to the new implementation. It was reported that in-class interactions had become more frequent and that students dared express their opinions and ask questions. The following excerpt reveals how Valérie perceived this reduction in shyness over time.

I think it's change a lot, before and now. Because, from when we start coming to [the university], and when we start learning French and we [are] like all quiet and not really talk and speak in class, and also not really interact with lecturer. At the first, maybe level one, level two, French 1, French 2, then after that we, when we start interact, then we feel like: "Ah, it's good." It's more [laugh], more noisy in our class, because we all already dare to speak up our opinion, dare to speak up our question (Valérie C5:3:186).

When applying the constant comparative method, all themes which carried the same meaning were merged into a single all-encompassing code. In spite of this, a large number of codes were identified. As prescribed by Creswell (2005), these codes were subsequently combined into categories. Figure 1 illustrates this process, and highlights how codes such as self-confidence, motivation, and joy were combined into the theme of positive affect; whereas shyness and anxiety were combined into the theme of negative affect. Figure 1 depicts how the open coding process enabled the reduction of ten codes into one manageable category. Yet, the open coding process did not reveal any relationship between codes or categories. This was achieved through axial coding.

Axial Coding

The purpose of axial coding is to reconstruct the data which have been deconstructed by the open coding process. With axial coding, categories were reorganized along the relational axes set by Strauss and Corbin (1990). Figure 2 depicts the axial coding diagram resulting from this process, and links affect to improvements. In this diagram affect was placed in a central position and was observed as a consequence of MAS2L within the context of foreign language learning. The theme of learning with friends was identified as the intervening condition to the phenomenon. Indeed, friends provided learning support which proved beneficial in terms of affect. The strategy which was put in place to cope with issues of affect was adaptation. Students adapted in various ways to the situation which affected them in order to surpass their fears, anxieties or low levels of motivation. As a consequence, students felt that they had made progress and improvements in their language proficiency. The themes of learning with friends, adaptation, and improvement are described hereafter with evidence taken from the interviews.

1) Learning with friends. On numerous occasions, students explained how they learned French with their friends from the group. These explanations triangulated with observations and with Adair-Hauck and Donato's (1994) description of learning French within the zone of proximal development (ZPD). More knowledgeable students provided support to those who did not have the same foreign language proficiency. As can be seen in the following triangulated quotations taken from the interviews, assistance was often related to vocabulary enquiries, grammar, and more specifically conjugating verbs. In other cases, assistance from friends took the form of encouragements, explanations, or corrections.

I think I'm the one who always say: "Faster go and study, faster go and study." I'm the one who play the role like this, and they will finally before go to sleep, they will at least they read a bit. But, always like they have, they have problem they will ask. [And then Laurence,] she is, she is the one who tell me: "Check, check again, I think this one wrong already." She will tell me like that (Valérie C4:1:199,202).

For example there is a new vocabulary, if I know then I will tell them, and also because I'm not so strong in grammar part, Valérie she is strong in grammar part then she will help us if for example we do not understand in which situation or sentences we should use what kind of tenses (Nolwenn C4:3:178).

Sometimes the word, the vocab that I forget, I will ask like Marie-Thérèse: "How to say this word? How to say that?" (Chantal C4:4:124).

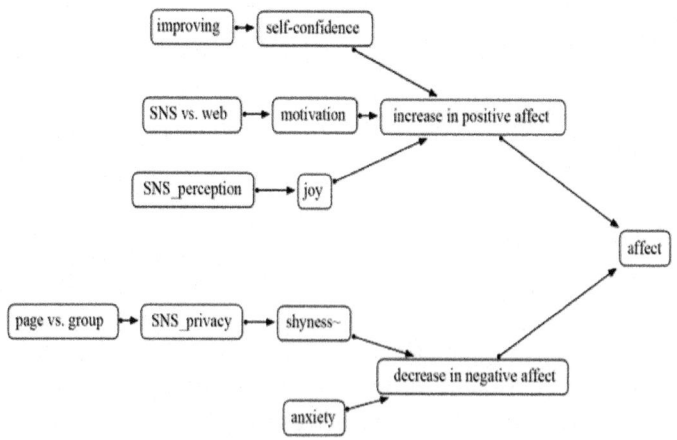

Figure 1. Open coding process of the affect category.

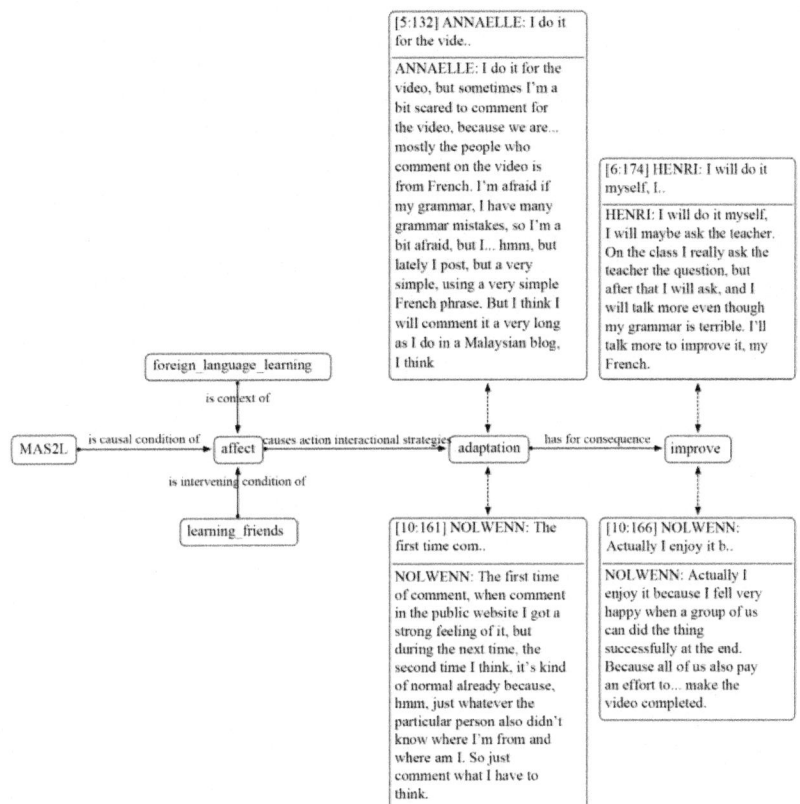

Figure 2. Axial coding of affect leading to improvement.

Sometimes, they ask me, they ask me also the vocabulary and conjugation (Marie-Thérèse C4:2:239).

I speak French with them and also when they ask me how to do the work, I will help. I will help them to finish the work (Ariane C4:5:123).

I will show Valérie my work, then she will correct it, she will explain it back to me, what is wrong, what is right, what is not wrong (Annaelle C4:9:152).

2) Adaptation. When language learning tasks were planned to provide the students with an opportunity to write comments on French news portals, it was envisioned that removing the student from the comfort zone of the SNS would challenge them to excel in applying their communicative skills. This was indeed the case. However, by removing them from their comfort zone, students experienced more anxiety. Annaelle and Nolwenn related their coping mechanisms which they put in place to overcome their distress. Annaelle recalled how she felt about posting

a comment on a YouTube video which had been uploaded by a French person. For her, writing a comment was perceived as a frightening task since it would be viewed by Internet users residing in France. Annaelle explained that she feared her grammar would not be correct, and thus would reveal her inadequacies. However, Annaelle adapted to this situation by focussing on simple grammatical structures which she felt she had mastered. With this coping mechanism, Annaelle envisioned posting a longer text, similarly to what she had been doing using her native language. Nolwenn's fears were comparable to Annaelle as she felt that her proficiency in French was insufficient to be mistaken for a French Internet user. Yet this feeling was only present during her first post. Nolwenn explained that as she realised that no one knew where she came from, she felt she could freely comment without worrying about such issues. For Henri adapting to issues of low self-confidence encountered during in-class tasks was made possible by focussing on a topic which he felt was interesting, and which he knew he could talk about. For Yolande, fear of taking an exam was resolved when she realised that she was familiar with the format of the evaluation, and that she had been sufficiently exposed to the target language. Yolande explained that this exposure had provided her with the confidence she needed to sit for an international French proficiency exam known as the DELF. Firth and Wagner (2007) view adaptation to a new communicative context as an essential part of the learning process. This view is based on the Doolittle and Hicks (2003) constructivist interpretation that cognition should be envisioned as an adaptive process which results in making the learners more viable in a changing environment. As such, it can be inferred that students participating in the present study adapted to change, and thus learned to communicate in a new and challenging context. The following excerpts provide evidence of this theme.

I do it for the video, but sometimes I'm a bit scared to comment for the video, because we are… mostly the people who comment on the video is from French. I'm afraid if my grammar, I have a very grammar, I have many grammar mistakes, so I'm a bit afraid, but I… hmm, but lately I post, but a very simple, using a very simple French phrase. But, I think I will comment it a very long as I do in a Malaysian blog, I think (Annaelle C6:5:132).

The first time of comment, when comment in the public website I got a strong feeling of it, but during the next time, the second time I think, it's kind of normal already because, hmm, just whatever the particular person also didn't know where I'm from and where am I. So just comment what I have to think (Nolwenn C6:10:161).

I think for the first in the debate I have the problem to talk because my French is not good. I think. I maybe lack of confidence, but the topic for when the debate is, is very interesting (Henri C6:6:205).

Before this I'm afraid to take DELF, but after you [...] expose to us, and post it in Facebook, then the exposure will give us the confidence. Then we, because I think if we are not, if we are not exposed to... to particular test, then we just go, go at that time to sit in the exam. We don't know anything. And, and especially for the, for the language that we don't recognise well, so I think the exposure before the test is good (Yolande C6:9:111).

3) Improvement. As students adapted and overcame their affective inhibitions, they realised that they could communicate in French. Freed from the affective filters described by Krashen (2009), students were able to increase their opportunities to expose themselves to, and practice their skills in the target language. In the following excerpt, Henri explains how in spite of perceived grammar difficulties, he pushed himself to practice his speaking skills. Moreover, he explains how although documents which he was exposed to were beyond his oral comprehension skills, he still persevered in order to grasp key information and improve his pronunciation. Improvements were also reported when students read comments on Facebook, and when they used the language outside of class. The following quotations substantiate the theme of improvement as perceived by the students.

I will talk more even though my grammar is terrible. I'll talk more to improve it, my French [...] Maybe from the Facebook, maybe some trailer from the film. Okay, I will listen to it, okay, how they speak in French? Maybe there are some problems because French native speakers are very fast when speak French, and sometimes I cannot catch what they are trying to say. I sometimes blur, and maybe I listen to it more, many times. Okay, okay, this is, this is, this is, what they are speaking, okay, I can use it to improve my pronunciation also, I think (Henri C6:6:174, 193).

Because if I, you tell us on Facebook, not only me know how to improve, but others also can read the comment, and can also to improve together (Chantal C6:4:111).

Through Facebook, hmm... maybe the way, hmm... because in the group we have to use French to... so even outside class we still have to communicate in French. So, it, it, it will improve our French language (Ariane C6:1:199).

Selective Coding

The selective coding process enabled the emergence of the model represented in Figure 3. This model links

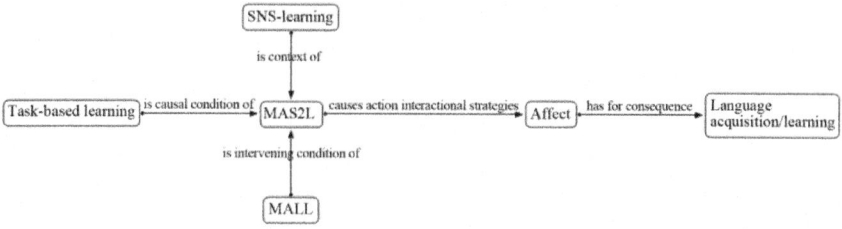

Figure 3. Selective coding diagram.

learning a foreign language on mobile phones and Facebook, to task-based learning, SNS-learning, mobile assisted language learning (MALL), affect, and language acquisition and learning.

Data segments identified the theme of task-based learning category as the causal condition. It is this category which the students perceived as the cause for the MAS2L implementation. This category encompasses themes such as peer correction, learning with friends, as well as college study groups. Students perceive learning as a collective activity which occurred in and out of the classroom. In-class activities which made use of the mobile phones to create documents which were uploaded to the SNS are included in this category. Out-of-class activities where students communicated on the SNS for their tasks, such as posting comments, are also classified in this category.

Both MALL and SNS-Learning were perceived as particularly relevant to the present study. Yet for the students, SNS-Learning appeared as more of a novelty, and as such was reported more predominantly. As an example, friends and families' views of the implementation were repeatedly reported in terms of SNS-Learning, yet MALL did not receive this mention. In this study, the students mainly perceived the MAS2L implementation through its SNS-Learning facet. For these reasons, SNS-Learning was linked to MAS2L as the context of the phenomenon. This category included themes such as SNS and privacy, SNS problems, the compulsive pattern of SNS-Learning, as well as relationships with friends. Similarly to the theme of task-based learning, SNS-Learn- ing includes a strong social constructivist element as students perceived this mode of learning as primarily collectivist.

On the other hand, MALL was associated with individualist learning. For the students, the m-Learning facet of the MAS2L implementation was linked to the delivery of learning material, to location, to selecting between a laptop and a phone, to the notion of ubiquity, and to phone problems, such as issues of connectivity. There was no apparent connection between task-based learning and MALL, in spite of the students using their mobile devices to shoot videos in French as part of their class activities. This task was perceived as relating to SNS- Learning as it involved the online peer-feedback element. This view contrasts with Kim and Mangenot's (2009) description of MALL which encompasses delivery as well as the use of tools on the phone for task-based learning. This suggests that the students perceived MALL as a mean to increase their mobility, rather than the techno-centric approach which tends to focus more on the devices.

The affect category was identified in the action/interactional strategies. It includes themes such as frustration, enjoyment, perceived ease, motivation, and self-confidence. It is noteworthy that the theme of anxiety was not included in this category. This theme was insufficiently grounded and did not have enough density. Although anxiety was experienced at times during this study, it appears that students did not perceive it as equally relevant as other themes linked to affect. Of all the themes included in this category, self-confidence was the most grounded with 107 occurrences. This suggests that MAS2L had a significant impact on this affective filter, though additional quantitative studies could evaluate this impact. Both increase in positive affect and decrease in negative affect were included in this category. This reflects the positive view which the students had of the implementation.

The consequence of the MAS2L implementation was identified as the language acquisition/learning category. Data pointed to three themes within this category: 1) foreign language learning, 2) exposure to foreign language, and 3) language acquisition. As was described in the data, students mainly perceived their learning experience through exposure to the target language, and through access to learning material. Language learning was continuously reported throughout the six cycles of implementation, yet students perceived it as more readily related to SNS-Learning and task-based learning than MALL. It was initially anticipated that recourse to the Monitor would be conducted through the mobile devices. In-class observations revealed that this was indeed the case, yet interview data did not significantly report this trend. Exposure to the target language was primarily linked to the delivery of lecture notes and to task-based learning. Acquisition was reported whenever students had perceived their improved language proficiency, but remained incapable of describing the processes they had undergone. This theme was linked to task-based learning as well as exposure to the target language.

CONCLUSION

Concerning affect, the MAS2L implementation was reported to have increased the students' motivation to access the platform, to learn and to communicate in the target language. Enjoyment was often cited when students described how they felt about using the MAS2L platform. This feeling was linked to communicating with their peers on the SNS, and to reviewing productions, posts, and comments which were regularly published. It was noted that students did not report any anxiety when using the technology. This was also the case with a technophobic student who managed to overcome his initial apprehensions. Using the MAS2L platform, students exhibited a certain level of self-confidence as their proficiency improved. This was particularly visible as students were disappointed that their productions in the target language would not be viewed by friends and family members outside the Facebook group.

For the students, sharing the same virtual network as their lecturers changed the perception of their relationship. Students reported that they felt closer to their lecturers, and that the relationship was comparable to the ones they had with their friends. This concurs with previous findings published by Pasfield-Neofitou (2008) who revealed that the SNS had enabled her to gain more insights on her students' lives and on the way they learned a foreign language. The present study implicated this relationship with reduced anxiety, and increased motivation. After the final cycle of implementation, the lecturers no longer taught the students in the cohort. These students still attended courses in the faculty where they completed their final semester. During this semester, the MAS2L platform was still used for administrative communications. The topic of these communications was mainly the upcoming DELF exams which several students passed successfully. Peer exchanges were still recorded two months after the end of the last cycle. In one such instance, the MAS2L platform was used to send a distress message to the group. Valérie, while out with three other classmates, happened to experience car difficulties when her fuel tank became empty. She promptly used her phone to post a message on the French course's platform, and requested for help. Replies from other classmates were shortly answered, and someone came to assist them. This event highlights the students' perception of the MAS2L platform as a mean to rapidly and effectively communicate with their peers. These exchanges revealed that all communications were conducted in French. It is noteworthy to emphasize that even after the end of the implementation, students still used the platform to communicate in the target language, even during an event which was considered as an emergency.

Four main limitations to this study need to be highlighted. First, due to the qualitative nature of the grounded action research and to the absence of a randomized sampling method, findings may not be generalized to the whole population. Second, although the duality of the role of the researcher as the cohort's lecturer was taken into account during the data analysis phase, interferences may have unknowingly occurred. Third, as a consequence of financial constraints, data collection was limited to a period of one and a half year. Fourth, the lack of students engaged in a bachelor degree in French in Malaysia limited the study to a single site.

In order to provide this qualitative study with quantifiable results, it is suggested that future studies could address the same issues through quantitative paradigm. These studies could measure the impact of using Facebook on mobile device on anxiety, self-confidence and motivation. Additionally, further studies could seek to validate the present study by changing specific variables such as the context, the language learned, the SNS used, or the age of the participants.

REFERENCES

1. Adair-Hauck, B., & Donato, R. (1994). Foreign Language Explanations within the Zone of Proximal Development. Canadian Modern Language Review, 50, 532-557.
2. Ally, M. (2007). Mobile Learning. International Review of Research in Open and Distance Learning, 8, 1-4.
3. Baskerville, R., & Pries-Heje, J. (1999). Grounded Action Research: A Method for Understanding IT in Practice. Accounting Management and Information Technologies, 9, 1-23. http://dx.doi.org/10.1016/S0959-8022(98)00017-4
4. Basoglu, E. B., & Akdemir, Ö. (2010). A Comparison of Undergraduate Students' English Vocabulary Learning: Using Mobile Phones and Flash Cards. The Turkish Online Journal of Educational Technology, 9, 1-7.
5. Chang, C.-K., & Hsu, C.-K. (2011). A Mobile-Assisted Synchronously Collaborative Translation-Annotation System for English as a Foreign Language (EFL) Reading Comprehension. Computer Assisted Language Learning, 24, 155-180. http://dx.doi.org/10.1080/09588221.2010.536952
6. Cheng, Y., Horwitz, E., & Schallert, D. (1999). Language Anxiety: Differentiating Writing and Speaking Components. Language Learning, 49, 417-446. http://dx.doi.org/10.1111/0023-8333.00095
7. Cochrane, T. D. (2010). Beyond the Yellow Brick Road: Mobile Web 2.0 Informing a New Institutional E-Learning Strategy. Research in Learning Technology, 18, 221-231.http://dx.doi.org/10.1080/09687769.2010.529110
8. Creswell, J. W. (2005). Educational Research: Planning, Conducting, and Evaluating Quantitative and Qualitative Research. Upper Saddle River, NJ: Pearson Education.

9. Daher, W. (2010). Building Mathematical Knowledge in an Authentic Mobile Phone Environment. Australasian Journal of Educational Technology, 26, 85-104.

10. Doolittle, P. E., & Hicks, D. (2003). Constructivism as a Theoretical Foundation for the Use of Technology in Social Studies. Theory & Research in Social Education, 31, 72-104. http://dx.doi.org/10.1080/00933104.2003.10473216

11. Dulay, H., & Burt, M. (1977). Remarks on Creativity in Language Acquisition. In M. Burt, H. Dulay & M. Finnochiaro (Eds.), Viewpoints on English as a Second Language (pp. 95-126). New York: Regents.

12. Ellis, R. (2000). Task-Based Research and Language Pedagogy. Language Teaching Research, 193, 193-220. http://dx.doi.org/10.1177/136216880000400302

13. Evers, J. C. (2011). From the Past into the Future. How Technological Developments Change Our Ways of Data Collection, Transcription and Analysis. Forum Qualitative Sozialforschung/Forum: Qualitative Social Research, 12.

14. Firth, A., & Wagner, J. (2007). Second/Foreign Language Learning as a Social Accomplishment: Elaborations on a Reconceptualized SLA. The Modern Language Journal, 91, 800-819. http://dx.doi.org/10.1111/j.1540-4781.2007.00670.x

15. Gabarre, S., & Gabarre, C. (2010). Shooting Short Videos in French with Mobile Phones. FULGOR, 4, 93-108.

16. García-Horta, J. B., & Guerra-Ramos, M. T. (2009). The Use of CAQDAS in Educational Research: Some Advantages, Limitations and Potential Risks. International Journal of Research & Method in Education, 32, 151-165. http://dx.doi.org/10.1080/17437270902946686

17. Godwin-Jones, R. (2011). Emerging Technologies: Mobile Apps for Language Learning. Language Learning & Technology, 15, 2-11.

18. Hung, J.-L., & Zhang, K. (2012). Examining Mobile Learning Trends 2003-2008: A Categorical Meta-Trend Analysis Using Text Mining. Journal of Computing in Higher Education, 24, 1-17. http://dx.doi.org/10.1007/s12528-011-9044-9

19. Hwang, W.-Y., & Chen, H. (2011). Users' Familiar Situational Contexts Facilitate the Practice of EFL in Elementary Schools with Mobile Devices. Computer Assisted Language Learning, 1-25.

20. Kabilan, M. K., Ahmad, N., & Abidin, M. J. Z. (2010). Facebook: An Online Environment for Learning of English in Institutions of Higher

Education? Internet and Higher Education, 13, 179-187. http://dx.doi.org/10.1016/j.iheduc.2010.07.003

21. Kemmis, S., & McTaggart, R. (1982). The Action Research Planner. Victoria: Deakin University Press.

22. Keskin, N. O., & Metcalf, D. (2011). The Current Perspectives, Theories and Practices of Mobile Learning. The Turkish Online Journal of Educational Technology, 10, 202-208.

23. Kim, H.-K., & Mangenot, F. (2009). Apprentissage Nomadeen Langue et Production Orale Asynchrone [Mobile Learning in Languages and Asynchronous Oral Production]. Proceedings of the Epal 2009 Conference, Grenoble, 4-6 June 2009, 1-17.

24. Krashen, S. D. (2009). Principles and Practice in Second Language Acquisition. Oxford: Pergamon Press Inc.

25. Lincoln, Y. S., & Guba, E. G. (1985). Naturalistic Inquiry. Thousand Oaks, CA: Sage.

26. Nah, K. C. (2011). Optimising the Use of Wireless Application Protocol (WAP) Sites for Listening Activities in a Korean English as a Foreign Language (EFL) Context. Computer Assisted Language Learning, 24, 103-116. http://dx.doi.org/10.1080/09588221.2010.526946

27. Olson, M. M. (2008). Using Grounded Action Methodology for Student Intervention-Driven Succeeding: A Grounded Action Study in Adult Education. Forum Qualitative Sozialforschung/Forum: Qualitative Social Research, 9, 1-21.

28. Oxford, R. (1999). Anxiety and the Language Learner: New Insights. In J. Arnold (Ed.), Affect in Language Learning (pp. 58-67). Cambridge, UK: Cambridge University Press.

29. Pasfield-Neofitou, S. E. (2008). Creative Applications of Social Networking for the Language Learning Class. The International Journal of Learning, 14, 235-239.

30. Silverman, D. (2000). Doing Qualitative Research. Thousand Oaks, CA: Sage.

31. Simmons, O. E., & Gregory, T. A. (2003). Grounded Action: Achieving Optimal and Sustainable Change. Forum Qualitative Sozialforschung/Forum: Qualitative Social Research, 4, 1-17.

32. Strauss, A. L., & Corbin, J. (1990). Basics of Qualitative Research: Grounded Theory Procedures and Techniques. Thousand Oaks, CA: Sage.

33. Tracy, S. J. (2010). Qualitative Quality: Eight "Big-Tent" Criteria for Excellent Qualitative Research. Qualitative Inquiry, 16, 837-851. http://dx.doi.org/10.1177/1077800410383121
34. Wang, M., & Shen, R. (2012). Message Design for Mobile Learning: Learning Theories, Human Cognition and Design Principles. British Journal of Educational Technology, 43, 561-575. http://dx.doi.org/10.1111/j.1467-8535.2011.01214.x
35. Yu, A. Y., Tian, S. W., Vogel, D., & Kwok, R. C.-W. (2010). Can Learning Be Virtually Boosted? An Investigation of Online Social Networking Impacts. Computers & Education, 55, 1494-1503. http://dx.doi.org/10.1016/j.compedu.2010.06.015

Chapter 3

A REVIEW OF MODELS IN EXPERIMENTAL STUDIES OF IMPLICIT LANGUAGE LEARNING

Si Liu, Huangmei Liu

School of Foreign Languages and Literatures, Lanzhou University, Lanzhou, China

ABSTRACT

The present review analyzes experimental research on implicit learning using linguistic stimuli, and proposes five key procedures of a framework for empirical studies of implicit learning. Our review begins with a brief overview of the current state of research on implicit learning, and then presents the procedures in detail: 1) choosing theoretical assumptions from psychology; 2) designing stimuli; 3) exposing subjects to information; 4) testing implicit learning; and 5) measuring subjects' state of awareness. This framework is intended to assist researchers in designing experiments on implicit learning both more comprehensively and with fewer flaws.

INTRODUCTION

Shanks (2005) uses nine examples of earlier research to give more explicit concept of implicit learning, and concludes that implicit learning can generally be characterized as learning that takes place both unintentionally and unconsciously. Interests in implicit learning have lasted about 50 years. Since Reber coined the term "implicit learning" for the first time in 1967, numerous experiments have been done in this field. Until now, it seems that the central issue of implicit learning studies has been proved that what researchers thought to have been learned implicitly really was acquired by implicit learning, and then to find the cognitive processes of implicit learning, rather than more fundamentally to prove whether implicit learning did in fact exist(Frensch & Rünger, 2003; Williams, 2009). Both psychologists and linguists are interested in the matter. Psychologists study it to learn more about human psychological mechanisms; linguists study it to learn more about human language developmental mechanisms. In this review, we would focus on clinical research with linguistic features.

Researchers like Williams (2004, 2005, 2009), endeavor to develop clinical methodologies and models that will make studies of implicit learning more reliable and persuasive. Clinical models are important gains from clinical studies. There are three general kinds of models: first, models based on offline methodology (Jiménez et al., 1996); second, models based on online methodology, mostly using RT, ERP or fMRI (Cleeremans & McClelland, 1991; Clegg et al., 1998; Leung & Williams, 2006; Williams, 2004, 2005); and third, models based on computational methodology, mostly constructed according to constructivist and emergentist views (Cleeremans & McClelland, 1991;Dienes, 1992; Estes, 1957; Hintzmann, 1986; Perruchet & Vinter, 1998). Following these three general models, there are detailed models developed by experimental practices. One of the most popular models using RT is the one developed by Williams in 2004, which examined implicit learning through a series of explicit training sessions that controlled subjects' attention, recording reaction time (RT) and drawing conclusions on which items had been learned implicitly (Chen et al., 2011; Leung & Williams, 2006; Williams, 2004, 2005).

Numerous models have been developed, but none of them is beyond dispute. On one hand, almost all contain some elements or procedures that make them less reliable; on the other hand, a more scientific criterion has not been found to guide researchers in planning their experimental procedures. In contrast, a surgeon follows a series of detailed and standardized preparation procedures before he or she enters the operating room. We, then, seek to give the best suggestions on developing and standardizing such necessary procedural steps for researchers in the clinical field of implicit learning.

METHOD OF OUR REVIEW

Literature Search Strategy

We tried to identify published studies through searches of Elsevier, Sciencedirect, Springer, Google Scholar and Google using keyword, title and abstract information. Each of these databases allows searches of articles before July of 2013. The following search terms were used: implicit learning, implicit knowledge, artificial grammar learning, sequence learning, unconscious learning and learning without attention. Manual searches were also important to consult for identifying other items from the references of other relevant reviews and book chapters.

Inclusion and Omission

Only English-language articles are included in the present review. To review critically and ensure manageability, our review focuses on clinical studies of implicit learning in relation to artificial grammar learning (AGL) and sequence learning (SL) but it is not exhaustive. Other paradigms, such as probability learning (Millward & Reber, 1968), melody learning (Rohmeier & Cross, 2010), visual search in complex stimulus environments (Chun & Jiang, 1999) and dynamic system control, have not been considered.

CONTROVERSIAL THEORETICAL ISSUES IN IMPLICIT LEARNING

Though this review focuses on the experimental models on implicit learning, this section will give a very brief summary about three theoretical issues that are quite controversial and need to be settled, because these theoretical issues seem to be the sources of the inconsistency of experimental results of implicit learning. The first issue is the definition of implicit learning. In the introduction section, we mentioned Shanks' conclusion about implicit learning as learning that takes place both unintentionally and unconsciously (Shanks, 2005). Definitions elsewhere (Cleeremans & McClelland, 1991; Clegg et al., 1998; Jiménez et al., 1996; Leung & Williams, 2006; Reber, 1967) also give descriptions like this. It is not difficult to find that the description itself is quite vague, because words like "unintentionally" and "unconsciously" are words without settled definition. Another difficulty in defining "implicit learning" is whether it should only include learning that occurs implicitly or all kinds of learning except ones occurring explicitly (Frensch & Rünger, 2003), since "implicit" does not absolutely equal to "unaware", and neither does "explicit" equal "aware". The inconsistency in defining implicit learning causes researchers to design experiments of implicit learning with different concepts of implicit learning in mind (Cleeremans & McClelland, 1991; Clegg et al., 1998; Jiménez et al., 1996; Leung & Williams, 2006), and consequentially makes the results of their experiments incomparable (Frensch & Rünger, 2003).

The second theoretical problem is that the processing mechanism of implicit learning and explicit learning is unsettled. There are disputes between the multiple-system hypothesis and single-system hypothesis (Frensch & Rünger, 2003). The former holds that implicit learning and explicit learning use different processing systems, whereas the latter holds that the two use the same processing system, and even some hypothesize that explicit learning should developed from implicit learning. This also makes the results of research incomparable with different concepts about processing mechanisms (please see Frensch & Rünger, 2003, for detail).

The third theoretical issue is also very troublesome: it is the uncertainty of attention mechanisms. In experiments, researchers need to make the acquisition of stimuli implicit or unaware by controlling subjects' attention. This problem will be given a more detailed discussion in Sections 4.1 and 4.3.

Though these theoretical issues do exist and do have passive consequences on the research of implicit learning, it is unlikely to be settled any time soon. However, to some extent, we might be able to complement this by adopting more controllable models in clinical studies.

A CRITICAL REVIEW ON EXPERIMENTAL MODELS IN CLINICAL STUDIES

After analytical work, we find that experimental models in clinical studies of implicit learning are usually involved in the following essential procedures: (1) choosing theoretical assumptions from psychology; (2) designing stimuli; (3) exposing subjects to information; (4) testing implicit learning; and (5) measuring subjects' state of awareness

Choosing Theoretical Assumptions from Psychology

Researchers have conceived of various presuppositions about implicit learning. The two most famous are the following: (1) the shadow theory (Searle, 1992), which holds that there is an unconscious mind and a conscious mind, and that the two are just the same, only with consciousness absent in the former; and (2) the not-reallyexisting theory (Shanks & St. John, 1994), which holds that results in experiments are about instances rather than rules, and thus learning about any kind of knowledge is explicit rather than implicit. Though there is still much to say about such presuppositions, we will not focus on them, instead, on psychological suppositions adopted in clinical experiments.

In designing experiments that test implicit learning, all or at least most researchers (Cleeremans & McClelland, 1991; Clegg et al., 1998) try to find their ground in the achievements of psychology, since implicit learning is thought to be an integral part of psychology. In the training section, researchers usually try to create conditions that promote implicit learning by controlling how subjects allocate attention, thus the most commonly cited supposition pertains to attention. "In psychology, the basic assumptions concerning attention have been that it is limited, that it is selective, that it is partially subjective to voluntary control, that attention controls access to consciousness, and that attention is essential for action control and for learning" (Schmidt, 2001: 11). These assumptions are basically used in the design of training, thus, we will review their roles in a later section on exposure.

Designing Stimuli

Usually, clinical research on implicit learning has essentially been focused on two stimulus paradigms: artificial grammar learning (AGL) and sequence learning (SL). The following sections will give more insight on the two paradigms with a critical view.

Artificial Grammar in Stimuli

Artificial grammar learning is arguably the most influential paradigm (Cleeremans & Dienes, 2008). In studies adopting artificial grammar, subjects are usually asked to memorize or look at a series of materials, and then to select from test materials the ones that conform to the materials they have seen before and to describe what rules they depend on to make the selection decisions. Reber (1967) was one of the first researchers to adopt AGL as experimental information in the study of implicit learning. He asked subjects to learn a series of letter strings within a limited time and then told them that these strings were all constructed according to a particular set of rules (an artificial grammar created by him). Later he conducted a test on the subjects with new strings and with such questions as which strings conformed to the rules earlier referred to. Subjects made decisions with better-than-chance accuracy; but results showed low correctness in description of the rules. Hence Reber concluded that the learning of the artificial rules was a phenomenon of implicit learning. Though Reber's conclusion was criticized heavily, since then, many researchers have taken to using artificial grammar to study implicit learning. Later versions of artificial grammar, however, have undergone many modifications (e.g. Reber, 1989; Berry & Dienes, 1993; Cleeremans et al., 1998; Pothos, 2007; Shanks, 2005; Wan et al., 2008).

What is arguably more worthy of note lies in the following experiments, which try to make the clinical stimuli closer to natural language. Williams (2004) used artificial nouns, artificial determiners and their artificial determiner-noun relationship as stimuli of implicit learning, but the determiners used had strong characteristics of gendered language determiners. Leung & Williams (2006) used artificial determiners, artificial syntax structure and the artificial determiner-agent/patient relationship as stimuli in Experiment 1. In Experiment 2, they used artificial nouns, artificial determiners and their artificial determiner-noun relationship as stimuli of implicit learning, having removed the features of gendered language determiner, using English nouns instead of artificial nouns, and using pictures to make up for the lack of context; Rebuschat & Williams (2009)adopted a semi-artificial grammar, which consists of English words and German syntax. Chen et al. (2011) conducted experiments in Chinese implicit learning, base on Williams' (2004) model, using extremely low-frequency Chinese characters as determiner, and Chinese nouns and an artificial determiner-noun relationship.

Although closer to natural language, these stimuli still have their own defects. The defect of Williams' (2004) stimuli is the gender features of the determiners; in Leung & Williams (2006), the stimulus defect results from its use of pictures, which might arouse other visual processing with the same effect as implicit learning. The stimuli in Rebuschat & Williams' (2009) experiments, from German syntax, may be too close to those of English. In Chen et al. (2011), the stimuli themselves seemed good, but Chen classified them in Chinese as "structure": in fact, the stimuli, though in the position of determiner, were more likely to be elements of adjectives belonging to a semantic field in Chinese that is completely ideographic. More modifications, therefore, are expected in future experiments. It is expected that one of the new directions will call for stimuli closer to natural language in a natural context with semantic and pragmatic features taken into consideration.

Sequence

In experiments in the paradigm of sequence learning, subjects are usually meant to learn the order of elements in a sequence during a training course that asks them to react as fast as possible to the elements that appear. If a subject has learned the sequential feature of the elements, he needs much less time to decide the features of the elements coming up (Clegg et al., 1998). Nissen and Bullemer (1987), the first adopted sequence learning in clinical study of implicit learning, demonstrated the effect of learning without awareness of the sequential rules. Cleeremans and McClelland (1991) used a sequence of stimuli whose locations were determined by a finite-state grammar. Fu et al. (2008, 2010) adopted two second-order conditional sequences of numbers in a target-location task, in which the location of each number was determined by the locations of the previous two numbers. Implicit sequence learning was also studied frequently in psychological studies of aging and other issues as a window through which to look inside human brain function (Rieckmann & Bäckman, 2009).

Artificial sequences are popular in today's implicit learning studies, but they are more or less too artificial to attract subjects, or unable to consider various meanings. This makes those experiments more likely to be in the situation of a mathematic or logic test. Even specialists in mathematics and logic believe that language is what we depend on to think. We believe that more linguistic features, particularly semantic and pragmatic features, should be added to the sequences in the future.

Models of Exposing Subjects to Information

Now we discuss two crucial methodology problems in the exposure phase. The first problem is the balance of exposure: researchers are expected to be able to ensure an environment that helps implicit learning happen while reducing the probability that implicit learning becomes explicit. That is to say, any break in the balance of exposure, too much or too little, would render the experiments questionable. The second problem is the control of attention allocation. As we discussed in Section 3.1, psychological presuppositions about attention are the theoretical foundation upon which researchers depend to design their training course. Attention and awareness are two inseparable sides of the same coin (Carr & Curran, 1994; James, 1890; Posner, 1994). Discussing the development of knowledge, Schmidt (2001) said, "perhaps the only role for attention is that, presumably, at least the crucial evidence that triggers changes in the unconscious system must be attended." That is to say, in clinical experiments, researchers need to control any kind of attention to implicit features, to reduce all likelihood of arousing attention to implicit features, or even to try to distract subjects' attention from implicit features. In terms of these two problems, we can see the strengths and the weaknesses of the most commonly adopted exposure paradigms.

Chiefly, there are four kinds of exposure paradigms: (1) implicit goal not mentioned + activities connected to implicit features; (2) explicit goal + explicit goal training + activities connected to implicit features + implicit goal not mentioned; (3) explicit goal + explicit goal training + implicit goal not mentioned; (4) only stimuli + implicit goal not mentioned.

Most sequence learning studies belong to the first type (Clegg et al., 1998; Cleeremans & McClelland, 1991; Nissen & Bullemer, 1987; Rieckmann & Bäckman, 2009): subjects are not told anything about the existence of rules, but only asked to react to questions as by pressing a fixed key when seeing an element or to memorize sequences in order. These kinds of inductive activities, however, are very likely to lead attention to orders and bring about the construction of hypotheses about sequence. For example, a person who had taken GRE test would easily tend to try to find rules in an exposure like of the one used by Fu et al. (2008). Likewise, clinical studies following the design of Reber (1967) which based on sequential rules might fall also this kind of trap.

Paradigms 2 and 3 have become popular since Williams (2004) adopted paradigm 3 in his experiment about implicit learning of a four-determiner-artificial grammar. Both Williams (2004) and Chen et al. (2011), which replicated models of Williams (2004), asked subjects to study four determiners' explicit features without mentioning anything about the implicit features of the stimuli. Between Williams (2004) and Chen et al. (2011), Leung & Williams (2006) replicated Williams (2004) by following Paradigm 2, adding activities about implicit features but still not mentioning the implicit goal. They used pictures to help subjects to build the implicit connection between the target words and the implicit features by asking them to decide whether the objects are in the pictures were near or far. This activity was connected strongly with the implicit feature in that experiments that targeted words also functioned as determining "near" and "far". In Paradigm 2, activities with connection to the implicit features might easily draw subjects' attention to implicit features, leading them to form hypotheses. Though the later debriefing still gave no obvious sign that hypotheses were formed, we are still not sure that the subjects knew about the existence of their subconscious hypotheses. We argue, however, that both Paradigms 2 and 3 seem more reasonable than Paradigm 1, because they set up an explicit goal to attract subjects' attention away from implicit features; and training about explicit features may leave subjects no room in attention recourse to be aware of implicit features. Would the paradigm work in the way the researchers expect? We doubt it, since to experimental subjects training is a passive way to obtain knowledge, and some of them, very weak in passive learning, might be inclined instead to explore knowledge by themselves. In this way, explicit training would fail as a distracter; a better way to attract subjects might be to let them allocate their attention to explicit features initially, by presenting more meaning-focused tasks in text form.

Paradigm 4 has been used more commonly in computational models (Elman, 1990; Perruchet & Vinter, 1998; Sun, 2002). Though computational models have proven the implicit learning ability of computer programs, we still wish to ask how one can determine whether a computational model provides a good explanation of human learning, a thing which is so complicated and multi-determined (Cleeremans & Dienes, 2008).

Models of Testing Implicit Learning

In this section, we discuss three main measures used in testing the effect of subjects' implicit learning: (1) classical tests, (2) SRT, and (3) measures in computational model.

Classical tests are the ones adopted very widely by researchers in clinical studies of implicit learning. Commonly, they test only students' accuracy of judgment on the use of implicit learning. For example, in clinical experiments with artificial grammars and sequences as stimuli, subjects' knowledge of the artificial rules or sequential rules was tested by their accuracy rate in picking out elements conforming to the rules from new strings shown to them as testing materials (e.g. Chen et al., 2011; Dienes & Altmann, 1997; Reber 1967; Wan et al., 2008; Williams, 2004). There are still a considerable number of experiments adopting the classical test model with modification. For example, Wan et al. (2008) added familiarity rating into tests; Kinder & Shanks (2003) added visual noise and string movements in their AGL experiment. These types of tests, however, would give subjects hints, or they might draw subjects' attention to implicit features, which would make test results less reliable.

Serial reaction time measurement results are considered more convincing than classical ones, since they allow retrieval cues observed when subjects take tests. Usually two facets of learning effects are recorded: accuracy rate and reaction time on test items (e.g. Cleeremans & McClelland, 1991; Clegg et al., 1998; Jiménez et al., 1996; Leung & Williams, 2006; Nissen & Bullemer, 1987). To prove that the results of reaction time reflects qualities of implicit learning, both controlled or grammatical items and violation or ungrammatical items are randomly distributed and tested in the test (Leung & Williams, 2006). If the reaction time of controlled items is significantly shorter than that of the violation items, the target implicit knowledge is thought to be learned. Whether it is learned implicitly depends on result measures of awareness, which we will discuss in the next section. Leung & Williams (2006) designed an artificial grammar expressing meaning as "near or far". The test section asked students to point out whether the phrases containing "near" or "far" elements of the artificial grammar conformed to the picture on the screen. If a phrase containing an element of "far" was shown under a picture whose target object was in the foreground, then it was a violation item, and the reaction time to it should have been longer than that of control items. The design in Leung & Williams (2006) was better, but it still left a future step to be more scientific and convincing: to add another dimension to distinguish explicit knowledge from implicit knowledge, rather than only learned from unlearned. How do we make this move? More experiments and researches need to be done. For example, researchers could conduct another experiment immediately after with a small group from the same subjects to find a time scale for an explicit reaction and an implicit reaction, and then do their analysis of implicit learning.

Another sub-model of RT was developed by adding familiarity as a variable to measure memory strength (e.g. Shanks & Perruchet, 2002; Shanks et al., 2003). Researchers following this model take the assumption that greater familiarity or priming effects would lead to faster reaction, thus, the test items that need less time are considered to be more familiar to subjects and are more likely to belong to the learned group. This assumption was proved by standard signal detection theory models for recognition judgments (Pike, 1973; Ratcliff & Murdock, 1976). However, if we do take measurement like this in a clinical study of implicit learning, we must admit firstly that it was graded rather than dichotomous between implicit and explicit (Cleeremans, 1997). Then the conclusions made by researchers under this model could be trapped in an embarrassing state.

Models of tests in computational studies usually focus on measuring the learnability of the computer programs. Most of the results are positive (e.g. Cleeremans & McClelland, 1991; Perruchet & Vinter, 1998; Sun, 2002), however, it is the design of a computational model which might put its result into doubt. Shanks (2005) argued that between two most dominant computational model of implicit learning, symbol processing models (O'Brien & Opie, 1999; Shanks, 1997) were more successful than distributed models (Dienes et al., 1999; Kinder & Shanks, 2001), since the former was able to give information to distinguish implicit representational state from explicit ones. Until now, however, experiments using distributed models have seemed more successful in learning, which might delay the development of symbol processing models.

Measuring Subjects' State of Awareness

This is usually the last phase of a clinical experiment on implicit learning, which unveils the subjects' awareness states. It is used to find whether the subjects learned the target implicit features implicitly or explicitly. The measurement models of awareness tests enjoy much more attention from researchers than models of the other phases discussed above, because of the join-in researchers in psychology in the literature. Models have been updated and renewed from time to time, and new models are published almost whenever new discoveries or related inventions come up. Researchers (Rebuschat, 2008) essentially divide the awareness measurement models into three groups. Table 1 presents a clear classification of these models.

Summary

We identify the five key procedures that are necessary to an implicit learning experiment. For each procedure, we had double-way analyses: finding flaws of a type of procedure's design and comparing different designs of different experiments. By doing this, we gave detailed comments of each procedure of the framework. Table 2 summarizes the main message of our comments.

CONCLUSION AND FUTURE DIRECTIONS

Merikle & Reingold (1991: 226) argue strongly that one measure is hardly enough to identify learning know

Table 1. Summary of awareness measurements models.

Model	Sub-model	Researches	Techniques	Strength	Weakness
Verbal reports	Free reporting	Abrams & Reber, 1988; Dienes et al., 1991; Leung & Williams, 2006; Payne, 1994; Williams, 2004	Interview; open questions	Subjects can say what they want; sounds like with no information omitted.	Dissociation between acquired knowledge and its verbalizability; insensitive and incomplete measure of awareness;
	Closed questionnaire	Berry & Broadbent, 1984; Broadbent, 1977	Multiple choice	Focus on the state features of subjects wanted by the research	
Objective test	Offline objective test	Holender, 1986; Stadler, 1998	Forced-choice test, or free generation task	Providing retrieval cues; more sensitive to conscious knowledge.	Lack of exclusivity; underestimating the influence of unconscious knowledge
	Computational objective test	O'Brien & Opie, 1999; Shanks, 1997	Symbol-processing system to distinct implicit and explicit knowledge	Completely objective and self-controlled	Not widely used and still under the way of polishing
Subjective test		Chen et al., 2011; Dienes, 2008; Dienes & Berry, 1997; Dienes & Scott, 2005	Confidence ratings; source attributions; binary confidence technique; SDT measure of sensitivity;	Exclusivity; sensitivity; more easily to absorb scientific or new techniques	Difficulty in selection of the type of confidence scale; lack of a standardized procedure

Note: Thanks are given to Berry & Dienes (1993), Dienes (2008), Dienes & Scott (2005), Merikle et al. (2001), Reingold & Merikle (1990), and Shanks & St. John (1994), and special thanks go to Rebuschat (2008), from which we get important information for this table.

Table 2. Summary of clinical procedure related findings in implicit learning.

Procedure	Models	Researches	Format	Comments & suggestions
Theoretical assumptions	Attention assumption	Chen et al., 2011; Leung & Williams, 2006; Williams, 2004; Williams, 2005	Not clear in most of researches.	Assumptions of each procedure had better be discussed.
Clinical stimuli	Artificial grammar	Starter: Reber, 1967; Variants: Berry & Dienes, 1993; Leung & Williams, 2006; Pothos, 2007; Reber, 1989; Shanks, 2005; Wan et al., 2008; Williams, 2004;	Computerized/pen & paper	More interesting to reduce subjects' nerve; more close to nature language in nature context with semantic and pragmatic features taken into consideration
	Sequence strings	Starter: Nissen and Bullemer, 1987; Variants: Cleeremans & McClelland, 1991; Clegg et al., 1998; Fu et al., 2008, 2010;	Computerized	
Exposure	Implicit goal not mentioned + activities with connection to implicit features	Clegg et al., 1998; Cleeremans & McClelland, 1991; Nissen & Bullemer, 1987; Rieckman & Bäckman, 2009	Computerized/pen & paper	Researchers need to ensure no attention to implicit feature, to reduce any kind of probability that might arouse attention to implicit features, or even to try to distract attention from implicit features; but all should be done with subjects in an initiative state.
	Explicit goal + explicit goal training + activities with connection to implicit features + implicit goal not mentioned	Leung & Williams, 2006	Computerized/pen & paper	
	Explicit goal + explicit goal training + implicit goal not mentioned	Williams (2004), and Chen et al. (2011)	Computerized/pen & paper	
	Only stimuli + implicit goal not mentioned	Elman, 1990; Perruchet & Vinter, 1998; Sun, 2002	Computerized/pen & paper	
Learning testing	Classical test	Chen et al., 2011; Dienes & Altmann, 1997; Reber, 1967; Wan et al., 2008; Williams, 2004	Computerized/pen & paper	Providing retrieval cues; avoiding being hints or drawing attention to implicit feature
	SRT	Cleeremans & McClelland, 1991; Clegg et al., 1998; Jimenez et al., 1996; Leung & Williams, 2006; Nissen & Bullemer, 1987	Computerized	Testing items should be more scientific avoid being hints or drawing attention to implicit feature; trying to distinct explicit knowledge form implicit one
	Computational model	Perruchet & Vinter, 1998; Sun, 2002	Computerized	Trying in symbol processing models

Awareness states	Verbal reports	Abrams & Reber, 1988; Berry & Broadbent, 1984; Broadbent, 1977; Dienes et al., 1991; Leung & Williams, 2006; Payne, 1994; Williams, 2004	Computerized/pen & paper/ recording	Reducing dissociation between acquired knowledge and its verbalizability; improving insensitivity to awareness
	Objective tests	Holender, 1986; O'Brien & Opie, 1999; Shanks, 1997; Stadler, 1998	Computerized/pen & paper	Increasing exclusivity; improving sensitivity to unconscious knowledge
	Subjective tests	Chen et al., 2011; Dienes, 2008; Dienes & Berry, 1997; Dienes & Scott, 2005	Computerized/pen & paper	Finding a proper and standardized confidence scale

ledge and awareness. This is true. It is exactly why we do need to maintain a whole framework to ensure that, although one step has a flaw, the steps before or after can make up for it. This is like what a food security department does when a pig becoming pieces of pork in meat stores: though the farm fails to find disease in one pig, the butchering factory may be still able to stop the pig from entering the market; if the butchering factory fails, the quarantine still has a chance. Of course, the framework of clinical experiments cannot be as standardized as that set up by official departments, because even today any tasks designed are not process-pure and completely exclusive, since a clear and comprehensive theory of awareness has not yet settled. However, at least a framework can be set up as guidance and advice for researchers to avoid design flaws or omissions. That is what we endeavor: to conduct a detailed comparison and search for a great amount of literature, though the comments and suggestions we bring forward still await empirical verification in which implicit learning can be studied exclusively and comprehensively.

Our recommendations to future studies on implicit learning are as follows: (1) developing a more valid control on attention allocation to ensure implicit learning to take place; (2) using materials or stimuli closer to natural language in natural context with semantic and pragmatic features taken into consideration to gain more understanding about human implicit learning in real situation; (3) adopting or developing new techniques to increase sensitivity to implicit learning and explicit learning; (4) allowing researchers in computational simulation fields still to have opportunities in symbol-processing models; (5) urging more efforts in online researches using ERP or fMRI technologies; (6) exploring implicit learning in second language acquisition.

In conclusion, by furthering a comprehensive understanding of procedural mechanisms that contribute to improvement in research designs, we may be able to gain a better understanding of implicit learning. In turn, new understanding gains may contribute to new suppositions that later help design more effective empirical studies. Thus, even though theoretical and empirical difficulties are far from resolution in the near future, there is an unprecedented opportunity for advancing our understanding of implicit learning.

REFERENCES

1. Abrams, M., & Reber, A. S. (1988). Implicit Learning: Robustness in the Face of Psychiatric Disorders. Journal of Psycholinguistic Research, 17, 425-439.
2. Berry, D. C., & Broadbent, D. (1984). On the Relationship between Task Performance and Associated Verbalisable Knowledge. Quarterly Journal of Experimental Psychology, 36, 209-231. http://dx.doi.org/10.1080/14640748408402156
3. Berry, D. C., & Dienes, Z. (1993). Implicit Learning: Theoretical and Empirical Issues. Hove, UK: Lawrence Erlbaum.
4. Broadbent, D. (1977). Levels, Hierarchies and the Locus of Control. Quarterly Journal of Experimental Psychology, 29, 181-201. http://dx.doi.org/10.1080/14640747708400596
5. Carr, T. H., & Curran, T. (1994). Cognitive Factors in Learning about Structured Sequences: Applications to Syntax. Studies in Second Language Acquisition, 16, 205-230. http://dx.doi.org/10.1017/S0272263100012882
6. Chen, G., Tang, Z., Yang, & Dienes (2011). Unconscious Structural Knowledge of Form-meaning Connections. Consciousness and Cognition, 20, 1751-1760. http://dx.doi.org/10.1016/j.concog.2011.03.003
7. Chun, M. M., & Jiang, Y. (1999). Top-Down Attentional Guidance Based on Implicit Learning of Visual Covariation. Psychological Science, 10, 360-365. http://dx.doi.org/10.1111/1467-9280.00168
8. Cleeremans, A. (1997). Principles for Implicit Learning. In D. Berry (Ed.), How Implicit Is Implicit Learning? (pp. 196-234). Oxford: Oxford University Press. http://dx.doi.org/10.1093/acprof:oso/9780198523512.003.0008
9. Cleeremans, A., Destrebecqz, A., & Boyer, M. (1998). Implicit Learning: News from the Front. Trends in Cognitive Sciences, 2, 406-416. http://dx.doi.org/10.1016/S1364-6613(98)01232-7
10. Cleeremans, A., & Dienes, Z. (2008). Computational Models of Implicit Learning. In R. Sun (Ed.), Cambridge Handbook of Computational Psychology (pp. 396-421). Cambridge: Cambridge University Press. http://dx.doi.org/10.1017/CBO9780511816772.018
11. Cleeremans, A., & McClelland, J. L. (1991). Learning the Structure of Event Sequences. Journal of Experimental Psychology: General, 120, 235-253. http://dx.doi.org/10.1037/0096-3445.120.3.235
12. Clegg, B. A., DiGirolamo, G. J., & Keele, S. W. (1998). Sequence

Learning. Trends in Cognitive Sciences, 2, 275-281. http://dx.doi.org/10.1016/S1364-6613(98)01202-9

13. Dienes, Z. (1992). Connectionist and Memory-Array Models of Artificial Grammar Learning. Cognitive Science, 16, 41-79. http://dx.doi.org/10.1207/s15516709cog1601_2

14. Dienes, Z. (2008). Subjective Measures of Unconscious Knowledge. Progress in Brain Research, 168, 49-64. http://dx.doi.org/10.1016/S0079-6123(07)68005-4

15. Dienes, Z., & Altmann, G. (1997). Transfer of Implicit Knowledge across Domains? How Implicit and How Abstract? In D. Berry (Ed.), How Implicit Is Implicit Learning? (pp. 107-123). Oxford: Oxford University Press.http://dx.doi.org/10.1093/acprof:oso/9780198523512.003.0005

16. Dienes, Z., Altmann, G. T. M., & Gao, S. J. (1999). Mapping across Domains without Feedback: A Neural Network Model of Transfer of Implicit Knowledge. Cognitive Science, 23, 53-82. http://dx.doi.org/10.1207/s15516709cog2301_3

17. Dienes, Z., & Berry, D. C. (1997). Implicit Learning: Below the Subjective Threshold. Psychonomic Bulletin and Review, 4, 3-23. http://dx.doi.org/10.3758/BF03210769

18. Dienes, Z., Broadbent, D. E., & Berry, D. C. (1991). Implicit and Explicit Knowledge Bases in Artificial Grammar Learning. Journal of Experimental Psychology: Learning, Memory, & Cognition, 17, 875-882. http://dx.doi.org/10.1037/0278-7393.17.5.875

19. Dienes, Z., & Scott, R. (2005). Measuring Unconscious Knowledge: Distinguishing Structural Knowledge and Judgment Knowledge. Psychological Research, 69, 338-351.http://dx.doi.org/10.1007/s00426-004-0208-3

20. Elman, J. L. (1990). Finding Structure in Time. Cognitive Science, 14, 179-211.http://dx.doi.org/10.1207/s15516709cog1402_1

21. Estes, W. K. (1957). Toward a Statistical Theory of Learning. Psychological Review, 57, 94-107. http://dx.doi.org/10.1037/h0058559

22. Frensch, P. A., & Rünger, D. (2003). Implicit Learning. Current Directions in Psychological Science, 12, 13-18. http://dx.doi.org/10.1111/1467-8721.01213

23. Fu, Q., Dienes, Z., & Fu, X. (2010). Can Unconscious Knowledge Allow Control in Sequence Learning? Consciousness & Cognition, 19, 462-475.http://dx.doi.org/10.1016/j.concog.2009.10.001

24. Fu, Q., Fu, X., & Dienes, Z. (2008). Implicit Sequence Learning and

Conscious Awareness. Consciousness and Cognition, 17, 185-202.http://dx.doi.org/10.1016/j.concog.2007.01.007

25. Hintzmann, D. (1986). "Schema Abstraction" in a Multiple-Trace Memory Model. Psychological Review, 93, 411-428. http://dx.doi.org/10.1037/0033-295X.93.4.411

26. Holender, D. (1986). Semantic Activation without Conscious Identification in Dichotic Listening, Parafoveal Vision, and Visual Masking: A Survey and Appraisal. Behavioral and Brain Sciences, 9, 1-23. http://dx.doi.org/10.1017/S0140525X00021269

27. James, W. (1890). Principles of Psychology. New York: Holt.http://dx.doi.org/10.1037/11059-000

28. Jiménez, L., Méndez, C., & Cleeremans, A. (1996). Comparing Direct and Indirect Measures of Implicit Learning. Journal of Experimental Psychology: Learning, Memory, and Cognition, 22, 948-969. http://dx.doi.org/10.1037/0278-7393.22.4.948

29. Kinder, A., & Shanks, D. R. (2001). Amnesia and the Declarative/Nondeclarative Distinction: A Recurrent Network Model of Classification, Recognition, and Repetition Priming. Journal of Cognitive Neuroscience, 13, 648-669.http://dx.doi.org/10.1162/089892901750363217

30. Kinder, A., & Shanks, D. R. (2003). Neuropsychological Dissociations between Priming and Recognition: A Single-System Connectionist Account. Psychological Review, 110, 728-744.http://dx.doi.org/10.1037/0033-295X.110.4.728

31. Leung, J., & Williams, J. (2006). Implicit Learning of Form-Meaning Connections. In R. Sun, & N. Miyake (Eds.), Proceedings of the Annual Meeting of the Cognitive Science Society (pp. 465-470). Mahwah, NJ: Lawrence Erlbaum Associates.

32. Merikle, P. M., & Reingold, E. M. (1991). Comparing Direct (Explicit) and Indirect (Implicit) Measures to Study Unconscious Memory. Journal of Experimental Psychology: Learning, Memory and Cognition, 17, 224-233. http://dx.doi.org/10.1037/0278-7393.17.2.224

33. Merikle, P. M., Smilek, D., & Eastwood, J. D. (2001). Perception without Awareness: Perspectives from Cognitive Psychology. Cognition, 79, 115-134.http://dx.doi.org/10.1016/S0010-0277(00)00126-8

34. Millward, R. B., & Reber, A. S. (1968). Event-Recall in Probability Learning. Journal of Verbal Learning and Verbal Behavior, 7, 980-989. http://dx.doi.org/10.1016/S0022-5371(68)80056-8

35. Nissen, M. J., & Bullemer, P. (1987). Attentional Requirement of

Learning: Evidence from Performance Measures. Cognitive Psychology, 19, 1-32. http://dx.doi.org/10.1016/0010-0285(87)90002-8

36. O'Brien, G., & Opie, J. (1999). A Connectionist Theory of Phenomenal Experience. Behavioral and Brain Sciences, 22, 127-196.http://dx.doi.org/10.1017/S0140525X9900179X

37. Payne, J. W. (1994). Thinking Aloud: Insights into Information Processing. Psychological Science, 5, 241-248. http://dx.doi.org/10.1111/j.1467-9280.1994.tb00620.x

38. Perruchet, P., & Vinter, A. (1998). PARSER: A Model for Word Segmentation. Journal of Memory and Language, 39, 246-263. http://dx.doi.org/10.1006/jmla.1998.2576

39. Pike, R. (1973). Response Latency Models for Signal Detection. Psychological Review, 80, 53-68. http://dx.doi.org/10.1037/h0033871

40. Posner, M. I. (1994). Attention in Cognitive Neuroscience: An Overview. In M. Gazzaniga (Ed.), The Cognitive Neurosciences (pp. 615-624). Cambridge, MA: MIT Press.

41. Pothos, E. M. (2007). Theories of Artificial Grammar Learning. Psychological Bulletin, 133, 227-244. http://dx.doi.org/10.1037/0033-2909.133.2.227

42. Ratcliff, R., & Murdock, B. B. (1976). Retrieval Processes in Recognition Memory. Psychological Review, 83, 190-214. http://dx.doi.org/10.1037/0033-295X.83.3.190

43. Reber, A. S. (1967). Implicit Learning of artificial Grammars. Journal of Verbal Learning and Verbal Behavior, 6, 855-863. http://dx.doi.org/10.1016/S0022-5371(67)80149-X

44. Reber, A. S. (1989). Implicit Learning and Tacit Knowledge. Journal of Experimental Psychology: General, 118, 219-235. http://dx.doi.org/10.1037/0096-3445.118.3.219

45. Rebuschat, P. (2008). Implicit Learning of Natural Language Syntax. Unpublished Doctoral Dissertation, Cambridge: University of Cambridge.

46. Rebuschat, P. & Williams, J. (2009). Implicit Learning of Word Order. In N. A. Taatgen & H. van Rijn (Eds.), Proceedings of the 31st Annual Conference of the Cognitive Science Society. Austin, TX: Cognitive Science Society.

47. Rieckmann, A & Bäckman, L. (2009). Implicit Learning in Aging: Extant Patterns and New Directions. Neuropsychology Review, 19, 490-503. http://dx.doi.org/10.1007/s11065-009-9117-y

48. Reingold, E. M., & Merikle, P. M. (1990). On the Interrelatedness of

Theory and Measurement in the Study of Unconscious Processes. Mind and Language, 5, 9-28.http://dx.doi.org/10.1111/j.1468-0017.1990.tb00150.x

49. Rohmeier, M., & Cross, I. (2010). Narmour's Principles Affect Implicit Learning of Melody. In Demorest et al. (Eds.), Proceedings of the 11th International Conference on Music Perception and Cognition (ICMPC 2010), Seattle, 23-27 August 2010.

50. Schmidt, R. (2001). Attention. In P. Robinson (Ed.), Cognition and Second Language Instruction (pp. 3-32). Cambridge: Cambridge University Press.http://dx.doi.org/10.1017/CBO9781139524780.003

51. Searle, J. R. (1992). The Rediscovery of the Mind. Cambridge, MA: MIT Press.

52. Shanks, D. R. (1997). Distributed Representations and Implicit Knowledge: A Brief Introduction. In K. Lamberts & D. Shanks (Eds.), Knowledge, Concepts and Categories (pp. 197-214). Hove: Psychology Press.

53. Shanks, D. R. (2005). Implicit Learning. In K. Lamberts & R. Goldstone (Eds.), Handbook of Cognition (pp. 202-220). London: Sage. http://dx.doi.org/10.4135/9781848608177.n8

54. Shanks, D. R., & Perruchet, P. (2002). Dissociation between Priming and Recognition in the Expression of Sequential Knowledge. Psychonomic Bulletin and Review, 9, 362-367.http://dx.doi.org/10.3758/BF03196294

55. Shanks, D. R., & St. John, M. F. (1994). Characteristics of Dissociable Human Learning Systems. Behavioral and Brain Sciences, 17, 367-447. http://dx.doi.org/10.1017/S0140525X00035032

56. Shanks, D. R., Wilkinson, L., & Channon, S. (2003). Relationship between Priming and Recognition in Deterministic and Probabilistic Sequence Learning. Journal of Experimental Psychology: Learning, Memory, and Cognition, 29, 248-261.http://dx.doi.org/10.1037/0278-7393.29.2.248

57. Stadler, M. A., & Roediger III, H. L. (1998). The Question of Awareness in Research on Implicit Learning. In M. A. Stadler & P. A. Frensch (Eds.), Handbook of Implicit Learning (pp. 105-132). Thousand Oaks, CA: Sage.

58. Sun, R. (2002). Duality of the Mind. Mahwah, NJ: Lawrence Erlbaum.

59. Wan, L. L., Dienes, Z., & Fu, X. L. (2008). Intentional Control Based on Familiarity in Artificial Grammar Learning. Consciousness & Cognition, 17, 1209-1218.http://dx.doi.org/10.1016/j.concog.2008.06.007

60. Williams, J. N. (2004). Implicit Learning of Form-Meaning Connections. In B. VanPatten, J. Williams, S. Rott, & M. Overstreet (Eds.), Form-Meaning Connections in Second Language Acquisition (pp. 203-218). Mahwah, NJ: Erlbaum.
61. Williams, J. N. (2005). Learning without Awareness. Studies in Second Language Acquisition, 27, 269-304. http://dx.doi.org/10.1017/S0272263105050138
62. Williams, J. N. (2009). Implicit Learning. In W. C. Ritchie, & T. K. Bhatia (Eds.), New Handbook of Second Language Acquisition (pp. 319-353). Bingley: Emerald Group Publishing Ltd.

Chapter 4

WHY ASYNCHRONOUS COMPUTER-MEDIATED COMMUNICATION (ACMC) IS A POWERFUL TOOL FOR LANGUAGE LEARNING

Mark Brooke

Department of Linguistics and Modern Languages, Hong Kong Institute of Education, Hong Kong, China

ABSTRACT

Tertiary institutions are increasingly using online virtual environments such as Blackboard to upload course content for students. However, there is still limited usage of the online blogging and discussion tools. This study describes the language used by tertiary students involved in blogging and discussions online. It also demonstrates learning processes observed through the interactions of participants over time. Findings suggest that this unique discourse mode is a potentially powerful tool for language learning.

INTRODUCTION

Gustafson, Hodgson and Tickner (2004: p. 5) state:

"We would like to stress the importance of discourse analysis as a tool/method for looking closer at dialogue patterns when researching networked learning environments and trying to explain the possible failures or successes of such environments."

By successes, the authors refer to the kind of learning that takes place in an online asynchronous environment. This research has analysed the discourse from thirty online forums, consisting of around one-hundred and fifty postings (ranging from fifty to three hundred words in length), to present the English language used by groups of advanced learners of English as a second language and to link this language with processes of learning identified online. It is hoped that this study describes why the online asynchronous learning environment is an effective one for learning English as an additional language. The first part of this article "SLA theories of language learning and the potential of ACMC" examines language learning theory based on Second Language Acquisition (SLA).

This provides the conceptual basis of the study.

The second part "processes of learning" uses empirical evidence to demonstrate 2 types of social learning identified. These are mutually-constructing meanings and incidental learning.

The third part of this article "ACMC language product" is a description of the linguistic diversity identified in this researcher's second language learning context. This section reveals that the ACMC is a uniquely rich language environment where differing text formats appear and spoken and written discourse as well as differing tenors can cohabite easily, even to the extent of coinciding within clauses.

CONCEPTUAL BASIS OF THE STUDY: SLA THEORIES OF LANGUAGE LEARNING AND THE POTENTIAL OF THE ACMC

Social and Deeper Learning

It is commonly known that Vygotskian (1962, 1978) premises focus primarily on the social construct of the human consciousness. Cognitive language growth is embedded in the dynamics of social interaction. Consequently, learners are rarely isolated, encapsulated knowers or doers and benefit more in the field of second language learning through social intercourse to enable them to use the language they learn in context. In addition, and according to constructivist thinking, groups can construct meanings together through negotiation and reach higher levels of consciousness leading to deeper learning than isolated individuals. A significant element to these notions is that the need for language retrieval for communicative purposes facilitates the learning of that language. This is inextricably linked with the notions of "Communicative Language Teaching' (see Howatt, 1984: 279). Another key element is that social learning enables the language learner to learn pragmatic uses of language or communicative functions such as agreement or persuasion, evaluation or argumentation. It was Wilkins (1976) who first published on this aspect of meaning-based syllabi coining the term of "notional syllabuses".

Noticing Language

Van Lier (1996: p. 11) states:

"To learn something new one must first notice it. This noticing is an awareness of its existence, obtained and enhanced by paying attention to it. Paying attention is focusing one's consciousness, or pointing one's perceptual powers in the right direction, and making mental 'energy' available for processing".

This "noticing" followed by a more focused "paying attention" encapsulates what Schmidt (1994) points out as two of the main functions of the intra-mental consciousness (in contrast to the inter-mental) in Vygotskian terminology: attention (noticeing and focusing on information) and intention (learning something intentionally rather than unintentionally while doing something else). In other words, learners will normally only learn a linguistic item when they are ready to do so, when their mental lexicon is able to absorb it. For second language educators, it is thus quintessential to seek to facilitate these processes by offering a communicative environment for their students which is language-rich. In other words, second language learners should be exposed to a variety of text types in both written and spoken mode, offering a wide range of language along the discourse mode and tenor continuum (Halliday, 1975, 2004). As Hatch (1996: p. 209) posits coherence in talk and writing is attained via overall system constraints on communication, by calling up generic scripts that fit the communication situation, by knowing the structure of speech events, and by recognizing the ways information may be formatted in various rhetorical genres.

Risk-Taking

Krashen (1982) refers to affective barriers to second language acquisition. These are commonly understood as the areas involving feelings, emotions, mood and temperament. It is believed that these elements are greatly reduced in the ACMWC environment (Lewis and Allan, 2005: p. 45). This is in part due to the fact that access can be closed but is particularly due to the discourse mode of asynchronous written communication (ACMWC). With asynchronicity, students have time to reflect upon and formulate their thoughts before expressing them and engaging in interaction. In contrast to spontaneous and timebound synchronous interaction, studies have revealed that this genre of communication enables students to produce a greater quantity and better quality of discourse than in an oral classroom (Ortega, 1997; Peters, 2000). They also lead to more equal participation between students (Warschauer, 1996) and ultimately deeper learning. In this way, it is suggested that students might be more absorbed in the tasks and less concerned with linguistic errors or deviances from the norm

THE STUDY

Material and Methods

The research objective was to:
- Analyze how an online environment's e-journaling (blogging) tool and forum tool might enhance groups of 3rd year Chinese BEd pre-service teachers' English as a second language learning capabilities. To meet this objective, the following questions were asked:
- What processes of language learning can be observed online? What language structures (genre types, language structures, and interactional patterns) emerge through language use online between participants?

Context

The research was conducted as part of the pre-service teacher education field experience practicum at the Hong Kong Institute of Education. Students are mother tongue Cantonese speakers who are training to be English language teachers in primary and secondary state schools. Students are placed in local state schools for 6 weeks during their 3rd year practicum. They are expected to manage and deliver English as a additional language courses to their students. The online asynchronous forums were set up primarily as a support line for these student teachers during practicum. By using the blogging and discussion forums, trainees could receive support from this researcher who was their mentor as well as support from each other by sharing their experiences online. Thus, the language production and learning that took place was observed as it emerged through communication. At no stage were participants informed that the site had been set up for language learning. In addition, the language analyses performed and described in this article were conducted at the end of the case studies. Thus, this researcher did not intentionally promote the language use described online. Rather, the data were observed through postcase study analysis. Further, participants were instructed to use the sites independently, without aid from native or near-native language users. Participants were fully aware that the use of the sites was not part of an assessment cycle rendering it a platform for natural, fluent language not requiring thoroughly proof-read postings.

Participants

Three case studies of eight weeks were conducted. Each case study consisted of eight third-year participants of a four-year BEd (EL) degree from both Hong Kong and mainland China aged between 20 and 25. There was a mix of male and female students aged between 20 and 25. Pseudonyms of participants are used.

Design

The research was performed by this researcher in his capacity as teacher educator—researcher using action research methodology. Action research as Lewin (1946: p. 206) posits, involves:

"A spiral of steps, each of which is composed of a circle of planning, action, and fact-finding about the result of the action".

Through experimentation and multiple observation of empirical evidence, data were collated in research observational note forms. Thus findings were constructed and continually refined over time. The virtual learning environment used was Blackboard and participants had closed access to the sites, offering some privacy as only those registered could write about their experiences and read those of their peers. This was believed to be a low risk environment to facilitate trainee critical and creative thinking as well as cooperative and collaborative learning. This prediction was substantiated at the end of each case study as participant interviewees reported that they were happy to share their views online.

PROCEDURE

Phase 1

A welcoming announcement was sent out to participants telling them that the site would be available for support and inviting them to introduce themselves online and to share any views about the practicum experience to follow. Participants were at no stage told that their language for blogging or discussion would be analyzed.

Phase 2

After the first week of teaching, participants began posting their weekly blogs.

Phase 3

Each week a new forum was added to the sites and this was used for weekly reports and discussions. This researcher acted as online moderator inviting participation and facilitating interaction if required.

Phase 4

At the end of each case study, threads were collected for textual analysis and research findings written up and evaluated.

RESULTS

In this section, the processes of language learning observed are presented. These processes relate to the SLA characteristics noted above e.g., social and deeper learning, noticing, and risk taking.

Processes of Learning

Mutually Constructing Meanings

Student A: "I wonder whether it is necessary for teachers to write lesson plans for EVERY SINGLE lesson. I know that it is helpful to spend time preparing learning materials for students and to plan beforehand the objectives and structure of lessons. Yet, is it a must to put down detailed steps and the time each step takes in a lesson plan"?

Student B: "I don't think for teachers who are already overwhelmed with their overloading work, writing lesson plans for every single lesson is not necessary. However, it is important for us—student teachers—to write enough lesson plans, so that we can learn to carefully plan what to do in a lesson, see whether it works out and reflect on how to improve it for the next time. I guess this is just a process every teacher has to go through. Once we feel that we don't need to write it anymore, we don't have to write it. But I guess it would still be good for experienced teacher to write some lesson plans from time to time for lesson improvements".

Student C: "I agree with Tian that we, student teachers, should write lesson plans in the preliminary stage of our teaching. Every time we revise our lesson plans based on our accumulated experience, we are making progress".

In this excerpt of interaction, it is possible to see the language construction process. The first student commences the topic of discussion. Then student B replies. Student B's response is in non-academic language. In contrast, student C encapsulates what B discusses by defining B's meanings: "preliminary stage" is used for "student teachers"; "revise" is used for "reflecting on how to improve it"; and "accumulated experience" is used for "a process every teacher has to go through". All of these terms used by student C are improving the conceptual and academic content of B's responses by summarizing them or remodelling them to improve them. This makes the dialogue a construction zone. This is therefore a good example of how participants can learn from each other online for second language acquisition to occur. The language used by B was non-academic. In contrast, C's language was academic and B's noticing of these language items has been facilitated through communication. This is further discussed below as part of "incidental learning". In a way, this is a form of scaffolding language as C is helping to raise B's awareness of more complex ways of communicating the same ideas. This therefore reveals C's awareness of B's zone of proximal development. C is guiding B to use more complex language. Other examples of refining language or retuning it to teach it were continuously remarked during the case studies.

Incidental Learning

The following originates from a discussion on teaching reading in the secondary school classroom. The online interaction takes place over a period of 2 days.

Day 1

Trainee 1 states: "I got a big problem—students found the reading I gave them too difficult. I looked up the words on odd number pages for them and I went through the 1st paragraph with them together in class too but they still found it too difficult."

What follows then is a discussion between her and her trainer during which the trainer states:

Trainer: "You can pre-teach any crucial vocabulary initially and inform them that it's not necessary to comprehend every single word to enjoy the story. If the language is problematic, the text might be too difficult but there's no harm in trying the book out—why don't you should select 2 or 3 short extracts for students to read over the holiday and then go through those as a shared reading when you're back"?

Day 2

A previously vicarious participant adds to the dialogue:

Trainee 2: "I told students they didn't need to know all the words. I don't think they had thought about it before. Then I gave them the essential vocabulary and I read students a page of a graded reader of Birthday Girl" by Haruki Murakami. They said they liked it even though it was difficult. So it can help to tell them they don't need to know everything J".

Trainee 1 replies on the same day: "I could try a graded reader if the level is too difficult."

This is then rounded off by trainee 2, also on day 2, who states: "Good idea! Didn't think of telling you about graded readers"!

Trainee 1 has been guided to try out a new idea for reading instruction through her peer's postings. However, as the peer admits, the mention of a graded reader was not meant to be a learning point. In other words, in an online environment such as this, unplanned learning can occur. This particular example of learning is not at the word level but rather at the ideational level. As long as classroom practice is discussed between stakeholders, learning of this kind seems to be facilitated on a regular basis because issues are discussed which each member can relate to. Incidental learning at the word or word group level did occur also. In the excerpt above, the term accumulated experience was used by B in a later posting. This was then followed up by this researcher at the end of the case study. Participant B was asked if she was aware of the term prior to the study. She stated that she had not been and was not aware that she had used it either. When asked about her prior knowledge of collocations that co-exist with "experience" in this way, the participant answered that she might have used "growing" or "previous" but would not have used "accumulated". The fact that she did use the term "accumulated experience" in a later posting suggests therefore that this was an example of noticing language and, the fact that she was not aware that she had used it, suggests that she had learned it incidentally.

Language Variety Observed in the CMC Environment

In the following section, the author will provide a description of the language generated online by participants. If the processes of learning in Section 1 of the results occur frequently, the language used during communication is very important because it is part of the language that learners are learning through their interactions. The first observation presents the text structures used for communication. The tenor for these structures can be both informal and formal.

The Text Types Used for the Organization of the Discourse

This first data presentation will focus on the kinds of texts used for communication over the 3 case studies as well as the formulaic expressions that pertain to these text types. The CMC is most often formatted in letter form or report form. However, within these forms, it also contains narrative, personal recount or procedural texts. In addition, there is frequently a much more interactive conversational style of discourse with much shorter turns taken, use of smileys and other examples of phatic communion.

The letter format

Some users prefer to use informal letter writing styles. Others prefer more formal letter writing style. The following are salutations and closings observed:

Informal salutations: Hi everyone; Howdy; Hello everyone; Hiya all; Hi there.

Formal salutations: Dear + name; Dear + fellow classmates; Dear + fellow course mates; Dear all/Dear everyone

Informal closings: Best wishes; Best; Thank you; Isn't it interesting? Haha!; Hope it helps J; Talk to all of you later!; Will keep you updated on this; Can't think of anything more at the moment—I will keep you updated asap; How are you all going?^^; Interested to know what others in the group think?; Want to know what happens next? It's coming soon!; Tbc wk 3; Gd Rdgs.

Formal closings: I am looking forward to your suggestions and sharing; I'm looking forward to hearing from you; I hope these ideas are useful and I look forward to hearing other people's ideas.

The report format

A posting may also take a report format with a title such as "Struggling with teaching". This might then be followed by sub-headings e.g., Classroom observations; Teaching grammar etc. In this case, no salutation or closing is used as with the letter format.

The Writing Genres Used for Blog Postings

The letter or report format might be used as the structure of the text but the actual language used is most commonly based on genre types such as personal recounts/narrative descriptions or expository texts analyzing an issue of significance or an argumentative explaining and justifying someone's view on something.

The narrative genre

As with narrative constructions, there tends to be an "orientation": "I still find some problems with my class that I am worried about"; a problem: "my supporting teacher suggested to me that I should teach activity sheets in class as they do". They are repetitive drilling exercise L I am afraid that abandoning those activity sheets will offend my supporting teacher", a solution: I will try to negotiate with my supporting teacher later about this issue, and a Coda: "those are my reflections. I would like to hear your advice."

The expository genre

As with expository texts, there tends to be topic priming: I have several concerns about teaching in a co-teaching mode, followed by a sequencing of points expanding on the priming: First of all, with co-teaching, every lesson must be taught by 2 people. Secondly, in terms of the organization of a lesson, whilst one person is lecturing, the other must play a role as the TA. Thirdly, the actual individual teaching time we have is less.

A Mixture of Conversational English and Written English

There appears to be a range of both spoken and written discourse features that can be used at any time in long or short utterances. No rules tend to apply.

Written discourse grammar

However I've got a lot of problems Nevertheless I will work harder cheers!
 ^   ^
 _

The teacher understanding the students' needs has been adopting a rather exam-oriented mode of teaching which provides students with loads of assignments.

Spoken discourse grammar

These can occur within a clause, a kind of code mixing: "We need to strike a balance between drilling and meaningful tasks. Ya the pretty blur term balance again."

Or from one clause to the next in a kind of code switching: "A prerequisite to becoming a teacher is to appreciate literature and music. The Phantom of the Opera is awesome."

The Interactional Communicative Functions

As is common with spoken discourse, the following meaning-based functions have been observed on a regular basis:

- Statement of opinion: "what bothers me is that this school is quite different from the school I went to last year. Frankly, we prepared more precisely for the observations".
- Giving advice: "additionally, you may try to stick some strips of question types and its Chinese meaning onto the wall to facilitate students" understanding to your questions."

- Self evaluation: "actually I didn't prepare very well last week and I was disappointed in my performance".
- Evaluating others: "regarding setting two versions of handouts for students, I am not sure if this is the most suitable way to do it".
- Asking questions: "is it OK to use Chinese in English teaching too facilitate lower level students?"
- Asking for advice: should I follow the traditional routine of teaching?
- Answering questions: "My supporting teacher told me that she sometimes uses Chinese to support those less confident students".
- Hypothesizing: "If I had to use English only in class, it would be difficult for me to make them understand my instructions."
- Agreeing and disagreeing: "You are so right to say that everything is so relative/I am not sure if the reality can be so ideal. Nevertheless, I would incline to Crystal's suggestion".
- Expressing gratitude: "Thanks for the encouraging message!"
- Expressing regret: "We wish that they would enjoy the lessons."
- Reporting others' advice or opinions (both spoken and written forms with recursive tense and without): "one teacher told me that the students I am going to teach are quite 'ACTIVE'. She told me that the students said I had taught too fast."
- Referring to others' points: "I totally understand your feelings when getting the wrong response from students."
- Rhetorical statements or questions: "I think most of you have already heard of this activity".

DISCUSSION

The results demonstrate how second language learners involved in ACMC construct meanings together or learn from each other when engaged in discussion online. They also reveal that online written communication might have the same potential for developing linguistic competence through negotiation of meaning as oral interaction does. Both noticing and incidental learning occur frequently and construction of meaning can be traced through the postings. In addition, the results demonstrate that the asynchronous written discourse environment is one which facilitates a range of written text formats, linguistic features specific to narrative and expository genres and communicative functions encompassing a great variety of interactional meaning-based expressions more common to spoken communication. The environment often presents language as a hybrid of spoken/written modes both within clauses, between clauses as well as in the form of greater chunks of spoken or written discourse at text level. These occurrences tended to depend on the type of interaction being used prior to a posting or on the psychological state of the participant and his/her relationship to the event/ topic of discussion i.e., if the topic was deemed to be a very serious one, it was more likely to be described in report format using more formal tenor; if it was a more jovial posting, it tended to be in letter format with more elements of spoken discourse features.

CONCLUSION

It is this author's opinion that the language learning processes and language varieties described from this study, reveal that this environment is an extremely powerful one for second language learning; in this author's context, for the learning of the English language. In addition, as a relatively new form of communication, it is evolving and creating its own characteristics. These characteristics tend to be what might be called "tenor-inclusive", encouraging discourse representing language along the continuum of formality. They also tend to combine both spoken and written discourse features at clause, sentence and text levels. Future research using more longitudinal studies with larger groups interacting together might reveal the evolution of new emerging discourse modes. These studies might also help to validate this research if the same instances of learning and language are observed.

REFERENCES

1. Chandler, P., & Sweller, J. (1991). Cognitive load theory and the format of instruction. Cognition and Instruction, 8, 293-332. doi:10.1207/s1532690xci0804_2
2. Chun, D. (1994). Using computer networking to facilitate the acquisition of interactive competence. System, 22, 17-31. doi:10.1016/0346-251X(94)90037-X
3. Gustafson, J., Hodgson, V., & Tickner, S. (2004). Identity construction and dialogue genres—How notions of dialogue may influence social presence in networked learning environments. Proceedings of the Fourth International Conference on Networked Learning, Lancaster, 5-7 April 2004.
4. Halliday, M. A. K. (1975). Learning to mean—Explorations in the development of language. London: Edward Arnold.
5. Halliday, M. A. K. (2004). An introduction to functional grammar (3rd ed.). London: Education and Lifelong Learning.

6. Hatch, E. (1992). Discourse and language education. New York: Cambridge University Press.
7. Kember, D. (1996). The intention to both memorise and understand: Another approach to learning. Higher Education, 31, 341-354. doi:10.1007/BF00128436
8. Kern, R. (1995). Restructuring classroom interaction with networked computers: Effects on quantity and quality of language production. Modern Language Journal, 79, 457-476. doi:10.1111/j.1540-4781.1995.tb05445.x
9. Krashen, S. (1982). Principles and practice in second language acquisition. London: Pergamon Press Inc.
10. Lewin, K. (1946). Action research and minority problems. Journal of Social Issues, 2, 34-46. doi:10.1111/j.1540-4560.1946.tb02295.x
11. Marton, F., & Saljo, R. (1976). On qualitative differences in learning II: Outcome as a function of the learner's conception of the task. British Journal of Educational Psychology, 46, 115-127. doi:10.1111/j.2044-8279.1976.tb02304.x
12. Ortega, L. (1997). Processes and outcomes in networked classroom interaction: Defining the research agenda for L2 computer-assisted classroom discussion. Language Learning & Technology, 1, 82-93.
13. Pellettieri, J. (2000). Negotiation in cyberspace: The role of chatting in the development of grammatical competence. In M. Warschauer, & R. Kern (Eds.), Network-based language teaching: Concepts and practice. Cambridge: Cambridge University Press.
14. Peters, K. (2000). Concrete steps for on-line discussion. URL (last checked 19 September 2000). http://booboo.webct.com/otln/Asynchronous_Strategies.htm
15. Prawat, R. S. (1996). Constructivisms: Modern and postmodern. Educational Psychologist, 31, 215-225.
16. Schmidt, R. W. (1994). Deconstructing consciousness: In search of useful definitions for Applied Linguistics. AILA Review, 11, 11-26.
17. Stevick, E. W. (1976). Memory, meaning and method. New York: Newbury House Publishers.
18. Vygotsky, L. S. (1962). Thought and language. Cambridge, MA: MIT Press.
19. Vygotsky, L. S. (1978). Mind in society. Cambridge, MA: Harvard University Press.

20. Warschauer, M. (1996). Computer-assisted language learning: An introduction. In S. Fotos (Ed.), Multimedia language teaching. Tokyo: Logos International.
21. Wilkins, D. (1976). Notional syllabuses. Oxford: Oxford University Press. doi:10.1037/11193-000

Chapter 5

UBIQUITOUS LEARNING ANALYTICS IN THE REAL-WORLD LANGUAGE LEARNING

Kousuke Mouri and Hiroaki Ogata
Faculty of Arts and Science and the Graduate School of Information Science and Electrical Engineering, University of Kyushu, Fukuoka, Japan

ABSTRACT

In recent years, ubiquitous learning systems based on Computer Supported Ubiquitous Learning (CSUL) and u-learning have been constructed using ubiquitous technologies such as mobile devices, RFID tags, QR codes and wireless networks. These types of learning include not only in-class learning but also in a variety of out-of-class learning in spaces such as homes, libraries and museums. However, the learning materials provided by ubiquitous learning systems are, in most cases, prepared by teachers or instructional designers, and it is difficult to find relationships between a learner and other learners in different contexts. In order to link learners in the real world and ubiquitous learning logs (ULLs) that are accumulated in cyber space by a ubiquitous learning system called System for Capturing and Reminding of Learning Log (SCROLL), this paper proposes an innovative visualization system that integrates network visualization technologies with Time-Map based on Ubiquitous Learning Analytics (ULA). In this paper, a Ubiquitous Learning Log (ULL) is defined as a recorded form of knowledge or learning experiences acquired in a learner's daily life. An experiment was conducted to evaluate whether the visualization system is of benefit in finding the relationships between learners and ULLs and whether the developed layout called the Ubiquitous Learning Graph (ULG) is easy to use compared with certain previous visualization layouts. In the experiment, learners found relationships between their own knowledge and ULLs, demonstrating that the system can increase learners' learning opportunities.

INTRODUCTION

In recent years, ubiquitous learning (u-learning) has been the focus of attention in educational research across the world. To develop context-aware and seamlessly integrated Internet environments, Computer Supported Ubiquitous Learning (CSUL) or u-learning has been carried out using ubiquitous technologies such as RFID tags and cards, wireless communication, mobile phones, Personal Digital Assistants (PDAs), and wearable computers (Ogata et al. 2004; Yin et al., 2010). These types of learning include not only in-class learning but also a variety of out-of-class learning in spaces such as homes, libraries, and museums. In addition, researchers in the u-learning or seamless-learning have been pointed out such as the need for effective in-class learning designs and the necessity of helping students learn across at-home and in-school contexts (Hwang 2014, 2015).

One of the application domains of u-learning or CSUL is language learning. For example, Ogata et al. (2011) introduced their u-learning system called System for Capturing and Reminding of Learning Log (SCROLL), which allows users to share information with others by recording what they have learned in a web browser or mobile device. In addition, some CSUL systems were constructed in the domains of Nature Science (Chu et al., 2010; Hwang et al., 2011) or complex science experiences (Hwang et al., 2009).

These learning logs are accumulated in cyber space by using such systems, and they include contextual data such as location and time information. Aljohani and Davis (2012) described learning analytics called Ubiquitous Learning Analytics (ULA) in order to analyze enormous learning data including contextual information. The value of ULA is discussed by considering two possible kinds of interactions. The first is the interaction between learners and their contexts, referred to as learners-to-context interaction. The second is the interaction between learners and context-based learning materials, referred to as learner-to-context-based learning materials interaction. Aljohani et al. suggested that the use of learners' contextual data can enhance the interaction between learners, mobile devices, and learning environments. In addition, analyzing or visualizing contextual data has the potential for improving knowledge of the patterns of learners' interactions with their contexts (Aljohani and Davis 2012). Similarly, Ogata et al. (2014a) reported that it is important for learners to recognize what and how they have learned by analyzing and visualizing past learning logs, so that they can improve their way of learning. However, little attention has been paid to this point. One of the issues of ULA is how to visualize learners-to-context and learner-to-context-based learning materials interactions. After that, it is necessary to present or recommend the results of the visualization on a mobile device or desktop PC.

To tackle these issues, we developed an innovative visualization system that combines network graphs with Time-Map, based on ULA. In this paper, we call graphs based on graph theory "network graphs". How can learners learn in certain kinds of learning situations by visualizing relationships between themselves and a context, and themselves and context-based learning materials? For example, if learners are at the botanical gardens in the morning, they do not have the means to learn knowledge related to the place (botanical gardens) or time information (morning). In addition, they do not know whether the knowledge can be applied to other learning environments or not. The visualization system enables learners to access such information.

The rest of this paper is constructed as follows. Section 'Related works' discusses related works. Section ‹Scroll› introduces how to use SCROLL in the real-world language learning. Section ‹Visualization method› describes the methods of the visualization system. Sections›Implementation› and ‹Evaluation› describe the design, implementation, and initial evaluation experiment on the visualization system. Section›Method› summarizes the contributions made by the work.

RELATED WORKS

Context-aware U-learning

Researchers on context-aware u-learning have constructed u-learning environments in which learners can study anywhere and anytime. They integrated knowledge and location information by using cutting-edge technologies such as RFID, QR-codes, NFC-tags, and GPS (Hsu et al., 2011; Lai et al., 2013; Lee and Kuo 2014). For example, Hwang et al. (2008) developed a context-aware u-learning system with an attached RFID tag for plants. The application domain of their studies is Nature Science. When a learner arrives in front of a plant, the system asks him or her questions about the plant's features, such as its trunk, shape, and color. Based on the learner's responses, the system presents a list of candidate plants. This allows the learner to understand the relationship between knowledge about the plant and the place where he or she learned it. However, the context-based learning materials provided by Hwang et al.'s system are, in most cases, prepared by teachers or instructional designers and it is difficult to find relationships between a learner and other learners in different contexts because the system provides only interaction between a learner and the context-based learning materials. For example, if a learner learns a word in an informal setting, the word might be able to be applied in various other learning environments. However, there is no means for him or her to know whether it can be applied to other learning environments or not.

On the other hand, SCROLL allows learners to record what they have learned in daily life with contextual data using GPS sensors in the real-world language learning (Li et al., 2012). This means learners can freely create context-based learning logs and share them each other. There is a possibility that the learners can apply what they have learned to other learning environments by finding the relationships between their own and others' context-based learning logs. In order to find these relationships, this paper describes our ideas based on some previous visualization methods in the next sections: Geographical Information System and Time-Map, and Collocational Network.

Geographical information system and time-Map

A geographic information system (GIS) is designed to capture, store, manipulate, analyze, manage, and present all types of spatial and geographical data. By mapping learning information on the map in the system, learners can easily reflect on what and where they have learned. However, previous GIS designs did not take time-lines into consideration for learners' reflection. To tackle this issue, Johnson and Wilson (2009) developed a visualization tool for handling temporal data within a GIS framework, called Time-Map. As shown in Fig. 1, Time-Map consists of a time-line and Google Maps. It represents the shift of learning history in accordance with the lapse of time.

Figure 1. Time-Map.

Learners might forget when and where they have learned before. Therefore, Time-Map reminds them of their learning log entries recorded during a specified period of time by showing them on the timeline (default: two months before and after the set time). The visualization method can find individual learners' information in the spatio-temporal dimensions, but our proposed system can find relationships in different contexts among learners by combining Time-Map with network graphs. In the next section, this paper introduces the difference between our visualization and the related researchers' methods utilizing a series of network graphs called a collocational network.

Collocational network

Collocational networks are two-dimensional networks that contain interlinked collocation, i.e. words that occur together in a text. Williams (1998) used the collocational network as a corpus linguistic tool in order to create specialized dictionaries. Magnusson and Vanharanta (2003) described that it is important to visualize the most central concept in the text. For linguists, the relationships between words are important information. However, for learners in the real-world language learning, it is also important to grasp information such as other learners' contextual data connected to the learning contents. Our proposed system links learners' current knowledge and contexts in the real world to past learners' knowledge and contextual data that are accumulated in cyber space, by using a collocational network.

SCROLL

With the evolution of mobile devices, people prefer to record learning contents using mobile devices instead of taking notes on paper. For many people, this is a simpler method of note taking, since the information can be stored in various ways such as texts, photos, audio, and videos. We call formal notes written by language learners "learning logs". In this paper, a Ubiquitous Learning Log (ULL) is defined as a recorded form of knowledge or learning experiences acquired in a learner's daily life. In order to support such formal note taking, we designed and implemented our u-learning system called SCROLL (Ogata et al. 2011). SCROLL has supported various fields of learning such as task-based language learning, science communicator and career support for international students (Mouri et al., 2013; Ogata et al., 2014b; Mouri et al. 2015).

To simplify the process of capturing learners' learning experiences, SCROLL provides a well-defined form to illustrate a ULL. For example, when learners face problems in daily life, they may acquire some knowledge by themselves or ask others for help. As shown in Fig. 2, they can record the ULL with photos using a mobile device and SCROLL. The ULL includes meta-data such as the author, language, time of learning, location (latitude and longitude), place (name of nearby buildings) and tag, and the learners can search target ULLs based on the meta-data.

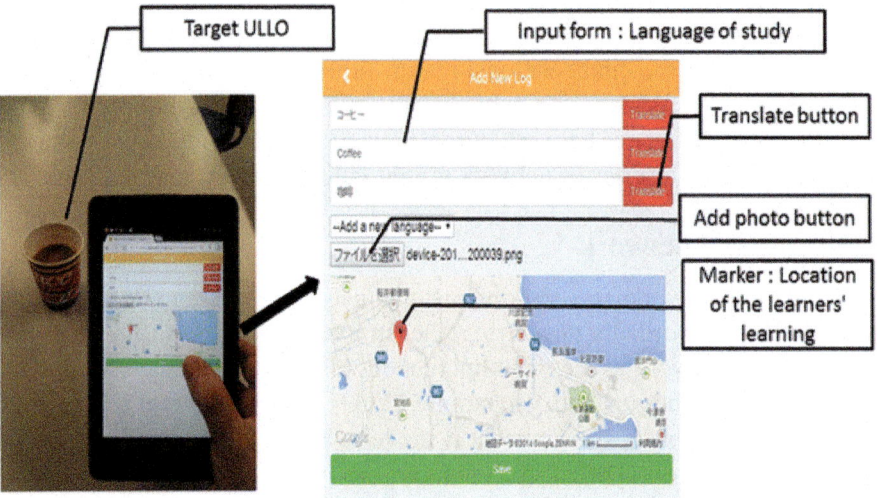

Figure 2. An example of adding a ULL.

To date, as shown in Table 1, there are 27,867 ULLs, 1772 users, 19 native languages, 30 kinds of places (e.g., supermarket or park) and 7 kinds of times (e.g., spring or summer). The proposed system visualizes relationships between learners and context-based knowledge, and learners and contextual data, based on the learning data outlined in Table 1.

Table 1. Learning data in SCROLL

Attribute	Description	Total
Knowledge	Content that they have learned. {e.g., natto, tofu, envelope}	27867
User	Author name (nickname on SCROLL) {e.g., Liu, Liam, James}	1772
Native Language	Learners' native language {e.g., Japanese, Chinese, Spanish, French}	19
Place	Location where the learning took place {e.g., supermarket, florist, park}	30
Time	Time when the learning took place {e.g., spring, summer, morning}	7

VISUALIZATION METHOD

A scenario of using the visualization system with SCROLL

Our visualization system mainly focuses on language learning fields. One way it can be used is to assist international students to learn Japanese. Language learners who face rich learning contexts every day can gain much knowledge from their daily lives, which include different kinds of situations such as shopping at the supermarket, visiting the doctor at the hospital, having a haircut in a barbershop, or visiting a museum (Li et al., 2013). The system can compare the past ULLs accumulated in cyber space in SCROLL with the learner's current context-based knowledge and contextual information, and present the relationships on his or her mobile device or desktop PC. As shown in Fig. 3, the workflow has the following four steps:

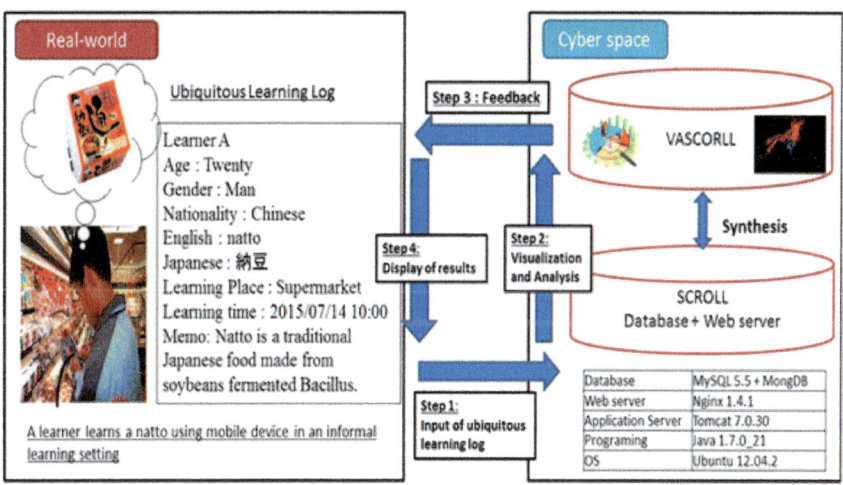

Figure 3. How visualization system and SCROLL works.

1. Step1: As shown in Fig. 3, learner A learns about natto (a traditional Japanese food made from fermented soybeans) at the supermarket, and he records his experience in a ULL in cyber space using a mobile device with SCROLL.

2. Step 2: The learner does not have the means to know whether the knowledge can be applied to other learning contexts or not. Using the system, he finds knowledge that can be applied in different contexts, by visualizing and analyzing a large amount of ULLs that are accumulated in cyber space with SCROLL.

3. Step 3: Based on the results of Step 2, the system identifies and presents important relationships such as 'learner-to-contexts' and 'learner-to-context-based knowledge interactions'.

4. Step 4: There are two ways the results of visualization can be shown, called "Display via context-based knowledge" and "Display via context".

    o Display via context-based knowledge: If learner A learns about natto at the supermarket, the system will provide him with contexts such as "restaurant" and "convenience store" related to natto. After that, the learner will visit the place using the learning log navigator function (Mouri et al., 2012) and learn more information directly from there. In addition, if he wants to learn indirectly about the experience, he can do so using a re-log on SCROLL.

    o Display via context: When learner A is at the supermarket in the daytime, the system will provide him with knowledge about "tofu" (a food made by curdling soymilk) and "edamame" (a preparation of immature soybeans in the pod, found in the cuisines of China, Japan, Korea, and Hawaii) related to "supermarket" and "daytime". After that, he will learn the knowledge related to the supermarket in the daytime using SCROLL.

The visualization method and the implementation we propose in the rest of this paper enable the two cases described above.

Visualizing ULLs based on a three-layer structure

To visualize and analyze several relationships between learners and ULLs, we uniquely defined them as three-layer structure, as shown in Fig. 4 (Mouri et al., 2014; Mouri et al., 2015).

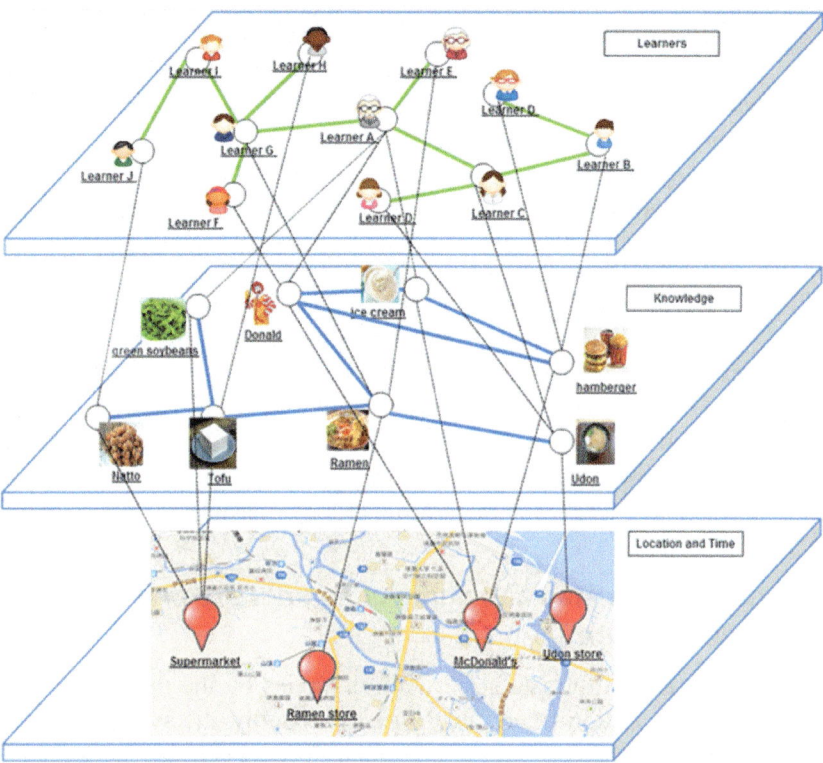

Figure 4. Three-layer structure in SCROLL.

The upper layer shows the individual learners. If a learner learns knowledge using SCROLL, there is a possibility that other learners have already learned it as well. The system finds these links to identify which learners have learned what kind of knowledge.

The intermediate layer contains the knowledge that learners have learned. In ULA, this means learner-to-context-based learning materials interaction. This paper calls it learner-to-context-based knowledge. In addition, some types of learning tasks can be included in this layer. For example, some task-based learning in u-learning environments can be carried out using knowledge with contexts (Sharon 2013). The scalability of the layers can be enhanced and the field of visualization can be widened by linking one's own ULLs to the knowledge learned by doing tasks.

The lowest layer contains contextual data such as location, place, and time. In ULA, this means learner-to-context interaction. The layer allows learners to grasp when and where they have learned by revealing knowledge related to certain places or times.

The analysis using the three-layer structure has the following advantages:

1. Places with a large number of links to related knowledge are places where learners can learn much knowledge. For example, if a certain supermarket or convenience store is related with various entries on natto, green soybeans, tofu, miso soup, and noodle cups, by the analyzing relationships between this knowledge and the location, the system can provide learners with valuable learning information.

2. Knowledge that is related to many places is knowledge that can be learned in various places. For example, if a learner experiences tea ceremony of a traditional Japanese culture at the university in Japan, a set of knowledge related tea ceremonies (e.g., tea, seiza: to sit in the correct manner on a Japanese tatami mat) can be learned in various other places. The tea can be purchased at the supermarket, and the seiza can be learned at the martial arts gymnasium.

How nodes are created and connecting lines are in the three-layer structure

Firstly, the system will create 1772 authors' nodes on the upper layer based on Table 1 in the section titled "SCROLL". Secondly, the system will create 27,867 knowledge nodes on the intermediate layer. Then, it will connect the authors' nodes to any related knowledge nodes representing things that learners have already learned. For example, if learner A learns about natto, tofu, and sushi, the system will connect the "learner A" of node on the upper layer to the "natto", "tofu" and "sushi" on the intermediate layer. In addition, it will connect the related knowledge to knowledge on the intermediate layer in order to identify learner A's next learning steps.

Thirdly, the system will create a contextual node on the lowest layer. Then, it will connect knowledge nodes on the intermediate layer to contextual nodes on the lowest layer. For example, if learner A has learned knowledge of natto at the supermarket in Japan, the system will connect "natto" on the intermediate layer to "supermarket" on the lowest layer.

LKPTE model

An important goal of our visualization system is to find the most important relationships between learners and context, and learners and context-based knowledge. For example, learners do not know the distance between learners' nodes such as "Mongolian Learner A" and "Chinese Learner A", and the natto of context-based knowledge as shown in Fig. 5 (left). In order to reveal the distance between nodes, this paper proposes a model called Learner-Knowledge-Place-Time-Experiences (LKPTE), shown in Table 2. Using this model, the system finds the most important relationships between learners and context-based knowledge, and learners and contexts, as shown in Fig. 5 (right).

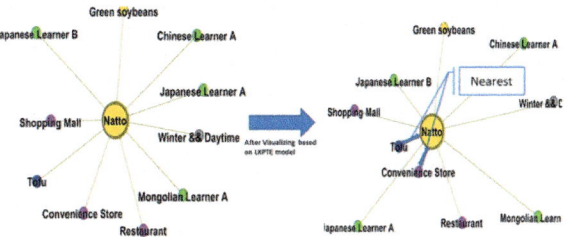

Figure 5. An example of visualization based on LKPTE model.

Table 2. LKPTE parameters

Parameter	Detail
L_g (Who)	Gender of learners
L_a (Who)	Age of learners
L_n (Who)	Native language of learners (e.g., Japanese, English, Chinese)
L_l (Who)	Level of learners (e.g., Japanese Language Proficiency Test)
K_l (What)	Level of knowledge (e.g., JLPT word level)
K_t (What)	Type of word (e.g., noun, verb, adverb, adjective)
P_l (Where)	Location of place (e.g. latitude and longitude)
P_n (Where)	Name of place (e.g. university, museum, supermarket)
T_s (When)	Season (spring, summer, fall, winter)
T_t (When)	Time of day (morning, daytime, night)
E_d (How)	Direct experience
Ei (How)	Indirect experience

Learners' parameter L (Who) shows their gender (L_g), age (L_a), native language (L_n), and Japanese Language Proficiency Test (JLPT) level (L_l). Using these parameters, the system can find other learners with similar traits.

Knowledge parameter K (What) shows the level of words (K_l) as indicated by the JLPT and word type (K_t), such as noun, verb, adverb, or adjective.

Parameter K is designed to indicate whether learners are at the right level of difficulty when learning from other learners' experiences.

Parameter P (Where) shows location (P_l) and place name (P_n). There is a possibility that ULLs in the same location contain different place names such as "university" and "restaurant". In addition, the same place names may contain different locations. Parameter P distinguishes ULLs in different contexts so that the system can detect learner contexts in the real world and ULLs in cyber space.

Parameter T (When) shows the season (T_s) and time of learning (T_f). For example, the most learners have learned about morning glory flowers in the morning. However, one learner has learned about them in the daytime. Generally, people regard morning glories as flowers that bloom in the morning, but there are kinds of that are in bloom during the daytime. For reasons like these, the system detects relationships between knowledge and place in different times. By seeing these relationships, learners can grasp information regarding the time of other learners' experiences.

Parameter E (How) shows direct experiences (E_d) and indirect experiences (Ei). Direct experience (E_d) denotes experience gained through sense perception. Indirect experience (Ei) denotes experience gained through others. Learners can save others' indirect experiences as "relog" using SCROLL. According to Kolb (1984), it is important to have direct experience. By revealing the relationships between direct experiences and indirect experiences, the system prompts learners to change from observers to doers by engaging in task-based learning (Mouri et al., 2013).

To reveal the distance between learners and ULLs, this paper measures the distance of connecting lines using cosine similarity (1). This paper defines the following vectors V_i (2) based on the parameters of LKPTE model.

$$similarity = \frac{\sum_{i=1}^{n} V1 \times V2}{\sqrt{\sum_{i=1}^{n}(V1)^2} \times \sqrt{\sum_{i=1}^{n}(V2)^2}} \quad (1)$$

$$V_i = \{L_g, L_a, L_n, L_l, K_l, K_t, P_l, P_n, T_s, T_f, E_d, E_i\} \quad (2)$$

IMPLEMENTATION

This section describes the implementation of the visualization system with the three-layer structure using network graphs with Time-Map.

The layout types of the network graph

This paper implemented the network layout as shown in Figs. 6 and 7. The network layout consists of using three basic layouts and the Ubiquitous Learning Graph (ULG) we developed.

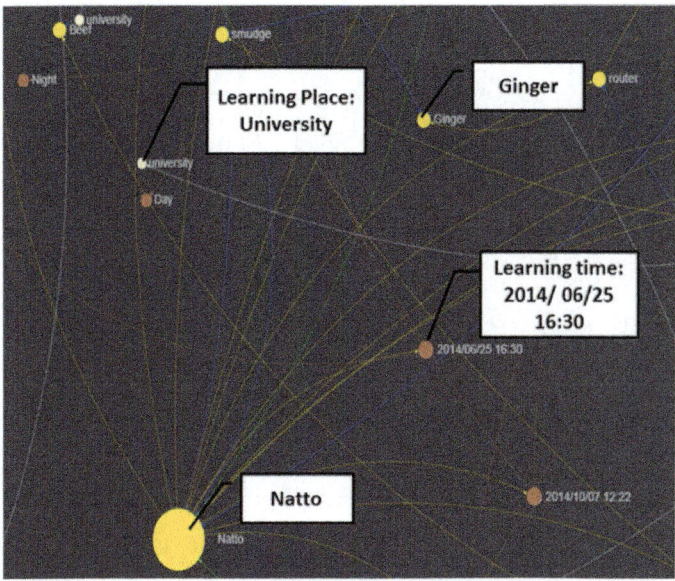

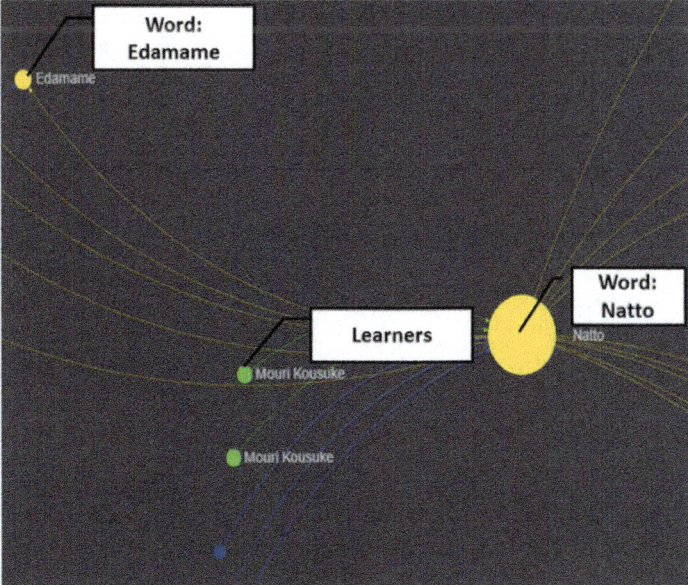

Figure 6. Random and force-directed layout.

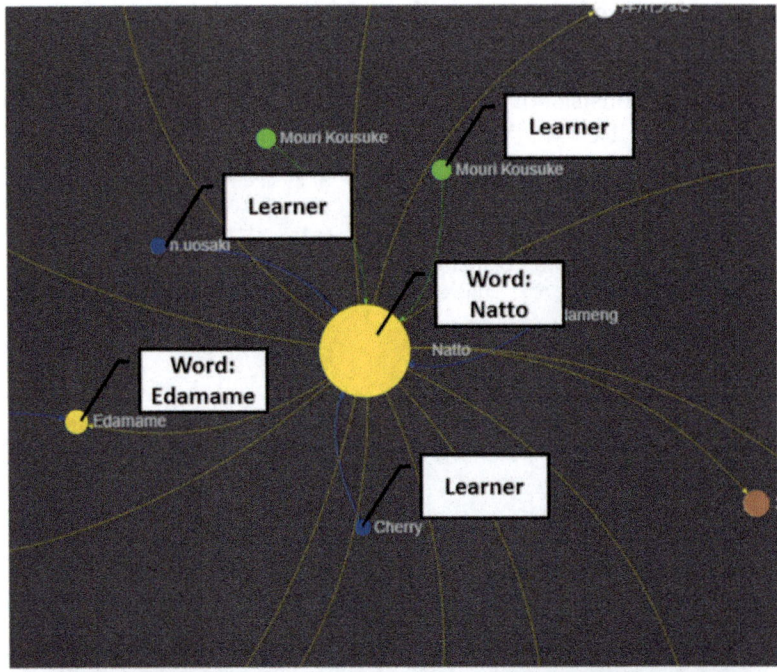
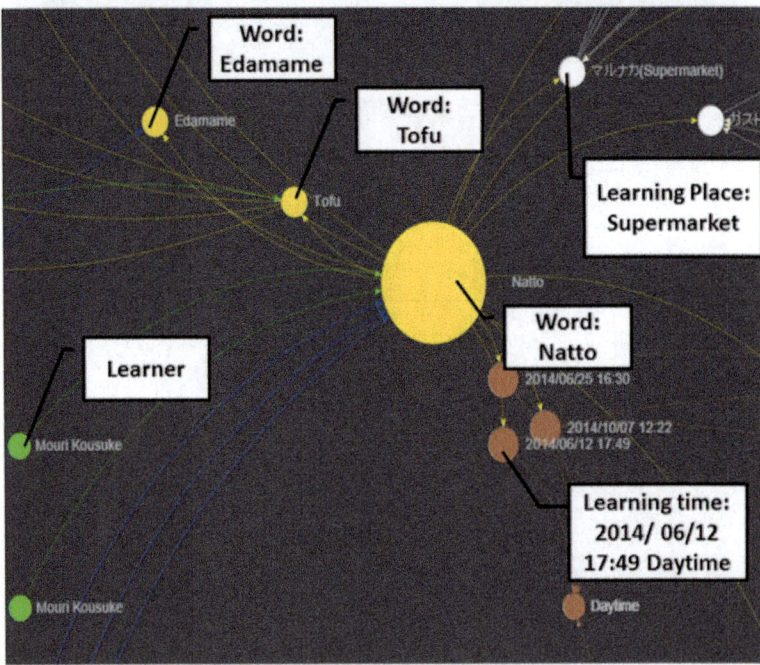

Figure 7. Yifan-fu-multilevel and ubiquitous learning graph layout.

The first layout consists of the random network shown in Fig. 6 (left). It uses a simple algorism that generates nodes randomly on the graph, and then the system links related nodes.

The second layout, shown in Fig. 6 (right), is a force-directed layout. It uses the force vector algorithm proposed in the Gephi software, appreciated for its simplicity and for the readability of the network it helps to visualize (Mathieu et al, 2014; Noack, 2009; Fruchterman and Reingold, 1991).

The third layout consists of the Yifan Hu Multilevel Layout, as shown in Fig. 7 (left). It uses a very fast algorithm to reduce complexity (Hu and Scolt 2001, 2005). The repulsive forces on one node from a cluster of distant nodes are approximated by a Barnes-Hut calculation, which treats them as one super-node (Barnes and Hut 1986).

The final layout, shown in Fig. 7 (right), consists of using the ULG we developed. The ULG is divided into four areas: top-left, top-right, bottom-left, and bottom-right. The center node on the network graph shows the central topic that learners want to know about. The top-left area shows others' knowledge related to this topic. In this case, learners can understand what other learners have learned about tofu and edamame right after learning about natto. The top-right area shows places related to the topic. For language learners, this is important information needed in order to apply their knowledge to other learning places, as described in the section titled "Collocational Network". The bottom-right area shows seasons or day of time such as "daytime", "spring" and "summer" related to the topic. Similarly, the bottom-left area shows places such as "university" and "supermarket" related to the topic.

Color coding of the visualized nodes

To avoid having learners feel confused when they see the past ULLs because there might be too many visualized nodes, it is definitely necessary to establish some criteria for the distinction of each node. To effectively distinguish each node, we created a color coding scheme for the nodes, shown in Table 3.

Table 3. Color coding to distinguish the kinds of nodes

Node	Layer	Node color
Learner's own name	Upper	Green
Names of other learners	Upper	Blue
Knowledge of learners	Intermediate	Yellow
Location of learners	Lowest	White
Time the knowledge was created	Lowest	Brown

Green nodes show the learner's own name on the upper layer. If a green node is connected to a yellow node on the intermediate layer, the connecting line is pink so that it can be easily recognized as the learner's own entry.

1. Blue nodes show the names of other learners on the upper layer. If a blue node is connected to a yellow node on the intermediate layer, the connecting line is blue.

2. Yellow nodes show both the learner's own knowledge and the knowledge of other learners. For example, the learner can recognize his own knowledge because the line connecting his name on the upper layer to the knowledge node on the intermediate layer is pink. In addition, the learner might discover the knowledge of other learners related to his own knowledge.

3. White nodes show the location of the learners on the lowest layer. These nodes include latitude, longitude, building names, and other location attributes

4. Brown nodes show the time that the knowledge was learned on the lowest layer. The time of learning is made up of attributes representing the time of day ("morning", "daytime", "night") and season ("spring" ,"summer","fall","winter").

Visualization system combined with network graphs and time-Map

The interface combining network graphs and Time-Map for visualizing the complex relationships between learners and ULLs is shown in Fig. 8 (left). It contains the following components:

Ubiquitous Learning Analytics in the Real-World Language Learning

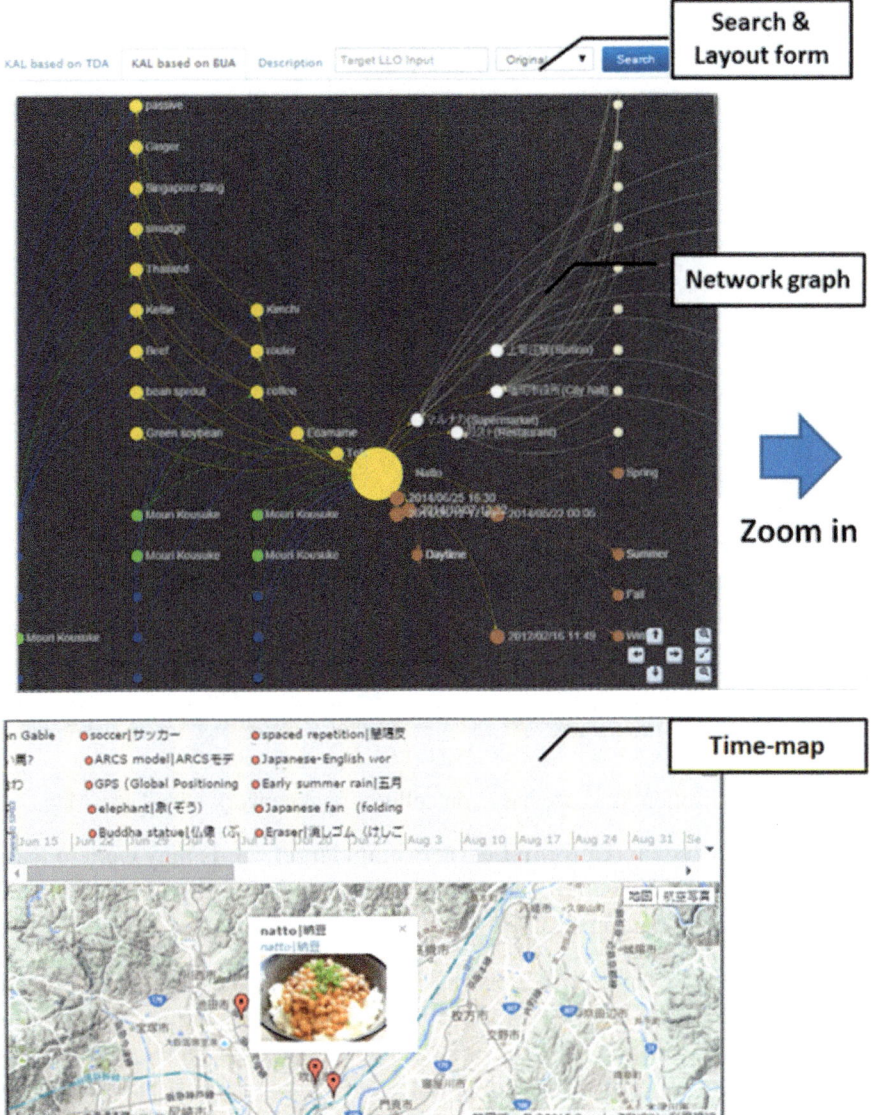

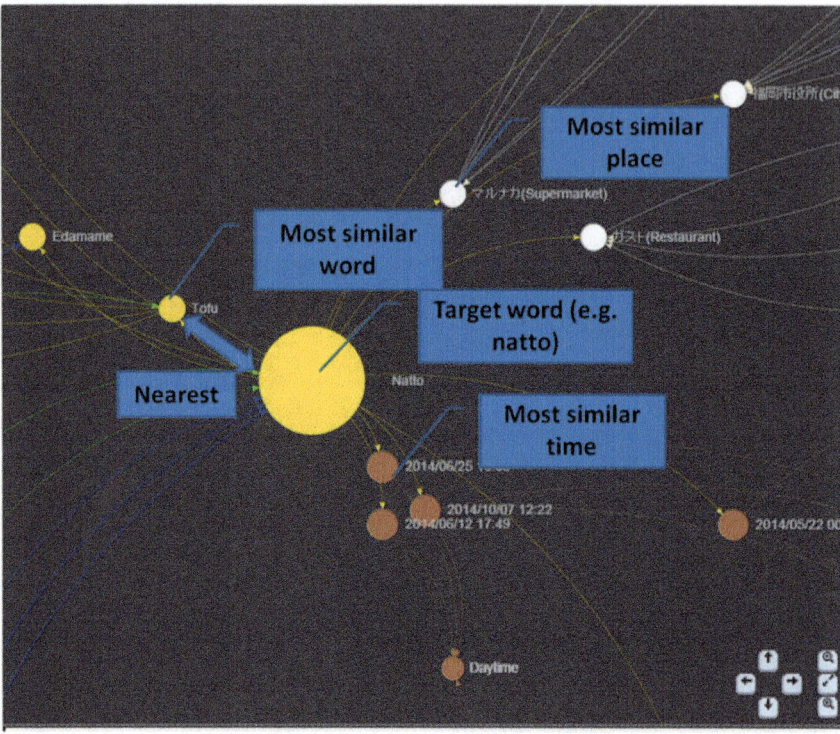

Figure 8. Visualization interface based on collocational network with Time-Map.

- Search and layout form: Learners input target words they want to learn about and choose a layout (Random layout, Force-directed layout, Yi-fan Hu layout, or ULG).

- Network graph: The network graph shows the layout calculated by the LKPTE model. Figure 8 (left) shows a sample of the ULG. Figure 8 (right) shows the enlarged network graph. In these two cases, learners can grasp that the target word (natto) is most similar to tofu based on the LKPTE model and cosine similarity. Similarly, they can see that natto is most similar to some contexts such as the supermarket (a place where they frequently learn about natto) and night (when they frequently learn about natto).

- Time-Map: Learners might forget their ULL entries or when and where they have learned before. Therefore, the system reminds them of their log entries recorded during a specified period of time by showing them on the timeline (default: two months before and after the set time).

Further, the network graph and time map functions are linked to each other. For example, if a learner clicks a certain node on the network graph, the time map will show the location and time corresponding to it. Therefore, learners can obtain its location and time information.

EVALUATION

Seventeen international students studying at the University of Tokushima and Kyushu University participated in the evaluation experiment. They were from China (10), Mongolia (6) and Malaysia (1) and aged 23 to 31. Their length of stay in Japan ranged from 1 month to 5years, and their JLPT levels were from 1 to 3 and no qualification. The evaluation experiment was designed to evaluate whether the visualization system would be of benefit in finding the relationships between the learners and ULLs and whether the newly developed ULG would be easy to use compared with previous visualization types such as the random layout, Yifan Hu layout, and force-directed layout.

METHOD

Before the evaluation began, we explained to the participants how to use the visualization system and SCROLL. In addition, since they had never used SCROLL before, they practiced using it for one day before using the system. After that, they recorded learning logs using SCROLL and then used it to visualize the relationships between themselves and their ULLs for two weeks. The participants used their own smart-phones (iPhone or Android device) to record their ULLs in formal and informal settings anytime and anywhere. The mobile devices used in the evaluation experiment were five iPhone 4s, eight iPhone 5s, and four Samsung Galaxy Note 3s. After the evaluation, the participants were asked to complete a questionnaire that used a five-point-scale to evaluate the system's performance and usability, as well as the ease of understanding the content and finding other ULLs using the system.

RESULTS AND DISCUSSION

The questionnaire results are presented in Table 4.

Table 4. Questionnaire results

Question	Mean	SD
1. Were the network graphs useful to find the relationships between you and others' contexts?	3.27	0.50
2. Were network graphs useful to find the relationships between your and others' knowledge?	3.52	0.48
3. Was Time-Map with the network graphs useful to grasp your or others' contexts?	3.92	0.59
4. Was Time-Map with the network graphs useful to grasp your or others' knowledge?	3.85	0.66

Q1 and Q2 ask about the usability and usefulness of the network graph. Q3 and Q4 ask about the importance and performance of the system.

The results of Q1 and Q2 revealed that the learners efficiently grasped their own or others' knowledge using the network graphs for visualizing ULLs. Through the evaluation we found out how the participants learned from others' knowledge and contexts. Many Chinese learners spent much time at the university in the summer during the evaluation experiment, and they had opportunities to find relationships between themselves as learners and the university. After visualizing knowledge such as "electric fan" (扇風機) and "air-conditioning" (空気調節) related to "university" and "summer" through the contextual data accumulated in cyber space in SCROLL, the system displayed the results of visualization on the learners' desktop PCs or mobile devices. Consequently, the learners could understand the relationships between their knowledge and the university in the summer.

The results of Q3 and Q4 indicated that the learners grasped their or others' context and knowledge. These questions were used to evaluate ULLs in the spatio-temporal dimension. For example, when a Chinese learner learned about natto at the supermarket, he or she used Time-Map to find more places, such as a "restaurant" or "shopping mall" where other learners had also learned about natto. Next, the learner was able to apply his or her knowledge about natto to other learning places such as restaurants and shopping malls.

We also evaluated the network layouts used in the previous studies and the ULG we developed. For the comparison, the participants used some of the conventional layouts during the experiment and completed the questionnaire shown in Table 5.

Table 5. The questionnaire about layouts

Question	
Q5. Which layout is the easiest to use?	
Q6. Which layout is the most effective for learning?	

The aim of Q5 was to evaluate the usability of the layouts, and aim of Q6 was to evaluate the learning effectiveness. Figure 9 shows the results of the questionnaires about layouts. The results indicated that for both usability and effectiveness, many participants preferred the ULG to the other layouts. They reported that they were able to grasp WHO was learning WHAT, WHEN, and WHERE in the ULG where these four categories were visualized. In regard with the usability and effectiveness, we interviewed the participants to compare the ULG with other layouts.

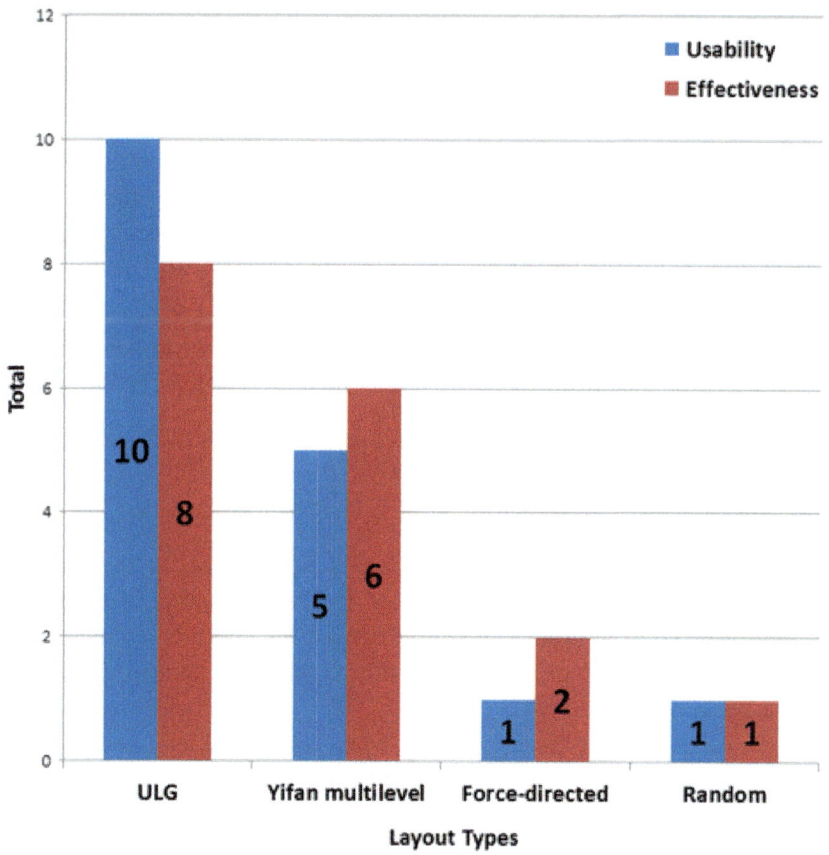

Figure 9. The number of selected layouts by each participant in the evaluation experiment.

1. ULG versus Random layout

The random layout enabled it to run faster than other layouts. However, the participants commented as below because the algorithm of the random layout generated nodes randomly on the graph.

- "When I used the random layout, it was difficult to find my knowledge and other contexts because I was not able to grasp the position of contexts on the graph."

- "In the point of usability and effectiveness for learning, it was worse than other graph layouts. But, it is good in terms of processing speed."

If comparing the ULG with the random layout, the processing speed of the ULG is slow, but it is very useful in finding the relationships between their own knowledge and other contexts. In addition, the random layout is not good layout for learning because the participants were not able to grasp the position of contexts on the graph.

2. ULG versus Force-directed layout versus Yifan multilevel Layout

As for the force-directed layout shown in Fig. 9, both usability and effectiveness for learning are lower than the ULG and Yifan multilevel layout. To compare the force-directed layout with the ULG and the Yifan multilevel layout, we asked the participants to comment "why did you prefer to the ULG and the Yifan multilevel layout than the force-directed layout?" The comments are as follows:

- "Yifan multilevel layout is easier to read than other layouts. Especially, the beautiful layout gave me the motivation for learning."

- "I think that the speed of visualization of the ULG is slow. But, if reviewing comprehensively in terms of easy of understanding the content and effectiveness for learning, I will select the ULG."

Though we had expected that the ULG would be useful layout in terms of the effectiveness for learning, it did not. But, if comparing usability of the ULG with the Yifan multilevel layout, the usability score is twice as high as that in the Yifan multilevel layout. That means the ULG is most useful layout for understanding the content.

After the experiment, we asked the participants to give comments and share their experiences of using the system. Examples of some positive comments are as follows:

- "It is very beneficial to find links between my knowledge and other learners' contexts. Especially, visualizing my current location or place is impressive for learning. When learning at the laboratory at the University of Tokushima, I often used to find relationships between the university and other learners' knowledge."

- "I'm from Mongolia. I always wanted to know about many learning events similar to what other Mongolian learners have learned. It is very helpful to know the learning spots where other Mongolian learners have been."
- "The advantage of the system for visualizing relationships between the word and the geographical data, for me, is that it gave me the motivation to learn Japanese."
- "It is very interesting to visualize other learners' vocabularies based on natto, a Japanese food."
- I thought that morning glories bloom in the morning, but actually, I noticed that there are kinds of morning glories that are in bloom even in the daytime, by using this system.

These positive comments and episodes show that the system helps find the relationships between learners and ULLs. Its advantage is that it helps learners grasp the relationships between what they have learned in their daily lives and other learners' contexts. However, there were also some negative comments.

- "Japanese words written in Kanji are quite difficult for people who don't know Japanese. The words visualized from other people's vocabularies were in Kanji. If the word details were in Hiragana, they could help beginners to learn the language."
- "I'm at JLPT level 1. The words visualized in two different locations were very simple words. There was almost no word to directly experience something or do a re-log. I wanted more difficult vocabulary and challenging learning situations."
- "It was little bit difficult to understand how to use the system. In addition, the function of saving learning logs is very good, but I prefer to write papers."
- "Sometimes the speed of visualizing learning logs in the system is too slow. (It took about $10\sim20s$)"

From these comments, the participants would suggest that the system developer take into account learners' Japanese levels. This means that the L_l parameter in the LKPTE model is not enough. In addition, we need to improve the system's speed in visualizing ULLs. In consideration of these issues, our future works are described in the next section.

CONCLUSION

This paper described a system for visualizing relationships between learners and ULLs. International students can add their knowledge to a ULL in SCROLL, and then SCROLL can present the learning contents to help them recall their knowledge based on their learning contexts.

By using SCROLL with the system that we proposed, the international students learned interesting knowledge that others had recorded. When the participants learned "electric fan (扇風機)" word in Japanese in the university or in a formal learning setting during evaluation experiment, our proposed system visualized to links the relationships "electric fan" and other contexts such as "electrical store" and "Shopping mall", and provided them. Also, six learners have learned "morning glory" in the morning while two learners have learned it in the daytime. It indicated that most morning glories bloom in the morning, but there are some varieties that bloom during the daytime. Our system was able to detect relationships between knowledge and time, and notify those who learned it in the morning that there exist ones which bloom in the daytime. In this way, learners were able to deepen their knowledge about "morning glory" through other learners' experiences.

The evaluation was conducted after the implementation of the function to visualize learners and ULLs. A questionnaire with a five-point-scale administered after the evaluation showed that the system supported the international students by visualizing ULLs. As mentioned in the section titled "Results and Discussion", the system needs improvement so that it can recommend more appropriate learning contexts or materials in accordance with learners' situations. In addition, we will consider making improvements because the L_l parameter in the LKPTE model was not sufficient.

In the future, the use and evaluation of the visualization system will continue, and we will improve the system as described above. Our next consideration is to support international students who are studying for the JLPT by having them use the system to enhance their Japanese language skills.

ACKNOWLEDGMENTS

This part of this research was supported by the Grant-in-Aid for Scientific Research No.25282059, No.26560122, No.25540091 and No.26350319 from the Ministry of Education, Culture, Sports, Science and Technology (MEXT) in Japan. The research results have been partly achieved by "Research and

Development on Fundamental and Utilization Technologies for Social Big Data" (178A03), the Commissioned Research of National Institute of Information and Communications Technology (NICT), Japan.

Open Access This article is distributed under the terms of the Creative Commons Attribution 4.0 International License (http://creativecommons.org/licenses/by/4.0/), which permits unrestricted use, distribution, and reproduction in any medium, provided you give appropriate credit to the original author(s) and the source, provide a link to the Creative Commons license, and indicate if changes were made.

Competing interests

The authors declare that they have no competing interests.

Authors' contributions

KM carried out design of the ubiquitous learning analytics study, collection and assembly of data, and analysis and interpretation of data. In addition, KM drafted this manuscript. HO performed the critical revision of this manuscript for important intellectual content, and final approval of this manuscript. This manuscript has not been published and is not under consideration for publication elsewhere. All authors read and approved the final manuscript.

REFERENCES

1. NR Aljohani, HC Davis, *Learning analytics in mobile and ubiquitous learning environments. In 11th World Conference on Mobile and Contextual Learning* (mLearn 2012, Helsinki, Finland, 2012)
2. J Barnes, P Hut, A Hierarchical O (n log n) Force-Calculation Algorithm. Nature **324**(4), 446–449 (1986)
3. HC Chu, GJ Hwang, CC Tsai, JCR Tseng, A two-tier test approach to developing location-aware mobile learning systems for natural science course. Comput Educ **55**(4), 1618–1627 (2010)
4. MEJ Fruchterman, EM Reingold, Graph drawing by force-directed placement. Sofw Pract. Exper. **21**(11), 1129–1164 (1991)
5. JM Hsu, YS Lai, PT Yu, U-plant: a RFID-based ubiquitous plant learning system for promoting self-regulation. Int J Internet Protoc Technol **6**(1), 112–122 (2011)
6. YF Hu, Efficient and high quality force-directed graph drawing. Math J **10**, 37–71 (2005)
7. Y.F. Hu, J.A. Scolt, A Multilevel Algorithm for Wavefront Reduction.

SIAM J. Sci. Comput. **23**(4), 1352–1375 (2001)

8. GJ Hwang, Definition, framework and research issues of smart learning environments – a context-aware ubiquitous learning perspective. Smart Learn Environ **1**(1), 1–14 (2014)

9. GJ Hwang, CC Tsai, SJH Yang, Criteria, strategies and research issues of context-aware ubiquitous learning. Educ Technol Soc **11**(2), 81–91 (2008)

10. GJ Hwang, TC Yang, CC Tsai, SJH Yang, A context-aware ubiquitous learning environment for conducting complex science experiments. Comput Educ **53**(2), 402–413 (2009)

11. GJ Hwang, HC Chu, YS Lin, CC Tsai, A knowledge acquisition approach to developing Mindtools for organizing and sharing differentiating knowledge in a ubiquitous learning environment. Comput Educ **57**(1), 1368–1377 (2011)

12. GJ Hwang, SY Wang, CL Lai, Seamless flipped learning- a mobile technology-enhanced flipped classroom with effective learning strategies. J Comput Educ **2**(4), 449–473 (2015)

13. I Johnson, A Wilson, The TimeMap Project: Developing Time-Based GIS Display for Cultural data. J GIS in Archaeol **1**, 123–135 (2009)

14. DA Kolb, *Experiential learning: Experience as the source of learning and development*, vol. 1 (Prentice-Hall, Englewood Cliffs, 1984)

15. HC Lai, CY Chang, WS Li, TL Fan, YT Wu, The implementation of mobile learning in outdoor education: Application of QR codes. Br J Educ Technol **44**(2), 57–62 (2013)

16. WH Lee, MC Kuo, An NFC E-Learning Platform for Interactive and Ubiquitous Learning, In proc of 2014 International Conference on Education Reform and Modern Management, ermm-14. Phuket, Thailand, 271-274, (2014). doi:10.2991/ermm-14.2014.74

17. M Li, H Ogata, B Hou, N Uosaki, Y Yano, Personalization in Context-aware Ubiquitous Learning-Log System, Proceedings of the 2012 IEEE Seventh International Conference on Wireless, Mobile and Ubiquitous Technology in Education, Takamatsu, Kagawa Japan, 41-48, (2012)

18. M Li, H Ogata, B Hou, N Uosaki, K Mouri, Context-aware and Personalization Method in Ubiquitous Learning Log. J Educ Technol Soc (SSCI) **16**(3), 362–373 (2013)

19. C Magnusson, H Vanharanta, *Visualizing sequences of texts using collocational networks*, In Proceedings of the 3 rd international conference on Machine learning and data mining in pattern recognition,

Leipzig (Springer, Germany, 2003), pp. 276–283

20. J Mathieu, V Tommaso, H Sebastien, B Mathieu, Forece Atlas2, a Continuous Graph Layout Algorithm for Handy Network Visualization Designed for the Gephi Software. PLOS One **9**(6), e98679 (2014). doi:10.1371/journal.pone.0098679, Jun10

21. K Mouri, H Ogata, M Li, B Hou, N Uosaki, Learning Log Navigator: Augmented awareness past learning experiences, In *proc of 2012 IIAI International Conference*, 159-162 (2012)

22. K Mouri, H Ogata, M Li, B Hou, N Uosaki, S Liu, Learning Log Navigator: Supporting Task-based Learning Using Ubiquitous Learning Logs. J Res Pract Technol Enhanc Learn (RPTEL) **8**(1), 117–128 (2013)

23. K Mouri, H Ogata, N Uosaki, S Liu, *Visualizaiton for analyzing Ubiquitous Learning Logs, Proceedings of the 22 nd International Conference on Computers in Education (ICCE 2014)*, 461-470, 2014

24. K Mouri, H Ogata, N Uosaki, Ubiquitous Learning Analytics in the Context of Real-world Language Learning, Proceedings of the 2015 International Conference on Learning Analytics and Knowledge (LAK 2015), Poughkeepsie, USA, 378-382, (2015)

25. A Noack, Modularity clustering is force-directed layout, Physical Reviewe E, **79**(2), 1-8, (2009)

26. H Ogata, Y Yano, Context-aware support for computer-supported ubiquitous learning. Proc. of IEEE International Workshop on Wireless and Mobile Technologies in Education, 27-34 (2004)

27. H Ogata, M Li, H Bin, N Uosaki, M El-Bishoutly, Y Yano, SCROLL: Supporting to share and reuse ubiquitous learning logs in the context of language learning. Res Pract Technol Enhanc Learn **6**(3), 69–82 (2011)

28. H Ogata, B Hou, M Li, N Uosaki, K Mouri, S Liu, Ubiquitous Learning Project Using Life-logging Technology in Japan. Educ Technol Soc J**17**(2), 85–100 (2014a)

29. H Ogata, K Mouri, M Bono, A Joh, K Takanashi, A Osaki, H Ochiai, Supporting Science Communication in a Museum using Ubiquitous Learning Logs, Proceedings of Workshop on Computational Approaches to Connecting Levels of Analysis in Networked Learning Communities, the 4th International Conference on Learning Analytics and Knowledge (LAK 2014), Indianapolis, USA, (2014b)

30. A Sharon, Storyline: A task-based approach for the young learner classroom. ETL J **67**(1), 41–51 (2013)

31. G Williams, Collocational Networks: Interlocking Pattern of Lexis in a Corpus of Plant Biology Research Articles. Int. J. Corpus Ling. **3**, 151–171 (1998)
32. C Yin, H Ogata, Y Tabata, Y Yano, Supporting the acquisition of Japanese polite expressions in context-aware ubiquitous learning. Int J Mobile Learn Organ **4**(2), 214–234 (2010)

Chapter 6

ONLINE E-LEARNING APPLICATION FOR PRACTICING FOREIGN LANGUAGE SKILLS WITH NATIVE SPEAKERS

Ilya V. Osipov, Alex A. Volinsky, Evgeny Nikulchev and Anna Y. Prasikova

Department of Mechanical Engineering, University of South Florida

ABSTRACT

Background

The paper describes an online e-learning web-based application for practicing foreign language skills with native speakers. Educational materials are a part of the application, along with the live audio–video feed between the participants.

Findings

The proposed technology is designed to supplement traditional methods of studying spoken language by bringing native speakers, students, and language-learning materials in one place. The main research question is whether strangers, first met on the internet can teach and learn languages using integrated training materials.

Conclusions

In the developed platform, any native speaker can perform a role of a teacher, i.e., facilitator of foreign language learning. Over 40,000 users registered in the system over a 6-month period. The system includes gamification as the part of user retention and virality mechanisms.

FINDINGS

Verbal communication is based on speech activity, which can be developed and applied during foreign language learning. Learning foreign languages is also associated with acquiring the knowledge of other cultures, which is impossible without practical speech communication. Necessary properties of online applications, which provide language communication practice are the possibility of audio and visual contacts; teaching methodology, including conversation scenarios, allowing participants to actually start and carry on a conversation on a given topic and motivation of the participants.

However, it was noted that traditional language learning does not provide enough training of direct verbal communication. Without conversational practice, mastering the language is slow and inefficient. Techniques, such as trips to foreign countries, living in a foreign family, and even socializing with foreigners on the street, all increase the language-learning outcomes. However, these methods are expensive and are not feasible for mass education. Live conversations with native speakers using Skype can also help, but it is hard to find a companion to speak in the desired language. Furthermore, this companion needs to have some training skills, while an average native speaker does not know the teaching methodology and simply does not know what to say.

Computer training system in the form of a game was developed, called i2istudy, to implement all the necessary components of spoken communication for training spoken foreign language skills. This game consists of the computer-aided conversation and communication with native speakers. For example, English-speaking users can learn Spanish from Spanish-speaking users, and vice versa. The i2istudy system allows native speakers to teach others without knowing how to teach and without knowing foreign languages. In other words, i2istudy allows all native speakers, not necessarily professional teachers, to teach their native language as a part of collegial network game (Buga et al. 2014; Zolfaghar and Aghaie 2012). The main feature of the system consists of providing a common space with educational materials, including specifically designed lessons, which are simple and understandable step-by-step educational instructions aiding communication. The platform, which allows live audio–video communication, is built into the web interface, based on the modern Web real-time communications (WebRTC) technology.

APPLICATION

The i2istudy.com is currently a free multilingual web service for studying foreign languages online. The main idea of the service is based on the "time banking" principle (Válek and Jašíková 2013; Seyfang and Longhurst 2013). For every minute that a person teaches in the mother tongue, s/he is rewarded with a minute that can be used to learn foreign languages. This approach currently allows using the system free of charge (Seufert 2014). The name "i2istudy" comes from the idea of the "eye-to-eye" learning, based on the peer-2-peer principle (Hsu et al.2007). A new model of studying with the native speaker according to a set of interactive courses was created. Every "lesson" is based on the split screen platform. On one side of the screen, live video feed with the native language speaker is shown, and on the other half is a set of audio and video slides (Fig. 1). Together with the native speaker, the learner goes through the predefined content. All the teacher has to do is read information presented in the slide in their native language. Therefore, there is no need for the professional teacher, and theoretically every person can teach their mother tongue within this format. The student is presented with similar materials, which can be translated into their native language, depending on the selected level. Furthermore, the i2istudy is a self-regulated system, as it allows every user to pick their own paste, time, level, gender, and plenty of other characteristics of their instructor, along with the lesson, thus everyone can find their "right" teacher.

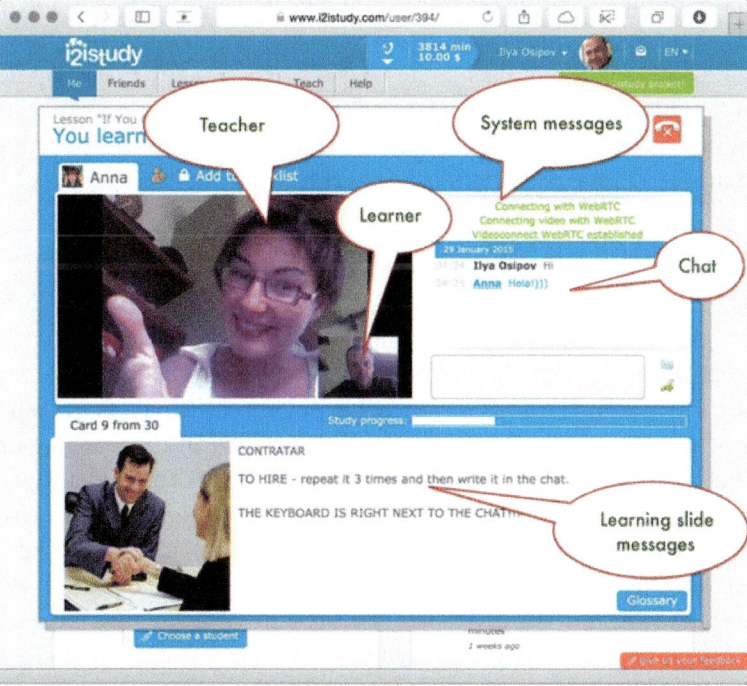

Figure 1. i2istudy lesson user interface.

The i2istudy is a social and informal approach to learning languages (Lai et al. 2013). It is not only a mere learning platform, but also a learning community that brings users together and builds relationships (Cohen 2014).

Learning foreign languages is a universal international activity uniting likeminded individuals all over the World. While studying, the system users enter into an intense live communication process with a native speaker, not only by studying the language, but also the culture, behavior, and manners. They not only discuss the set topics, but can also enter into a more personal communication. Currently, the system supports four languages: English, Spanish, Russian, and German; however, more languages can be added without significant technical changes of the system (Osipov et al. 2015).

This capacity is provided through the combination of three components for the user interactions with each other. One component provides real-time audio–visual communication for users, the next component displays text and a scenario of topics used for communication in languages understood by the users, and the third component allows communicating by sending and receiving instant text messages in the chat. The system–user interface is shown in Fig. 1. The system automatically tracks the time, which is reported in user accounts for the purpose of time banking (Marks 2012). The user interface, user interaction, and the script are presented by means of individual cards (slides), connected by a mutual discussion topic. Each slide consists of a separate text, graphics, and video in an interface, which is clear and understandable to each user, in their own native language. Each slide consists of a set of common fields provided in two languages, or in each individual language.

USER INTERACTIONS

The system also allows for the connection of multiple users with individual roles in the educational process. The logic of assigning roles within the framework of the system is that each user separately determines their own solutions. For example, to organize teaching of several students by a specialist in a particular knowledge, along with the monitoring of the teaching process, it may be necessary to have the roles of a teacher, a student, and a supervising controller. The teacher conveys the material to one or more students. However, the decision concerning the successful presentation and mastering of the material, for example, whether to jump to the next course or not, is taken by the controller (Fig. 2). The controller oversees the educational process.

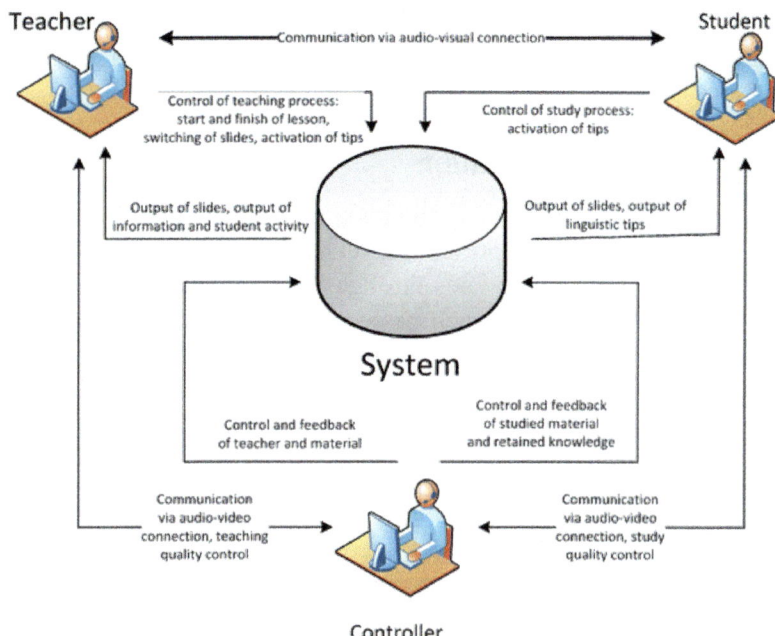

Figure 2. Teacher–student–controller interaction.

For example, decisions on whether the students can independently take the interactive tests available in the system, along with assessing the competency level of the teacher, are taken by the controller. Currently, for the study of foreign languages in the form of a game, the system allows only two roles: the teacher and the student.

GAMIFICATION

The developed application implements the following gamification methods:

The time banking principle

When user acts as a student by taking lessons, virtual system currency in minutes is spent from the user account. One minute of learning is debited from the account, while 1 min of teaching is credited to the account. Thus, the user acting as a teacher earns minutes, and the same user spends minutes as a student. In this way, all users participate in the virtual economy. Users are motivated to earn minutes, pushing the user to periodically assume the role of a teacher. Each user currently gets 30 min in the system as a part of the registration process. If all minutes are spent in the account, the system does not allow to study, but offers to teach to earn more minutes. Accumulated minutes are shown on the top of the interface screen in Fig. 1. The implemented time banking goal is to motivate users to teach in addition to learning (Osipov et al. 2015).

Sequential lessons presentation

Most computer games utilize gamification principles when the next game level becomes available after previous level has been completed. New lessons become available as the user goes through the previous lessons. Moreover, there is a grade displayed for each passed lesson as a single, dual, or triple star, reflecting how well the student passed the test at the end of each lesson. Sequential opening of the lessons in batches intrigues the user to find out what's coming next, and boosts user engagement. Explicit visibility of the grade encourages user to retake lessons with poor grades.

Achievements and badges

The user acquires nominal status, positioned as an achievement, for learning and teaching in the system. The user gets status notifications by email, while other users also see these "achievements and badges," and can select their learning partner based on this information. Basic list of "achievements and badges" includes "The First-grader; Middle school student, and High school student." To make it short, these are presented by the first two letters of the achievement, displayed in the corresponding language next to the user name, and are called badges. Shortened badges are used to save the space in the list, and will be replaced with medals in the future for better visibility. The goal is to motivate users to receive awards as an external evaluation, thus motivating them to come back and spend more time in the system.

Peer evaluation

For positive behavior reinforcement and encouraging polite communication between the users, peer evaluation is implemented. After each lesson, both the teacher and the student can evaluate each other. There are two types in this kind of evaluation. The fist is simple like/dislike, which are accumulated for each user and displayed in the personal profile. This information is also visible to other users in the lists of teachers and students. Thus, polite and positive users are clearly visible, based on the large number of likes, while impolite and unpleasant users are also apparent due to dominating dislikes. In addition, there is an option to report indecent user behavior to the system moderator. However, this option is a part of system moderation, rather than gamification (Osipov et al. 2015).

EXPERIMENTAL RESULTS

As a result of the conducted experiment, 39,729 users registered in the system in 6 months. 28,180 users indicated that they want to learn English, 8711 Spanish, 1028 Russian, and 1791 German languages (Table 1). About 20 % of all the 40,000 registered users participated in the experiment. As seen in Table 2, 20 % of the registered users have been involved in communicating with foreigners as a student or a teacher. The rest were either shy to speak with strangers, or decided not to spend their time. Some users failed to configure their microphone and web camera needed for the real-time audio–video connection, or their browser did not support the WebRTC protocol.

Table 1. Newly registered users' distribution by the native language.

New users by languages									
Month	01.12–31.12	01.01–31.01	01.02–28.02	01.03–31.03	01.04–30.04	01.05–31.05	01.06–30.06	01.07–31.07	01.08–31.08
Russian language, users	1069	3671	191	94	746	2186	3220	4329	1762
English language, users	178	746	68	25	295	978	4005	5582	2539
German language, users	15	22	3	3	6	22	29	38	14
Spanish language, users	17	43	12	3	79	760	903	1644	372

Table 2. Newly registered users' involvement in the learning/teaching process

Involvement									
Month	01.12–31.12	01.01–31.01	01.02–28.02	01.03–31.03	01.04–30.04	01.05–31.05	01.06–30.06	01.07–31.07	01.08–31.08
Number of just registered users who made a call in period	93	734	61	15	251	1026	2037	2072	722
Percent of just reg. users who made a call in period	7	16	22	12	22	26	25	18	15

As a result of the conducted experiments, it was established that two users, who were previously unfamiliar with each other, and who met in the developed application for the first time, could carry on a conversation following the suggested scenario, helping each other to learn foreign languages. Moreover, some users did not have a common language to use for communication. Average connection time was 11.9 min (189,207 min or 3153 h), divided by the number of successful connections (15,842). Table 3 shows the distribution of monthly successful connections.

Table 3. Successful connections, based on the duration and quantity for each month

Real connects									
Month	01.12–31.12	01.01–31.01	01.02–28.02	01.03–31.03	01.04–30.04	01.05–31.05	01.06–30.06	01.07–31.07	01.08–31.08
Successful connects duration, min	151	10,835	5021	3645	6202	37037	47,140	54,974	38,202
Number of successful connects	19	1228	492	131	587	3093	3868	3763	2661
Average duration, min	7.95	8.82	10.21	27.82	10.57	11.97	12.19	14.61	14.36

Any kind of interaction interruption was taken into account, including closing the browser or turning off the computer, or successfully finishing the lesson materials. Regardless of the fact that the average connection time is not very long, the experiment showed that two unfamiliar and unprepared users can carry on a conversation in a foreign language for quite long. Besides, the average connection time continued to increase with the number of registered users, and reached 14.4 min in August 2014. Moreover, the most loyal and active users became apparent, spending more hours learning and teaching, and even repeating the same lessons (Osipov et al. 2015).

The users registered as a result of advertising placed in social networks and conducted lessons either as a teacher or a student, learned the system interface on their own, without any special training. There were users not specifically recruited to conduct initial proof of concept experiments. The users accepted roles of the teacher and the student on their own. The corresponding ratio of 6.4 "teacher" users to 10.6 "student" users indicates that an average user is not afraid to play the role of a teacher in the developed system.

CONCLUSIONS

Online foreign language learning application was developed, where native speakers can act as teachers using teaching materials and scenarios available in the system. Over 40,000 users registered in the system. Combining modern information technology, spoken language teaching methods and gamification allowed developing an effective and quite popular tool for improving speaking skills in the study of foreign languages. The system allows finding a partner for practicing foreign language. The system can be used for developing foreign language communication skills and accelerated learning of foreign languages. The combination of online communications technology, educational content delivery, and gamification methods allowed maintaining average session duration at 14 min, which is longer than an average conversation in a store or on the street between strangers. Further development the system should be based on maintaining user interest through interesting content and gamification techniques and will probably allow achieving greater involvement and retention of users.

DECLARATIONS

Authors' contributions

IVO: Gamification; Experimental results; Literature review; Conclusions. AAV: Application, User interactions; Literature review; Conclusions. EN: Findings, Literature review; Conclusions. AYP: User interactions, Gamification; Experimental results. All authors read and approved the final manuscript.

Acknowledgements

The authors would like to thank the i2istudy.com team members for their dedicated efforts: Vadim Grishin, Ilya Poletaev, Andrei Poltanov, Elena Bogdanova, Vildan Garifulin, and Franziska Rinke.

Competing interests

The authors declare that they have no competing interests.

REFERENCES

1. Buga R, Căpeneață I, Chirasnel C, Popa A (2014) Facebook in foreign language teaching—a tool to improve communication competences. Procedia Social Behav Sci 128:93–98
2. Cohen EL (2014) What makes good games go viral? The role of technology use, efficacy, emotion and enjoyment in players' decision to share a prosocial digital game. Comput Human Behav 33:321–329
3. Hsu M-H, Jub TL, Yen CH, Chang C-M (2007) Knowledge sharing behavior in virtual communities: the relationship between trust, self-efficacy, and outcome expectations. Int J Human-Comput Stud 65(2):153–169
4. Lai K-W, Khaddage F, Knezek G (2013) Blending student technology experiences in formal and informal learning. J Comput Assist Learn 29(5):414–425
5. Marks M (2012) Time banking service exchange systems: a review of

the research and policy and practice implications in support of youth in transition. Child Youth Serv Rev 34(7):1230

6. Osipov IV, Volinsky AA, Grishin VV (2015a) Gamification, virality and retention in educational online platform. Int J Adv Comput Sci Appl 6(4):11–18. doi:10.14569/IJACSA.2015.060402
7. Osipov IV, Volinsky AA, Nikulchev E, Plokhov D (2015b) Study of monetization as a way of motivating freemium service users. Contemp Eng Sci 8(20):911–918. doi:10.12988/ces.2015.57212
8. Osipov IV, Nikulchev E, Volinsky AA, Prasikova AY (2015c) Study of gamification effectiveness in online e-learning systems. Int J Adv Comput Sci Appl 6(2):71–77. doi:10.14569/IJACSA.2015.060211
9. Osipov IV, Prasikova AY, Volinsky AA (2015d) Participant behavior and content of the online foreign languages learning and teaching platform. Comput Human Behav 50:476–488. doi:10.1016/j.chb.2015.04.028
10. Seufert EB (2014) Freemium Economics: Leveraging analytics and user segmentation to drive revenue (The Savvy Manager's Guides). Morgan Kaufmann, Waltham
11. Seyfang G, Longhurst N (2013) Growing green money? Mapping community currencies for sustainable development. Ecol Econ 86:65
12. Válek L, Jašíková V (2013) Time bank and sustainability: the permaculture approach. Procedia Social Behav Sci 92:986
13. Zolfaghar K, Aghaie A (2012) A syntactical approach for interpersonal trust prediction in social web applications: combining contextual and structural data. Knowl-Based Syst 26:93–102

Chapter 7

THE EFFECTS OF AN ONLINE STUDENT QUESTION-GENERATION STRATEGY ON ELEMENTARY SCHOOL STUDENT ENGLISH LEARNING

Fu-Yun Yu, Yu-Ling Chang and Hui-Ling Wu

Institute of Education, National Cheng Kung University

ABSTRACT

Recognizing the potential of online student question-generation to engage language learners in communicative activities and use the target language in a personally meaningful way for language and learning motivation development, an experimental study examining the English learning effects of this approach, in comparison to an online drill-and-practice strategy, was conducted. A quasi-experimental research design was adopted. Four sixth-grade classes ($N=106$) participated in this study and were randomly assigned to different treatment groups. An online learning system supporting the various learning activities was adopted. The results of analysis of covariance (ANCOVAs) showed that students in the online student question-generation group performed significantly better in English assessments and exhibited higher learning motivation than those in the contrast group. The significance of this study and suggestions for instructional implementation and future works are also presented.

INTRODUCTION

The importance of English language learning in a global society of lifelong learners

English has become one of the most popular languages in the world and is recognized as the most widespread language for communication in education, technology, business, diplomacy, science, and sports, as well as the high-tech and service-oriented industries, and many other fields (Zhang 2011). According to a report published by the British Council (2013), English is spoken at a useful level by some 1.75 billion people worldwide (i.e., one in every four people). Moreover, it is estimated that English has official or special status in at least 75 countries, that more than two thirds of the world's scientists and researchers use English as a second language, that 80 % of the world's electronically stored information is in English (Davies and Patsko 2013), and that two billion people will be using it or learning to use it by 2020 (British Council 2013).

The importance of encouraging people to learn English is widely acknowledged throughout Asia, in order to improve both national and individual competitiveness in an increasingly globalized world. Moreover, English has gradually become either the official or dominant foreign language in many Asian countries (Feng 2011). For example, in the 1980s, only approximately 4~5 % of Indians spoke English (Crystal 2004), but in recent years, it has been estimated that more than one third of the population of India (i.e., 350 million people) are able to use English in conversation (Graddol 2010). Overall, roughly 22.8 % of the population in Asia is able to speak English (Bolton 2008).

In light of the increasingly high demand for English proficiency, in 2001, the Ministry of Education in Taiwan launched the Nine-Year Joint Curricula Plan to revise the Elementary and Junior High School education system (Chern 2002). One of the major changes was that English became a required course for all fifth grade students and onwards, as opposed to such classes only starting in junior high schools (Wang2008). Two years later, in 2003, the age at which formal English language education began for Taiwanese elementary school children was further lowered to the third grade (Chou 2008).

The efforts to promote English proficiency in Taiwan were also expanded to tertiary education and in-service professional development. For instance, starting from 2002, the Ministry of Education encouraged universities to develop regulations for students to pass a certain level of standardized English proficiency tests as part of their graduation criteria (Hsu 2009; Wu & Wu 2010). Some government employees are also required to demonstrate a minimum A2 level in the Common European Framework of Reference for Languages (CEFR) (Wu & Wu 2010).

In spite of these reforms, Taiwanese students' performances in international English standardized tests still fall behind those of comparable Asian countries. According to a report by Educational Testing Services, the TOEFL scores of Taiwanese test-takers have been the lowest among those from Mainland China, Korea, Hong Kong, and Singapore since 2004 (Cheng 2011; Educational Testing Services 2010). As such, devising ways to improve English language teaching with substantiated learning effects remains a key concern for English scholars, educators, and government officials in Taiwan.

Teaching approaches to language education: from behavioristic to communicative paradigm shifts

According to Warschauer and Meskill (2000), language instruction has shifted from behavioristic to communicative paradigms over the last few decades. For many years before this, language instructors mainly focused on behavioristic instruction, using methods such as grammar translation and audio-lingual approaches, which utilize repetitious drills and practices in order to help students to memorize the focal language. In grammar translation lessons, teachers present students with large amounts of vocabulary and grammatical rules (Wang 2009), with the idea being that memorizing these can aid in the translation of sentences and longer texts (Kong 2011). To this end, students often engage in the tedious memorization of seemingly endless lists of grammar rules and vocabulary items (Liu & Shi 2007). Similarly, instructors who adopt audio-lingual methods to teach a second language tend to demonstrate correct models of sentences first, and students then repeat the accurate pronunciation and intonation of the target language verbally in order to memorize these (Felder & Henriques 1995; Wang 2009). These traditional teaching methods, in accordance with behaviorism, emphasize that instruction is composed of creating "a process of mechanical habit formation" by providing many opportunities for students to practice (Richards 2005).

However, over the last decade, a growing number of scholars have opposed the extensive use of these traditional language teaching strategies, with their focus on drills and practices. In their opinion, these approaches are mainly aimed at helping students to pass reading and writing examinations, rather than being able to communicate naturally in real-world contexts (Butler 2005; Su 2006; Yang & Lyster 2010). Moreover, traditional language teaching methods also prevent students from taking responsibility for their own learning (Ellis 2008).

In light of these weaknesses, many scholars have proposed alternative language instruction methods, such as total physical response, the natural approach, silent way, or suggestopedia, which have been applied since the 1970s (Brandl 2007). These approaches avoid rote learning, and instead focus more on the learners and their cognitive processes when learning a language, with learning being seen as a social process for conveying meaning (Jacobs & Farrell 2003; Nunan 2004). In simple terms, many scholars now see the ultimate goal of learning a language as being able to communicate effectively (Brandl 2007). As a result, a growing number of researchers now recommend that educators use communicative approaches, which encourage students to apply the target language to create meanings in various contexts (Wang 2009).

The emphasis on communicative approaches to language instruction (i.e., communicative language teaching, CLT), as both the means and ultimate goal of language learning, fits well with the principles of constructionism (Ruschoff & Ritter 2001). It is suggested that learners exposed to CLT (e.g., task-based instruction, output-based production tasks) are more inclined to engage in meaningful externalization and internalization of their own linguistic resources, rather than attempting to memorize the accurate models of the language (Richards 2005; Swain 1993). The process of using language to realize one's communicative intent helps learners to pay attention to both the accuracy of forms and the meanings of language simultaneously (Izumi & Bigelow 2000), engage in deeper and more elaborate processing of the forms (Izumi 2002), and seek solutions to any communicative problems encountered autonomously, once any gaps between their linguistic knowledge and intended goals are noticed (Hanaoka 2007; Swain & Lapkin 1995). As a result, CLT enables learners to increase their linguistic awareness and build their capabilities through actively and continuously using the language to communicate in meaningful contexts or around purposefully designed tasks (Richards 2005; Swain 1993).

In sum, CLT emphasizes learner-centeredness in language education (Song 2009). Also highlighted are the notions of providing learning opportunities for active engagement and some control of the learning process to facilitate greater self-competency, which in turn results in greater personal meaning and affective gains (Chang & Ho 2009). Consonant with the ideas of CLT, the current study applies a student question-generation strategy to language instruction, and its effects on language performance and learning motivation in English are examined.

Student question-generation: empirical evidence supporting its educational value and as an alternative approach to CLT for English learning

Research that applies the student question-generation (SQG) strategy in various fields has generally found positive effects with regard to outcomes such as comprehension (Brown & Walter 2005; Drake & Barlow 2008), motivation (Chin et al. 2002), positive attitudes toward the subject matter studied (Keil 1965; Perez 1985), problem-solving abilities (Dori & Herscovitz 1999), cognitive and metacognitive strategy development (Yu & Liu 2008), intra-group communication (Yu & Liu 2005), and more diverse and flexible thinking (Andre & Anderson 1978-79; Brown & Walter 2005; English 1997). While there is a growing body of empirical evidence substantiating the educational value of SQG, a majority of related studies deal with math and natural science subjects, and there are still a limited number of works exploring its effects in language instruction (Yu & Lai 2014).

As noted above, and consistent with the notions of CLT, SQG may prompt students to use English for meaningful oral and written communication. By requiring students to generate questions and corresponding answers based on the English learning content, as if they were test item designers, it is assumed that SQG can help students to develop language proficiency by consciously directing their attention to the forms and meanings of the target language simultaneously during SQG activities. To elaborate, when students engage in question-generation, the opportunities this provides to record questions by themselves may direct their attention to the correct pronunciation of the target language. To ensure that their speech is audible and clear, it is likely that students will engage in numerous rehearsals before recording, as well as listening to their recordings to make sure that they are of acceptable quality. In addition, in order to provide the correct answers to the questions they compose, students are likely to review the related learning materials so that they can better understand the content. This process may further direct students to review their questions and engage in editing and re-writing, as needed. In short, instead of attempting to memorize the target language, as seen in more traditional approaches, SQG can enhance the integrated development of listening, speaking, reading, and writing proficiency in language instruction, with its focus on using the target language for real communication, rather than simply passing tests.

Research purposes and questions

This study examines the effects of SQG and traditional drill-and-practice strategies on English performance. In order to encourage the students to engage in all four skills of listening, speaking, reading, and writing (and thus not only the latter two), this work carried out SQG in a computer-supported context, with online SQG chosen as the focal task. Furthermore, since learning motivation is very important for second language learners (Dörnyei & Ushioda 2011; Murray et al. 2011), and the communicative use of language has been suggested to increase this (Sanchez 2004), this work also examines the effects of online SQG on the student learning motivation.

In short, this study examines the effects of online SQG on English learning in comparison to the online drill-and-practice (D&P) strategy, guided by the following two research questions:
- Are there any significant differences between the online SQG and D&P strategies with regard to their effects on student academic performance in English?

- Are there any significant differences between the online SQG and D&P strategies with regard to their effects on student learning motivation in English?

METHODS

Participants and instructional materials

Four classes of sixth-grade students ($N=106$; 46 male, 60 female) taught by the same instructor from one primary school in Taiwan participated in this study. Because the participating students had started taking computer classes since they were in the third grade (one 40-min instructional session per week), they possessed the skills needed to participate in the online learning activities designed in this study, including word processing, imaging editing, multimedia file uploading, and web surfing. Additionally, since the students had been taking English classes since the third grade (two 40-min instructional sessions per week), they possessed the basic English abilities needed to engage in the focal activities. More specifically, all the participants had already learned the English alphabet and phonics, as well as the vocabulary and basic sentence structures frequently encountered in daily life.

The instructional materials adopted by the participating school, volume 7 of *Hi English* (Hess International Educational Group 2008), were used in this study. The vocabulary, sentence patterns, and phonics covered in the three units used in this work are listed in Table 1. Students should be able to use these sentence patterns to ask and answer questions in verbal and written forms after receiving the instruction. They should also be capable of differentiating and naming the various phonics in both verbal and written forms. Finally, the students should be able to use the taught vocabulary to describe their feelings or certain objects.

Table 1. Main topics covered in the English class during the study

Unit number/title	Vocabulary	Sentence Pattern	Phonics
1: Do you see any lions?	Lion, elephant, tiger, pig, snake	How many… do you see?	Sm—small, smart
		Do you see any …?	Sn—snack, snake
		Yes, I do.	Sw—sweater, swing
		No, I don't.	

2: Look! There's an elephant.	Big, small, clean, dirty, long, short	It looks …	Sk—skirt, sky
		They look…	Sp—spoon, spider
		There is a …	St—star, stairs
		There are …	
3: I feel tired.	Excited, tired, sick, bored, sleepy	How do you feel?	
		I feel…	
		How do you feel?	
		I feel …	
		I want to …	

Online learning system

An online learning system called QuARKS (Question-Authoring and Reasoning Knowledge System) (Yu 2009) was adopted in this study. Like all similar online systems, multimedia contents, including pictures, audio, and video, can be embedded as part of the questions that the students generate or answer. Texts with different fonts, styles, colors, and sizes can also be used for differentiation or highlighting purposes. Moreover, the question types that are often employed at all levels of the educational system are supported in QuARKS. Nevertheless, since multiple-choice, true-or-false, and matching questions are most frequently used by elementary English teachers in Taiwan, these were chosen to be generated for the online SQG and practiced in the D&P activities, which are described in more detail below.

For the online SQG, after selecting the type of questions to generate (by clicking on the respective icons, Fig. 1), the students were directed to the related space for the question-generation activities (Fig. 2). The students then needed to enter information into all the required fields for a successful submission. Specifically, for multiple-choice questions, the students needed to provide a question stem, two to five alternative answers, an answer key, and an annotation briefly explaining the main ideas tested in the question for each item (see Fig. 2). For yes/no questions, the students needed to provide a question, an answer key (yes or no), and an annotation for each item. Similarly, for matching questions, the students needed to give a question, two to ten options, and an answer key for each of the options to be matched. Once questions are submitted, they can be retrieved, revised, and deleted by the question-author (see Fig. 3).

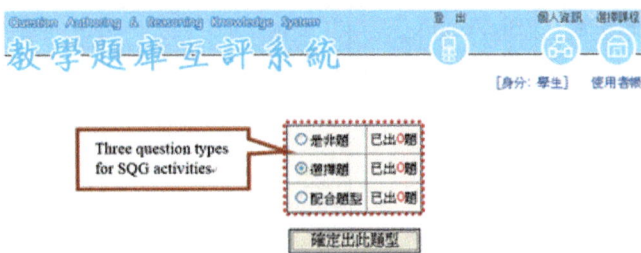

Figure 1. Selection of a question type to generate in the online SQG system.

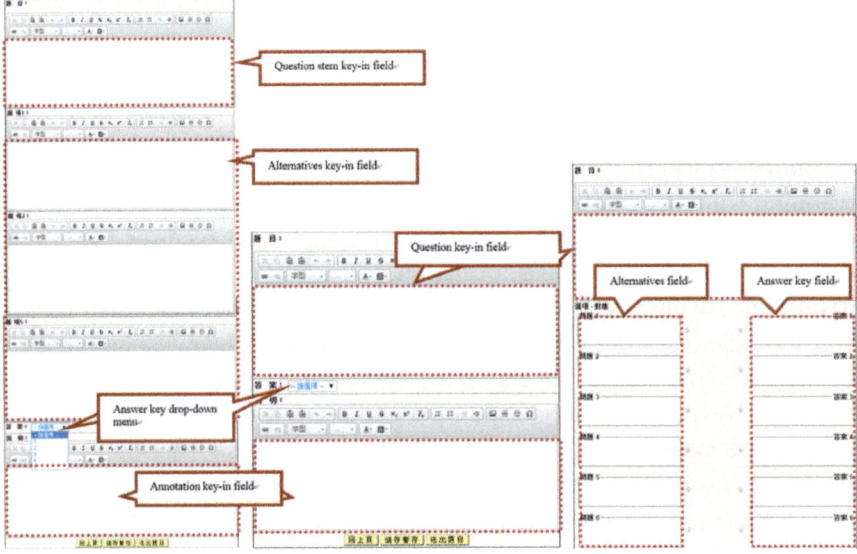

Figure 2. Online SQG space: multiple-choice (*left*), yes/no (*middle*), and matching (*right*) questions.

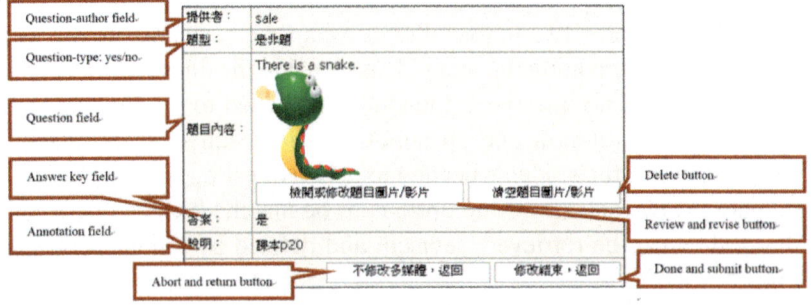

Figure 3. Retrieval of questions generated for review, revision and deletion.

For online D&P, the students first keyed in the number of items they would like to answer in the boxes beside the respective different question types (see Fig. 4) and were then directed to the related D&P spaces (see Fig. 5). After completion, the students could review all the questions they had answered during the D&P session, along with the related answer keys (see Fig. 6). If there was enough time, the students could then choose to do the drill-and-practice activity again by re-entering the number of questions to answer. The system would then randomly re-select the specified number of questions from the online database and put them in a different order, with the various options for multiple-choice items also re-sequenced.

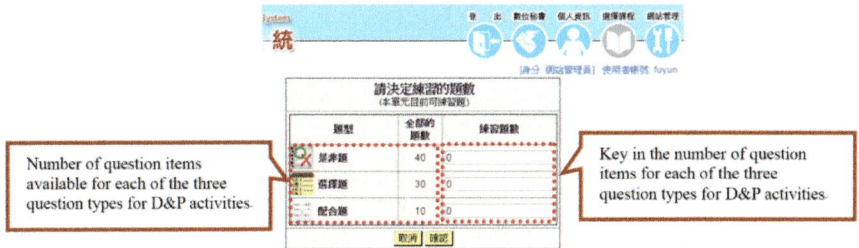

Figure 4. Specification of the number of questions in the online D&P window.

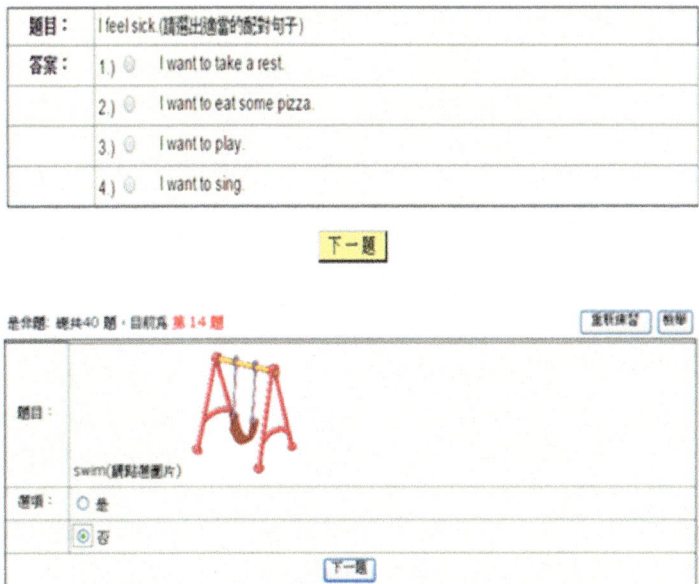

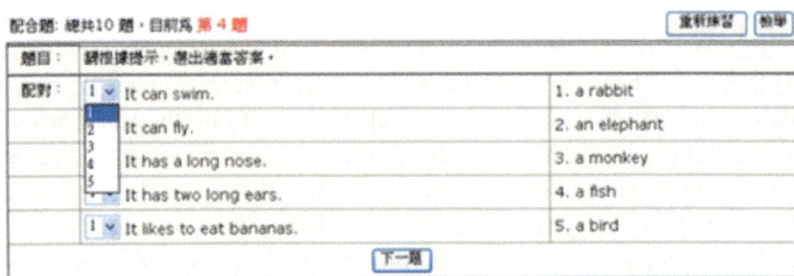

Figure 5. Online D&P activities: multiple-choice (*left*), yes/no (*middle*), and matching (*right*) questions.

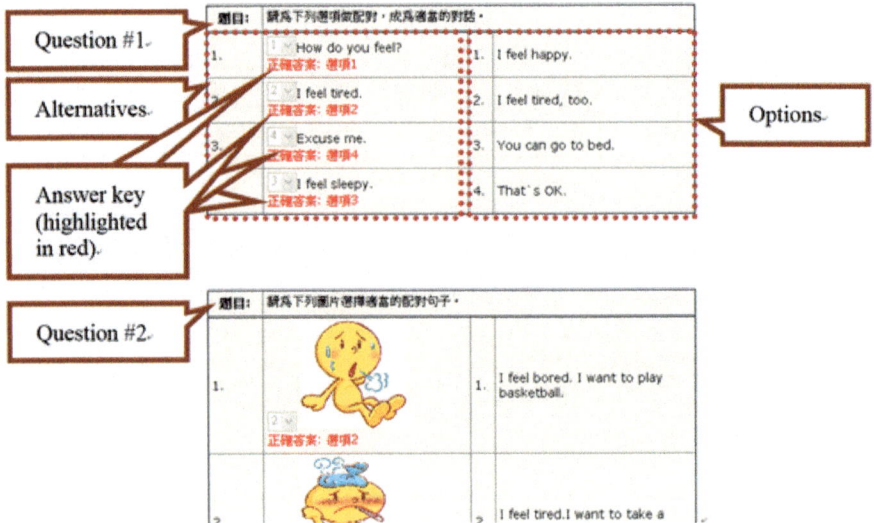

Figure 6. Online D&P review with correct answer shown (matching question type).

Research design and the experimental treatment groups

This study adopted a pretest-posttest quasi-experimental research design that lasted for 11 weeks. Each of the four intact classes used the adopted system for participation and was randomly assigned to one of the two treatment conditions: online SQG (the experimental group, $N=54$) and online D&P (the contrast group, $N=52$).

The students assigned to the online SQG group were directed to compose questions with answers in their assigned groups in accordance with that week's instructional content in text or multimedia forms. Students could choose to select the files already stored by the instructor in the multimedia database, or upload any files they found on the internet or created themselves (e.g., photos taken with their smartphones or digital cameras). They could also record audio of themselves asking questions.

In contrast, students in the online D&P group engaged in rote learning activities by answering a series of questions similar to those in the traditional English practice sessions with their assigned groups on computers. All questions were purposively selected by the instructor from the item bank provided by the textbook publisher.

Experimental procedures

To ensure the appropriateness of the implementation procedures, the smoothness of the adopted online system, and the clarity of the instrument, two pilot tests were conducted prior to the actual study in the previous semester. The main aims of the first pilot test were to ensure that the instruction and performance criteria for question-generation for different question types were understandable and clear to the students with different levels of English proficiency. Six sixth-grade students with below-average, average, and above-average English proficiency were thus purposefully selected and invited to participate in this pilot test. Some adjustments were made based on the participants' feedback with regard to the activity (i.e., more question models given to illustrate the performance criteria of SQG).

Furthermore, to ensure the operational smoothness of the adopted system in a large class setting, the appropriateness of the time allocated for different instructional events (i.e., training, hands-on practice with the system, and feedback on student performance in the last session), and the comprehensibility of the motivation scale, a second pilot test was conducted. Two fifth-grade classes ($N=59$) participated in this, one for the online SQG and the other for the online D&P. The results of the pilot study confirmed the system's stability and instrument's clarity. Also, based on data collected during the second pilot study, the maximum numbers of items included for different question types for each online D&P activity were as follows: 30 items for multiple-choice questions, 40 for true/false, and ten for matching.

Afterwards, the actual study was conducted in the students' regular English instructional sessions in the English classroom. In view of the value of collaborative learning for knowledge creation (Paavola & Hakkarainen 2005), the participants were assigned to groups of three or four to work collaboratively during the study. In accordance with the suggestions of most CL researchers (e.g., Johnson & Johnson 2009), heterogeneous groups, based on the students' English grade in the previous semester were formed. Specifically, for groups of three, there was one student from the lower quartile, one from the upper quartile, and one from the interquartile range. In constrast, for groups of four, there was one from the lower quartile, one from the upper quartile, and two from the interquartile range. As a result, eight groups were formed in each participating class.

As a routine during the study, the students participated in the online learning activities in the last 20 min of the second instructional session each week for 11 weeks. In the first week, a training session was given by the instructor to help the students get acquainted with the general operational procedures of the system, and they then completed the motivation scale, and their English grades from the previous semester were collected. One of the three question types was then targeted every two weeks (i.e., weeks 2 to 3 for multiple-choice, weeks 4 to 5 for yes/no, and weeks 6 to 7 for matching).

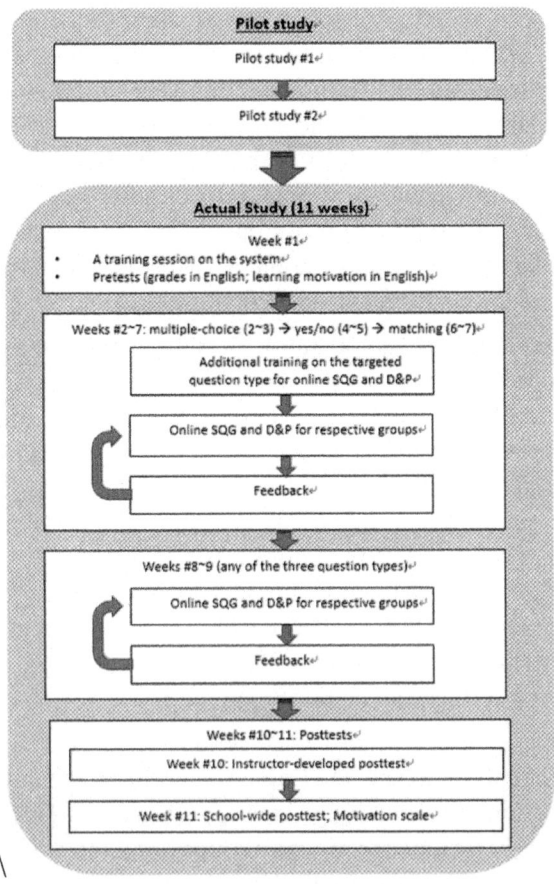

Figure 7. Experimental procedures used in this study.

To ensure the students had the necessary skills, a brief training session on generating or answering the target question type on the adopted system was arranged before the students took part in the related online activities (i.e., online SQG for the experimental group and online D&P for the contrast group). Feedback on student performance was arranged the following week, in which exemplary student work was highlighted and discussed. After gaining experience in generating or answering each of the three question types using the system, in weeks 8 and 9, the students were allowed to choose their preferred question types to generate or answer during the activities. In total, the students engaged in eight sessions of online SQG or online D&P activities in their respective groups. The instructor-developed posttest was then administered in the tenth week, while in the 11th week, all the participants took the school-wide posttest and completed the motivation scale. A flow diagram summarizing the major experimental procedures used in this study is shown in Fig. 7.

Instruments

English academic achievement tests

The students took instructor-developed and school-wide administered academic achievement tests after participating in eight online learning activities to measure their English performance. The instructor-developed test was composed of 28 multiple-choice, ten true/false, and three matching questions (with 12 options/answers). The school-wide administered test was composed of ten multiple-choice, eight true/false, and four matching questions (with 32 options/answers). Multimedia files were included to assess student recognition and use of the learned English (and thus not merely their memorization). Audio recordings were also included to assess student listening comprehension.

All items underwent item analyses procedures and needed to meet the criteria set for item discrimination (.25) and item difficulty (.40) before they were included for data analysis. For the instructor-developed test, all the items except one yes/no question met the set criteria, and thus only one item was excluded from the data analysis. For the school-wide administered test, since all test items met the set criteria, all were included in the data analysis. Finally, the Cronbach's α for the instructor-developed and school-wide tests were 0.93 and 0.98, respectively, indicating their high reliability.

Learning motivation in English

Due to the context sensitive nature of motivation (Duncan & McKeachie 2005), Pintrich, Smith, and McKeachie's Motivated Strategies for Learning

Questionnaire (MSLQ) was modified by Shiu (2002) to assess student learning motivation in English, and was adopted in this study. The scale contains 35 items which assess the respondent's learning goal orientation, task value, control beliefs, self-efficacy, expectations of success, and test anxiety in English. For each item, the students rated themselves on a five-point Likert scale, from strongly disagree (1) to strongly agree (5). After the scores of negative items were reversed (i.e., items on test anxiety), they were added to the scores of all other items to represent the respondent's learning motivation in English in the data analysis. The higher the score was, the greater the learning motivation the students had with regard to English.

After passing the expert content validity procedure, exploratory factor analysis was conducted. With all items having at least a factor loading of 0.45 on the corresponding factor, and all constructs accounting for a total of 81.6 % of the variance, the scale thus had satisfactory validity. Finally, the Cronbach's α of .92 indicated the consistency of this scale.

RESULTS

English academic achievement

Tests of analysis of covariance (ANCOVA) were conducted to examine the comparative effects of the online SQG and D&P strategies on student academic achievement in English, with student grades in English from the previous semester as the covariate. The assumption of the homogeneity of regression slopes was satisfied for both the instructor-developed test, $F(1, 102)$, 1.714, $p > .05$, and school-wide administered test, $F(1, 102) = 1.527$, $p > .05$, before proceeding to ANCOVA. The results of ANCOVA indicated that there were significant differences in English performance between the two groups, $F(1, 103) = 5.461$, $p < .05$, $F(1, 103) = 5.004$, $p < .05$, for the instructor-developed and school-wide administered tests, respectively, after controlling for student English performance in the prior semester. As shown in Table 2, students in the online SQG group had a significantly higher adjusted mean test score in both the instructor-developed and school-wide administered tests than those in the online D&P group.

Table 2. Descriptive statistics of the experimental treatment groups for the observed variables

Observed variables	Two treatment groups		Online SQG ($n=54$)	Online D&P ($n=52$)
English academic achievement	Pretest[a]			
		Mean (SD)	76.37 (21.13)	79.09 (20.25)
	Posttest (instructor-developed)			
		Mean (SD)	78.71 (20.66)	75.81 (22.73)
		Adjusted Mean	79.94	74.53
	Posttest (school-wide)			
		Mean (SD)	82.61 (21.29)	73.19 (27.26)
		Adjusted Mean	84.63	71.86
English learning motivation	Pretest[b]			
		Mean (SD)	123.15 (20.77)	111.06 (21.83)
	Posttest			
		Mean (SD)	126.29 (19.18)	110.00 (21.93)
		Adjusted Mean	122.13	114.02

[a] Grades in English from the previous semester
[b] Score on the modified MSLQ

Learning motivation in English

ANCOVA was also conducted to compare the learning motivation effects of online SQG and D&P, with the student pretest scores on the modified MSLQ as the covariate. The homogeneity of regression tests showed no violation of the assumption, $F(1, 102)=1.805$, $p>.05$. The results of ANCOVA revealed that there were significant differences between the two groups in learning motivation after the influence of the pretest was controlled, $F(1, 103)=7.326$, $p<.05$. As shown in Table 2, students in the online SQG group scored higher in the modified MSLQ (adjusted mean=122.13) than those in the online D&P group (adjusted mean=114.02).

DISCUSSION

Online SQG promoted English performance to a greater extent than online D&P

The findings of this study indicated that online SQG was a more effective strategy to enhance student English performance than the online D&P approach. In order to come up with test-worthy ideas and present them in an appropriate form of questions (i.e., text-only or text with audio and pictures), students who engaged in the SQG activities would be more likely to put the learned language into actual use and practice listening, speaking, reading, and writing with it, as compared to those who completed the online D&P exercises. In fact, there was little if any need and few opportunities for the D&P group to practice speaking English. Moreover, different ways of connecting and combining the vocabulary items and sentence patterns learned from the current unit, as well as different units, were more likely to be tried during the SQG process.

As seen in the questions generated by students, many items contained audio recordings or photos produced by the participants themselves and used to describe the abstract concepts covered in the units (e.g., excited, tired, sick, bored, sleepy, big, small, clean, dirty, long, and short). Some even included vocabulary and sentence structures covered in prior units. Such an elaboration process, according to King (1995), helps to build a complex cognitive network and reflects what McCrindle and Christensen (1995) emphasized as a powerful and effective way to enhance meaningful learning. In this regard, similar to what CLT can offer, the SQG activities would direct students to pay more and closer attention to the forms and meanings of the language, rather than merely fixating on the correctness of grammar, spelling, and pronunciation, as seen in the more behaviorist approaches to language teaching (e.g., grammar translation and audio-lingual method). The results of this study also supported the output hypothesis, as the process of output production allowed students to be more conscious of their linguistic states (Swain 2005).

In contrast, the online D&P activities had weaker effects on English performance. The teacher's informal in-class observations revealed that students in the D&P group mainly engaged in repeated practice. When encountering problems, these students were less often seen to adopt cognitive or metacognitive strategies, such as searching for resources, discussing things with peers, or asking the teacher questions, than those in the SQG group. This anecdotal observation is in consonance with the finding of McLoughlin and Oliver (1998) that students rarely use high-level cognitive processes in D&P activities. Instead, they tend to focus on practicing tasks in a repetitive manner until mastery is achieved.

In sum, the different levels of cognitive processing involved in SQG and D&P may result in the different learning effects obtained in this study. The various cognitive processes mobilized and enacted by SQG (e.g., reflecting on the learning experience, making sense of the learning materials, searching one's existing knowledge reservoir for possible connections and appropriate use of the language, seeking additional information for possible alternative answers and options for questions, connecting newly learned ideas with prior knowledge) were found in this study to enhance student English performance in different language areas (i.e., reading, writing, and listening), to a greater extent than was seen with D&P.

Online SQG enhanced learning motivation to a greater degree than online D&P

Students' responses to the learning motivation scale indicated that those assigned to the online SQG group, as compared to those to the online D&P, were more motivated to learn English, and tended to agree more with statements such as: learning the content covered in English class is very important to me; it is my own fault if I do not learn the materials presented in English class; and I am confident that I can understand the most complex material delivered by the instructor in this course. In other words, through the experience of constructing rather than simply answering questions online, students were generally more appreciative of the task value of the focal activity, were more intrinsically than extrinsically motivated, were more positive about their performance in English, were less anxious about English tests, and felt more that they themselves should be responsible of their own learning.

Although D&P strategies have traditionally dominated language learning activities, over the last few decades, the focus has shifted from a teacher-oriented to learner-centered pedagogy (Hoven 1999). Instead of using repetitive D&P to strengthen student memorization of the target language, a learner-centered pedagogy stresses the importance of encouraging learners to communicate in a meaningful context. The online SQG strategy was thus proposed to better meet the needs of the communicative approach. In this, students are given reasons to communicate using the target language and opportunities to produce something concrete in different forms (such as text-based or multimedia items) during the SQG process. As a consequence, the online SQG strategy was found to be more effective in promoting student learning motivation than the online D&P approach. This result is consistent with the suggestion of Sanchez (2004) that communicative use of the target language can increase learning motivation.

CONCLUSION

Since second language learners do not fully understand the language they are learning, and often do not need to actively use it for daily communicative purposes, as would be the case when learning a first language, the learning process tends to be less effective, and students have less motivation to engage in learning (Masgoret & Gardner 2003). It is thus necessary to cultivate an environment that can encourage the communicative use of the second language to increase both learner motivation and language competencies. This is even more urgent for students in East Asian countries where there are few opportunities for speaking and writing English in daily life, and the learning experiences of students in such contexts are often rather negative (Hwang et al. 2010).

In an attempt to cope with these limitations, this study proposed an online SQG strategy as an alternative approach to creating communicative needs and purposes for learning language. According to CLT, when learners are encouraged to construct their knowledge and control their learning on their own, this will encourage them to no longer process language by simply memorizing the spelling, pronunciation, and meaning of the target words. Instead, they are more likely to use English to communicate their needs and intentions, which may result in more positive learning experiences and thus improved learning performance and motivation (Chang 2005).

Significance of this study and the proposed strategy—SQG for English language learning

The results of the current study confirmed the effectiveness of the online SQG strategy for enhancing student performance and learning motivation in English. This approach went some way to mitigating the difficulties associated with traditional language teaching methods, especially the communication problems identified by Hwang et al. (2010). In addition, the online SQG strategy was able to meet the call of many scholars to use the target language to create meanings in various contexts (Wang 2009), and encourage the learners to focus on both the meanings and forms of the words they are using (Sanchez 2004). Furthermore, the online SQG strategy meets the criteria and conditions of setting up favorable second language instructional and learning contexts, as identified by Sanchez (2004). These include providing opportunities for learners to be exposed to the language, using it in a communicative context, and being motivated to do so for listening, speaking, writing, and reading. Due to online SQG's proven potential for second language learning, based on the learning effects obtained in this study, it is suggested that this approach be added to the current CLT strategy reservoir (e.g., along with task-based instruction and output-based production tasks), as an effective communicative approach to learning English as a second language.

Limitations of this study and suggestions for future works

The present study expands our current knowledge about SQG by confirming its effectiveness with regard to enhancing English performance in relation to the targeted vocabulary items, sentence patterns, and phonics, as well as learning motivation. However, this study investigated the learning effects of sixth-grade students with less than 4 years of formal English learning experience, who worked collaboratively on computers in Taiwan over a period of 11 weeks. The generalizability of the results to other contexts should consequently be exercised with care. Interested researchers are thus advised to extend the current findings by examining the influence of the SQG strategy in second language learning contexts other than English, and involve learners with different language learning experience, at different educational levels, and from different cultures. Moreover, if this strategy is implemented for a longer period of time, it is anticipated that the effects of SQG on all four language areas (i.e., reading, writing, speaking and listening) could be more clearly plotted and understood.

DECLARATIONS

Acknowledgements

This work was supported by the National Science Council and the Ministry of Science and Technology, Taiwan, ROC [NSC 99-2511-S-006-015-MY3; NSC 102-2511-S-006-003-MY3].

REFERENCES

1. Andre, M., & Anderson, T. (1978-79). The development and evaluation of a self-questioning study technique. *Reading Research Quarterly, 14*(4), 605-622.
2. Bolton, K. (2008). English in Asia, Asian Englishes, and the issue of proficiency. *English Today, 24*(2), 3–12.
3. Brandl, K. (2007). *Communicative language teaching in action: putting principles to work*. NJ: Prentice Hall.
4. British Council. (2013). *The English effect*. Retrieved March 22, 2015, from https://www.britishcouncil.org/sites/default/files/english-effect-report-v2.pdf.
5. Brown, S. I., & Walter, M. I. (2005). *The art of problem posing* (3rd ed.). Hillsdale, NJ: Lawrence Erlbaum Associates.
6. Butler, Y. (2005). Comparative perspectives towards communicative

activities among elementary school teachers in South Korea, Japan and Taiwan. *Language Teaching Research, 9*(4), 423–446.

7. Chang, M.-M. (2005). Apply self-regulated learning strategies in a web-based instruction—an investigation of motivation perception.*Computer Assisted Language Learning, 18*(3), 217–230.

8. Chang, M.-M., & Ho, C. M. (2009). Effects of locus of control and learner-control on web-based language learning. *Computer Assisted Language Learning, 22*(3), 189–206.

9. Cheng, T.-Y. (2011). The ability of Taiwanese college freshmen to read and interpret graphics in English. *The Asian EFL Journal Quarterly, 13*(1), 321–347.

10. Chern, C.-L. (2002). English language teaching in Taiwan. *Asia-Pacific Journal of Education, 22*(2), 97–105.

11. Chin, C., Brown, D. E., & Bruce, B. C. (2002). Student-generated questions: a meaningful aspect of learning in science. *International Journal of Science Education, 24*(5), 521–549.

12. Chou, C.-H. (2008). Exploring elementary English teachers' practical knowledge: a case study of EFL teachers in Taiwan. *Asia Pacific Education Review, 9*(4), 529–541.

13. Crystal, D. (2004). *Subcontinent raises its voice*. Retrieved February 22, 2015, from http://www.guardian.co.uk/education/2004/nov/19/tefl.

14. Davies, K. S., & Patsko, L. (2013). *How to teach English as a lingua franca (ELF)*. Retrieved March 22, 2015, from http://www.britishcouncil.org/blog/how-teach-english-lingua-franca-elf.

15. Dori, Y. J., & Herscovitz, O. (1999). Question-posing capability as an alternative evaluation method: analysis of an environmental case study. *Journal of Research in Science Teaching, 36*, 411–430.

16. Dörnyei, Z., & Ushioda, E. (2011). *Teaching and researching motivation*. Harlow, England: Pearson Education Limited.

17. Drake, J. M., & Barlow, A. T. (2008). Assessing students' levels of understanding multiplication through problem writing. *Teaching Children Mathematics, 14*(5), 272–277.

18. Duncan, T. G., & McKeachie, W. J. (2005). The making of the motivated strategies for learning questionnaire. *Educational Psychologist, 40*(2), 117–128.

19. Educational Testing Services. (2010). *Test and score data summary for TOEFL® internet-based and paper-based tests: 2010 test data*. Retrieved March 23, 2015, from http://www.ets.org/Media/Research/pdf/TOEFL-

SUM-2010.pdf.
20. Ellis, R. (2008). Explicit knowledge and second language learning and pedagogy. In J. Cenoz & N. H. Hornberger (Eds.), *Encyclopedia of language and education. Vol 6: knowledge about language* (2nd ed., pp. 143–153). New York: Springer Science Business Media LLC.
21. English, L. D. (1997). Promoting a problem-posing classroom. *Teaching Children Mathematics, 4*(3), 172–179.
22. Felder, R., & Henriques, E. R. (1995). Learning and teaching styles in foreign and second language education. *Foreign Language Annals, 28*(1), 21–31.
23. Feng, A. (2011). *English language education across greater China*. Bristol, UK: Multilingual Matters.
24. Graddol, D. (2010). *English next India: the future of English in India*. Milton Keynes, UK: The English Company (UK) Ltd.
25. Hanaoka, O. (2007). Output, noticing, and learning: an investigation into the role of spontaneous attention to form in a four-stage writing task. *Language Teaching Research, 11*(4), 459–479.
26. Hess International Educational Group. (2008). *Hi English* (Vol. 7). Taipei: Hess International Educational Group.
27. Hoven, D. (1999). A model for listening and viewing comprehension in multimedia environments. *Language Learning & Technology, 3*(1), 88–103.
28. Hsu, H.-F. (2009). *The impact of implementing English proficiency tests as a graduation requirement at Taiwanese universities of technology*. Unpublished doctoral dissertation, University of York, York, United Kingdom.
29. Hwang, W.-Y., Shadiev, R., & Haung, S.-M. (2010). Effect of multimedia annotation system on improving English writing and speaking performance. In X. Zhang et al. (Eds.), *Entertainment for education: digital techniques and systems* (pp. 1–12). Berlin, Heidelberg: Springer.
30. Izumi, S. (2002). Output, input enhancement, and the noticing hypothesis. *Studies in Second Language Acquisition, 24*, 541–577.
31. Izumi, S., & Bigelow, M. (2000). Does output promote noticing and second language acquisition? *TESOL Quarterly, 34*(2), 239–278.
32. Jacobs, G. M., & Farrell, T. S. C. (2003). Understanding and implementing the CLT (communicative language teaching) paradigm. *RELC Journal, 34*(1), 5–30.
33. Johnson, R. T., & Johnson, D. W. (2009). An educational psychology

success story: social interdependence theory and cooperative learning. *Educational Researcher, 38*(5), 365–379.
34. Keil, G. E. (1965). *Writing and solving original problems as a means of improving verbal arithmetic problem solving ability.* Unpublished doctoral dissertation, Indiana University, IN, USA.
35. King, A. (1991). Improving lecture comprehension: effects of a metacognitive strategy. *Applied Cognitive Psychology, 5*, 331–346.
36. King, A. (1995). Designing the instructional process to enhance critical thinking across the curriculum. *Teaching of Psychology, 22*(1), 13–17.
37. Kong, N. (2011). Establishing a comprehensive English teaching pattern combining the communicative teaching method and the grammar-translation method. *English Language Teaching, 4*(1), 76–78.
38. Lingoda GmbH. (2015). *English as a second language.* Retrieved March 21, 2015, from https://www.lingoda.com/english-as-a-second-language.
39. Liu, Q., & Shi, J. (2007). An analysis of language teaching approaches and methods: effectiveness and weakness. *US-China Education Review, 4*(1), 69–71.
40. Masgoret, A. M., & Gardner, R. C. (2003). Attitudes, motivation, and second language learning: a meta-analysis of studies conducted by Gardner and associates. *Language Learning, 53*, 123–163.
41. McCrindle, A., & Christensen, C. (1995). The impact of learning journals on metacognitive and cognitive processes on learning performance. *Learning and Instruction, 5*, 167–185.
42. McLoughlin, C., & Oliver, R. (1998). Maximising the language and learning link in computer learning environments. *British Journal of Educational Technology, 29*(2), 125–136.
43. Murray, G., Gao, X., & Lamb, T. (2011). *Identity, motivation and autonomy in language learning.* Bristol, UK: Multilingual Matters.
44. Nunan, D. (2004). *Task-based language teaching.* Cambridge, UK: Cambridge University Press.
45. Paavola, S., & Hakkarainen, K. (2005). The knowledge creation metaphor—an emergent epistemological approach to learning. *Science and Education, 14*, 535–557.
46. Perez, J. A. (1985). *Effects of student-generated problems on problem solving performance.* Unpublished doctoral dissertation, Teachers College, Columbia University, NY, USA.
47. Richards, J. C. (2005). *Communicative language teaching today.* New York: Cambridge University Press.

48. Ruschoff, B., & Ritter, M. (2001). Technology-enhanced language learning: construction of knowledge and template-based learning in the foreign language classroom. *Computer Assisted Language Learning, 14*(3-4), 219–232.
49. Sanchez, A. (2004). The task-based approach in language teaching. *International Journal of English Studies, 4*(1), 39–71.
50. Shiu, J.-D. (2002). *The effects of Internet-assisted instruction and the cognitive styles of sixth graders on English achievement and motivation for learning English*. Unpublished master's thesis, National Pingtung University of Education, Taiwan.
51. Song, Y. (2009). How can Chinese English teachers meet the challenge of creating a learner-centered communicative, intercultural classroom to achieve optimal student learning outcomes? *Canadian Social Science, 5*(6), 81–91.
52. Su, Y. (2006). EFL teachers' perceptions of English language policy at the elementary level in Taiwan. *Educational Studies, 32*(3), 265–283.
53. Swain, M. (1993). The output hypothesis: just speaking and writing aren't enough. *Canadian Modern Language, 50*, 158–164.
54. Swain, M. (2005). The output hypothesis: theory and research. In E. Hinkel (Ed.), *Handbook of research in second language teaching* (pp. 471–484). Mahwah, NJ: Lawrence Erlbaum Associates.
55. Swain, M., & Lapkin, S. (1995). Problems in output and the cognitive processes they generate: a step towards second language learning.*Applied Linguistics, 16*, 371–391.
56. Wang, Y.-C. (2008). *An investigation into communication strategy usage and the pragmatic competence of Taiwanese learners of English within a computer mediated activity*. Unpublished doctoral dissertation, University of Leicester, UK.
57. Wang, X. (2009). Second language theories and their influences on EFL in China. *English Language Teaching, 2*(4), 149–153.
58. Warschauer, M., & Meskill, C. (2000). Technology and second language learning. In J. Rosenthal (Ed.), *Handbook of undergraduate second language education* (pp. 303–318). Mahwah, New Jersey: Lawrence Erlbaum.
59. Wu, J. R.-W., & Wu, R. Y.-F. (2010). Relating the GEPT reading comprehension tests to the CEFR. In W. Martyniuk (Ed.), *Aligning tests with the CEFR: reflections on using the council of Europe's draft manual* (pp. 204–224). Cambridge, UK: Cambridge University Press.

60. Yang, Y., & Lyster, R. (2010). Effects of form-focused practice and feedback on Chinese EFL learners' acquisition of regular and irregular past tense forms. *Studies in Second Language Acquisition, 32*, 235–263.
61. Yu, F. Y. (2009). Scaffolding student-generated questions: design and development of a customizable online learning system. *Computers in Human Behavior, 25*(5), 1129–1138.
62. Yu, F. Y., & Lai, Y.-S. (2014). Effects of online student question-generation with multiple procedural guides for elementary students' use of cognitive strategies and academic achievement. *Journal of Educational Media and Library Sciences, 51*(4), 525–560.
63. Yu, F. Y., & Liu, Y. H. (2005). Potential values of incorporating multiple-choice question-construction for physics experimentation instruction. *International Journal of Science Education, 27*(11), 1319–1335.
64. Yu, F. Y., & Liu, Y. H. (2008). The comparative effects of student question-posing and question-answering strategies on promoting college students' academic achievement, cognitive and metacognitive strategies use. *Journal of Education and Psychology, 31*(3), 25–52.
65. Zhang, S. (2011). English as a global language in Chinese context. *Theory and Practice in Language Studies, 1*(2), 167–176.

Chapter 8

LEARNING 2.0: COLLABORATIVE TECHNOLOGIES RESHAPING LEARNING PATHWAYS

Popovici Veronica

"Ovidius" University of Constanta Romania

INTRODUCTION

The development of the Internet into the highly versatile, dynamic and democratized medium it is today has brought with it incredible transformations and opportunities in practically all fields of human activity. A new set of Internet-based technological tools, all gathered together under the roof of one broad term - Web 2.0 – are describing the increasing use of the Internet as a technology platform to enhance functionality, communication and collaboration. It encompasses the explosion of Web-delivered content, interconnectivity, new applications and social networking. The term "Web 2.0" actually describes the changing trends in the use of World Wide Web technology and web design that aim to enhance creativity, secure information sharing, collaboration and functionality of the web. Web 2.0 applications like blogs, wikis, online social networking sites, photo- and videosharing sites and virtual worlds have known an exponentially increasing development and popularity over the past few years. Research evidence suggests that these revolutionary online tools have not only had an impact on people's private and professional lives, but have also started to affect large organizations and institutional structures, leading them towards more collaborative and synergetic approaches. This process - intrinsically based upon the latest online technologies - is extremely interesting to observe in the educational sector, as an enhanced efficiency at this level is further on naturally disseminated in all segments and fields of activity.

Moreover, taking into account all the great advantages of using such tools in providing high quality, modern educational services and catalyzing learning processes, we believe this is an extremely interesting topic, of utmost importance for the future of education and the development of generations to come. After all, we are witnessing the dawn of a new era pertaining entirely to "digital natives" (Mason & Rennie, 2007), as today's children are using Web 2.0 technologies comfortably and efficiently and they will continue to do so ever more naturally. The reason why using these tools in educational settings is so crucial, particularly at this point in time, reveals itself from two different aspects merging together. On one hand, the younger generation will always need help from their older, wiser fellows in order to learn what they need to be successful in the complicated structures of the society they will grow up to be a part of. But, on the other hand, until these digital natives will start becoming those fellows, here we are still the representatives of those few „transition"generations in different stages of technical ability that are bound to adapt quickly to the imminent trends and find efficient measures to support imposing multiple innovations of the educational system, that will eventually permit a functional blend between the "old" and "new" tools and patterns for learning, as well as a smooth evolution of the entire system.

Bringing together the two realms of Web 2.0 and learning, in any form or type of organization around the globe, we will address the phenomenon under discussion with the term of „Learning 2.0", as it already appears in a few pioneering research papers. Since the concept of collaborative technologies is only a few years old itself, discussions around the topic of its fusion with the educational sector are an even bigger novelty. Therefore research on Learning 2.0 is still scarce, the only comprehensive project in this area of study, apart from some disparate articles and studies on different, very restricted aspects of Learning 2.0, being one initiated by the Institute for Prospective Technological Studies (IPTS) and the European Commission Directorate Education and Culture (DG EAC) in 2008. "Learning 2.0 – the Impact of Web 2.0 Innovations on Education and Training in Europe"(Redecker et all, 2009) aims at gathering concrete evidence on the take up of social computing by European education and training institutions, to understand its impact on innovations in educational practices and its potential for a more inclusive European knowledge society. At the same time, this research project also envisioned identifying challenges and bottlenecks so as to devise policy options for European decision makers, all in all proposing a very complex approach to understanding the role of collaborative technologies in European education and training institutions.

Although the final report issued at the end of this study is a very important informative tool for anyone plunging into this field, there are two disadvantages entailed. First of all, the results are biased by concentrating only on European institutions, which although was one of the major premises of the project, nevertheless cannot be ignored as a restrictive feature, and second of all our entire discussion takes place on very rapidly changing grounds, the Web 2.0 movement having suffered tremendous developments during the last couple of years. Having pointed out so far only the main limitations of this front-runner contribution in the Learning 2.0 field, we would like to mention a couple of other aspects that could be added into the same category. In our opinion, this study focuses primarily upon organizational innovation measures that need to be implemented in order to assure the efficiency of Web 2.0 tools within education and training institutions, in the detriment of other key aspects of the analyzed issue. One of these could consist into the main advantages of using Web 2.0 tools in educational contexts (such as their crucial contribution in distance education, informal learning and decoding tacit knowledge, as well as in the process of developing essential character and personality treats of future citizens of the world), which we believe it is a noticeably underdeveloped aspect in this study and also one that we will try to enrich with our research endeavours.

This is why, building upon existent research, we are proposing a more general, up-to-date and logically structured overview of the Learning 2.0 field, in which we intend to emphasize all the fundamental advantages of Learning 2.0 practices and the most severe challenges laying ahead for them. Our hopes are high that a clear outline of this phenomenon and its determining landmarks – one of the priority goals of this chapter – will foster deeper interest and further research into this very lively and current topic. In order to reach this we will begin with a detailed exposure of the Internet's development into what it has become nowadays, providing also a general view of the web-based tools accountable for its nomenclature. The purpose of all this will be to sketch the basic context in which we will take a deeper look at the multiple ways of Web 2.0 applications transforming learning patterns and pathways, or more exactly at all the advantages, opportunities and challenges brought by using such technologies for learning and at the ways in which current structures must metamorphose in order to best accommodate the positive aspects, while eliminating the negative ones.

THE DEVELOPMENT OF THE INTERNET INTO WEB 2.0

We would not be able to talk about innovative collaboration technologies nowadays without having witnessed over the past few decades one of the most influential global scale phenomenon, which will have definitively reshaped the history of human kind – the rise of the Internet. According to official statistics, the growth of the World Wide Web in terms of number of users and their interconnected networks has been exponential for almost two decades.1 The reach of the Internet is global - although it began in the US and is unquestionably a western technology, its presence and growth is no longer limited to western cultures. In fact, highest growth rates are registered in other regions such as Africa, the Middle East and Latin America, all of which points out to a more and more interconnected world. And the rationale behind this continuously increased interconnectedness is nothing else but the omnipresent ambition of overcoming geographic distances as primary barriers to information and knowledge access at a global scale.

The incredible growth rate of the Internet in such a short period of time has also made it evolve into a more user-friendly medium, which allows us to define it today according to both a technical and a social model. Therefore, the major impact of its growth may not be in the connectivity itself (which is significant, as mentioned above), but in the secondary changes in behaviour and values that such connectivity seems to stimulate (Mason and Hart, 2007). The emerging technical model means that the evolutionary development of web technology enables new capabilities for users. Higher bandwidths mean that images and videos are more readily available, thus increasing the richness of the media accessible on the web. Additionally, users can label, or "tag" pages and information units. Consequently, the web becomes increasingly dense in terms of primary content (the text web pages, the images and the video), the metadata of tags, and the linkages among sites and pages. Collectively, all three (primary content, metadata, and linkages) create a set of extraordinarily rich sources of information, so that becoming aware of the combination of the three dimensions presents opportunities for learning and for innovative connections among previously unrelated assemblages of facts and relationships (Mason and Hart, 2007). The emerging social model is enabled by how people choose to use the evolving technical capabilities. These permit and even encourage the formation of new social networks focused on particular interests or other shared characteristics, ranging from such simple concepts as attending the same school to more complex associations such as a shared interest in particular types of books or hobbies.

The significance of these examples of Internet deployment - one oriented toward software development, one purely social - suggests that what we are seeing is a new approach to using the giant network. It has become the meeting space - a virtual "third space" for gathering, beyond the physical ones like the workplace and the home - that goes beyond simply searching for and accessing information. The Internet is changing how we interact with each other, if it's either for learning from each other, for working together or for new ways of recreation. What it does is actually gathering a wide range of intertwined advanced and emerging technologies into the so-called second phase of the evolution of the online world. This is also the reason why the term "Web 2.0" has become so popular for defining these new technologies of the

Internet, representing – as shown above – only the suggestion of an upgraded network, of an Internet naturally developed into a new stage of existence and functionality.

According to Tim O'Reilly (2005), the one who introduced this term, Web 2.0 is the business revolution in the computer industry caused by the move to the Internet as a platform, and an attempt to understand the rules for success on that new platform. O'Reilly said that the "2.0" refers to the historical context of web businesses "coming back" after the 2001 collapse of the dot-com bubble, in addition to the distinguishing characteristics of the projects that survived the bust or thrived thereafter. The Internet era prior to that, the one pertaining to web developers and specialists only, is known as the Web 1.0 period, while Web 2.0 is what we call the democratized Internet or the Internet for everybody, since anyone in the world can easily go online and create their own contents there. What stays behind this empowerment of the masses, of this engagement in mass participation is the fact that all the Web 2.0 technologies under the loop here make it almost effortless for individuals to contribute to the web based discussion and provide an extremely convenient support for social interaction and exchange of one form or another. Since these tools have transformed the Internet into a place for networking, community building and sharing collective experience, some have been led to describe this new phenomenon of massively distributed collective intelligence as "the wisdom of crowds" (Ballantyne & Quinn, 2006), giving a first hint towards the bigger idea developed throughout this chapter of people sharing knowledge, learning together and exploring new ways of capturing and disseminating their intelligence, all processes enabled by innovative technologies of the Internet.

To enter more concretely into the world of Web 2.0 tools and paint a fairly comprehensive picture of these technologies without making use of an excessively technical vocabulary, here are the most popular ones of these tools and what they capture in essence:

- Weblogs or blogs are freeform digital canvases used to communicate in an open setting or well-defined group to capture topic-specific content in the form of articles (posts) listed in reversed chronological order; blogs can encompass all sorts of content, from visual, audio and video, as well as links to other blogs, information about the author and readers' comments; the term blogosphere has been born with the explosion of blogs around the world - there are currently around 100.000 new blogs created daily (Pascu, 2008) - describing the online world of these public writing environments;
- Wikis are web-based tools designed for collaborative, unstructured interactions among formal and informal groups, popular with project

teams for coordinating work, team editing and capturing project updates; the most well-known example of a wiki is Wikipedia, a collaboratively-created online encyclopaedia with more than 75000 active contributors working on more than 10 million articles in 250 languages (http://wikipedia.org/).
- Tagging, social bookmarking and folksonomies represent basically assigning categories/names to Web and other content, such as articles, books (Amazon), pictures (Flickr), videos (YouTube), blogs (Technorati) and wiki entries, or institutional and team documents;
- Social networking/online communities refer to Web-based sites or internal platforms that supports interaction among users of all kinds;
- Social filtering means letting users rate content to create collective opinion of its relevance and value;
- Mash-ups are the result of combining data from two applications (usually with open application programming interfaces) that weren't originally intended to work together.
- Virtual worlds are nothing else but virtual environments like Second Life or similar online 3D virtual worlds where users can socialize, connect and create using free voice and text chat.

All of these tools and others have slowly made their way into most every aspect of human life. We use them to stay connected with each other, to work more efficiently, to extend our network of peers, to enhance marketing and management activities and basically to share everything – from personal to field-specific information, from comments and opinions to institutional knowledge. Further on we are going to see how they are used also in enabling learning processes - formal or informal - what are the premises for such innovations in the realm of education and what amazing opportunities they bring along from this very specific and interesting point of view.

FROM WEB 2.0 TO LEARNING 2.0

Having a fairly clear image about some of the most largely used Web 2.0 tools and how the Internet developed into incorporating such innovative technologies, we can now reach the nucleus of our endeavour and address their role in learning and educative processes. We are basically referring to emerging initiatives of integrating Web 2.0 applications in educational contexts, a phenomenon unsurprisingly labelled as Learning 2.0. As it was mentioned before, there have been a lot of discussions about the effect that web technologies are having on commerce, media and business in general but a much more little coverage on the impact they are having on education. Like the web itself, technology enabled learning processes have gone through profound transformations as well. It actually all started with e-learning, comprising all forms of electronically supported learning and teaching, content being delivered via the Internet, intranet/extranet, audio or video tape, satellite TV, and CD-ROM, enabling the transfer of skills and knowledge.

The early promise of e-learning though - that of empowerment - has not been fully realized, as for many the experience of e-learning has been no more than a hand-out published online, coupled with a simple multiple-choice quiz, which is hardly inspiring, let alone empowering. This happened because the traditional approach to e-learning has been to employ the use of a Virtual Learning Environment (VLE), software that is often cumbersome and expensive - and which tends to be structured around courses, timetables, and testing (Becta, 2007).

This is an approach that is too often driven by the needs of the institution rather than the individual learner. Teachers sensed this major flaw of e-learning materials and have started to explore the potential of blogs, media-sharing services and other social software - which, although not designed specifically for e-learning, can be used to empower students and create exciting new learning opportunities. And these is how, by using this new web services, e-learning has tapped into its potential of becoming far more personal, sociable and flexible – in other words, of becoming Learning 2.0. One of the pioneers that intuitively recognized the beginning of this transition is Stephen Downes[2], a senior researcher with the National Research Council of Canada based in Moncton, New Brunswick at the Institute for Information Technology's e-Learning Research Group, who firstly coined the phenomenon as e-learning 2.0 and described it as an approach that combines the use of discrete but complementary tools and web services such as blogs, wikis, and other social software to support the creation of ad-hoc learning communities. In order to better understand how this happens specifically, we are further on going to look into the use of each of the major Web 2.0 tools in part for educational purposes.

We are going to start with blogs, as they are very easy and flexible tools for using, with various educational advantages, as shown by the increasing number of research studies in their educational usage. Blogs not only remove the technical barriers to writing and publishing online, but the „journal" format encourages students to keep a record of their thinking over time. Blogs of course also facilitate critical feedback, by letting readers add comments, which could be from teachers, peers or a wider audience. So it is suggested that blogs enhance writing skills, facilitate reflection, encourage critical thinking with collaborative learning, and provide feedback and active learning (Ellison & Wu, 2008). Blogs are well suited to serve as online personal journals because they enable students sharing files and resources, giving them the possibility of writing for readers beyond their classmates (Bruns, 2008). In addition, blogs can be used as e-portfolios that keep records of personal development process, reflections and achievement (Alexander, 2007). The beauty of it is that a blog needn't be limited to a single author - it can mix different kinds of voices, including fellow students, teachers and mentors, or subject specialists (experts of the dicussed matter or even personalities of the world outside immediate education circles, such as authors of studied novels or creators of studied art pieces), becoming a very interactive medium for learning with all these different peers being able to bring their input on a specific curricular subject in a certain virtual space. As blogs, wikis have also attracted attention in educational field for their advantages and usability, and studies about using wikis in education have increased in number. Wikis are considered to be effective tools for learning and teaching as they facilitate collaborative learning, provide collaborative writing, support project based learning, promote creativity, encourage critical searching, support inquiry based and social constructivist learning (Konieczny, 2007). Some of other educational usage of wikis are also suggested as classroom websites, easy course administration and timetabling, easy online updating content, online dictionary, student feedback and self assessment, bibliographically organized class or group projects, virtual classes for online collaboration, creating frequently asked questions (FAQ) for classroom or students (Augar et all, 2004; Konieczny, 2007).

Podcasting has aslo become a popular technology in education, in part because it provides a way of pushing educational content to learners. For example, Stanford University has teamed up with Apple to create the Stanford iTunes University3, which provides a range of digital content (some closed and some publicly accessible) that students can subscribe to using Apple's iTunes software. Especially as podcasting is being used with mobile devices, it can be viewed as another variant of mobile learning. Although podcasting is not a synchronous activity, it provides students information that will help them feel connected to the learning community. Moreover, as with blogging, podcasting provides students with a sense of audience - and they are highly motivated to podcast because the skills required seem relevant to today's world (Lee et all, 2008). Social networks can also be viewed as pedagogical tools that stem from their affordances of information discovery and sharing, attracting and supporting networks of people and facilitating connections between them, engaging users in informal learning and creative, expressive forms of behaviour and identity seeking.

Even media sharing sites like Flickr or YouTube have found their use within education. Flickr provides a valuable resource for students and educators looking for images for use in presentations, learning materials or coursework, and the tagging of images makes it much easier to find relevant content. Just as well, YouTube can be used in several interactive assignments where the final result can be viewed/appreciated/commented on in video format online by classmates and the wider YouTube community. So far we have managed to get only a brief glance into the use of Web 2.0 tool for education and learning, the topic being enriched with new practical examples or best practices every day. At the same pace increase also the research efforts of studying the impact of each and every one of these new media in educational contexts, which is a gratifying thing, bringing us more and more evidence of Web 2.0 technologies clearly reshaping learning pathways at the moment. To quickly summarise all of the above, being slowly introduced also in the educational system, such applications:

- facilitate access to information for everyone, making institutional processes more transparent and the distribution of educational material more efficient;
- integrate learning into a wider community, reaching out to virtually meet people from other age-groups and socio-cultural backgrounds, linking to experts, researchers or practitioners in a certain field of study and thus opening up alternative channels for gaining knowledge and enhancing skills;
- support the exchange of knowledge and material and facilitate community building and collaboration among learners and teachers;
- increase academic achievement with the help of motivating, personalised and engaging learning tools and environments;
- implement pedagogical strategies intended to support, facilitate, enhance and improve learning processes (Redecker et all, 2009).

Thus, such emerging technologies and changing pedagogies bring out the necessity for more effective two way communication, promoting interaction and collaborative working, sharing and flexible participation between all participants in the education and learning environment. We can honestly say now that we understand the Learning 2.0 phenomenon as one of utmost importance and actuality, announcing what might become a crucial impact on the future of educational pathways worldwide. Bearing this acknowledgement in mind, we will further embark on an attempt to better grasping the implications of Learning 2.0 developments, by underlining the core positive aspects they bring in, as well as the biggest challenges and bottlenecks.

DISCUSSING LEARNING 2.0

Opportunities and Advantages

The most obvious advantage of using Web 2.0 tools within educational and training contexts of all kind would be their contribution in terms of fostering worldwide innovation and modernization of this field. As the already undertaken research suggests and as the figure below very clearly depicts, Learning 2.0 strategies would contribute in particular to three dimensions of innovation – technological, pedagogical and organizational innovation. The self-explanatory matrix in Figure 1 pictures the way in which Learning 2.0 strategies bring together several core aspects of our lives, providing the technological premises (new ways, tools and methods) for learning, then drawing the attention upon the basic need of organizational transformations (re-creating teaching and learning practice), so that in the end all the preconditions are there for pedagogical innovation and empowerment of the learner. Establishing this incremental pace, Learning 2.0 strategies first of all imply the existence and usability of collaborative technologies, that would increase the accessibility and availability of learning content and would of course provide new, more efficient frameworks for knowledge acquisition, dissemination and management. Building on our introductory arguments, Web 2.0 tools allow embedding learning activities in more engaging multimedia environments, with a high degree of quality and interoperability, where dynamic or individualised learning resources are easily created. Moreover, the simple fact that Learning 2.0 helps overcoming the limitations of face-to-face instruction through versatile tools for knowledge exchange and collaboration is a great achievement per se and something that could be made the most of in remote areas where there is an unbalanced ratio between the number of learners and available teachers.

Moving forward to the next innovation dimension, namely the organizational innovation, Learning 2.0 both requires and promotes this type of transformations and it can contribute to making educational organizations more dynamic, flexible and open. Through collaborative technologies institutions in this sector can become reflective organizations that critically evaluate and revise their corporate strategies in order to support innovative pedagogies. But in order for this to happen first of all the necessary infrastructure in which social media tools are accessible to all learners and teachers needs to be provided. In addition to this, educational institutions need to make efforts towards creating an atmosphere of support for Learning 2.0, in which new teaching and learning models are fostered and new assessment and grading strategies are integrated.

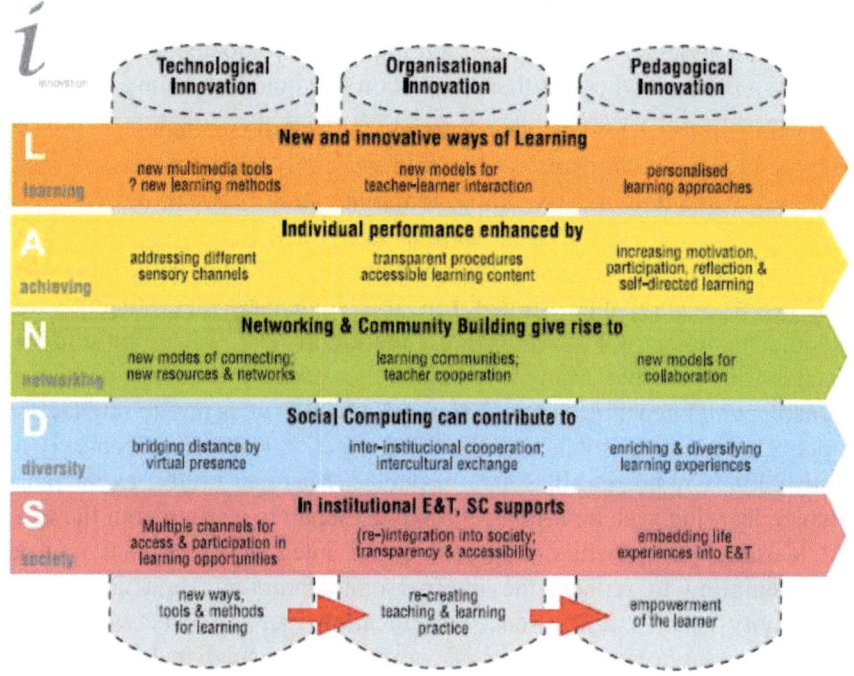

Figure 1. Te innovative potential of Learning 2.0

Once all these developments are mobilized, the primary sine-qua-non conditions are set for learning approaches using social media to promote pedagogical innovation, which basically presumes encouraging teaching and learning processes that are based on personalisation and collaboration. The main consequence of pedagogical innovation lays in a redefining shift within interaction patterns between and among students and teachers. This way teachers become much more than just instructors or lecturers – they embrace their roles as coordinators, moderators, mediators and mentors. At the same time students' roles evolve as well, from taking responsibility for their own learning progress to also having to support each other in their learning endeavours, and jointly creating the learning content and context. Hence, Learning 2.0 offers the entire playfield where learners can and are encouraged to assume a pro-active role in the learning process and develop their own – individual and collective – rules and strategies for learning.

Much more than just enhancing innovation at these three interrelated levels, social media support engages playful approaches, provides new formats for creative expression and encourages learners and teachers to experiment with different, innovative ways of articulating their thoughts and ideas. The Learning 2.0 landscape itself is shaped by experimentation, collaboration and empowerment, and allows learners and teachers to discover new ways of actively and creatively developing their individual competences, which in turn provides a rich soil where further innovation and quality learning can flourish.

Taking all this into consideration and the general fact demonstrated so far that emerging technology plays a key role especially for promoting interaction, delivering education and providing communication between individuals, we turn now to the crucial role of Learning 2.0 strategies in distance education. Several studies underlined the significance of interaction and the actual necessity of several interaction forms like student-teacher, student-student, studentcontent etc., contributing to the feeling of quality learning in distance education in particular. Many research studies reveal technology perceived as an enabler and intensifier of interaction, which leads at its turn to satisfaction of students, eliminating isolation feeling and effective learning outcomes (Chang et all, 2008; Cramer et all, 2007). Usluel & Mazman (2009) explained that distance learning systems use technology to separate learner from the teacher and learning group while maintaining the integrity of education process and attempting to replace the interpersonal communication and the inter subjectivity which is the essence of education transaction between teachers and learners, by a personal form of communication mediated by technology. Interaction in distance education is not limited to audio and video, or solely to teacher-student interactions, it must also represent the connectivity, the students' feel with the distance teacher, aides, peers etc., otherwise without interaction students become autonomous, isolated and procrastinate and drop out (Usluel & Mazman, 2009).

Therefore we can observe emerging technologies bringing out the necessity for more effective two way communication, promoting interaction and collaborative working, sharing and flexible participation, and also supporting the transition towards a distance learning system dominated by all these positive aspects. Moreover, emerging technologies not only have an impact on new ways of learning in distance education, but also on new models of teaching (Rennie & Mason, 2004). It is suggested that by the interactive technologies and medias which are provided by Web 2.0, these new pedagogic approaches that imply a closer relationship with students through active participation and effective twoways communication on virtual open platforms such as blogs or wikis are also supported.

Considering distance education in very broad terms, everything we brought into discussion above is actually an only natural development in the field of education in general, following similar systematic developments in other domains as well. If we think about the many ways in which all sorts of human activities between peers situated in geographically dispersed locations have been enabled by new technologies of the Internet, we can definitely say it was only a matter of time before these technologies began to be widely utilised in long distance education. Web 2.0 tools improve the quality of the pedagogical act in such contexts, supporting it in interactive and multivalent environments, and offering a wide palette of applications to display learning content and materials, projects and assignments, groupwork and examinations, which will all enrich the experience of learners engaged in long distance education by making the entire process more lively, dynamic and engaging. Beyond this, Web 2.0 technologies offer the learner itself a vast array of supports for expression and exercise of the learned content, which highly upgrade its level of preparation before examinations. If before such tools were introduced long distance students were usually "served" course materials on a certain static online location where they would access it, accumulate it and then deliver it within organized examination sessions, things are totally different now, with the new media hosting all sorts of applications whose role is to make the course materials more accessible and to help students better understand the practical utilization of what they are learning, while also serving as support for various types of projects and assignments.

But this type of increased interaction and versatility that emerging technologies are praised for bringing into the field of distance education are also the reason why Web 2.0's advantages should be considered on a much larger scale. Around the world people engage in learning activities that are not necessarily structured or organized in any way, but appear as a natural flow of continuously modulated information, made available on the web by millions and millions of peers following their passions, interests, fears, uncertainties, etc. and tapping into the "wisdom of crowds" they end up enriching themselves. What we are basically referring to is the concept of informal learning, involving all that is learned throughout life in the day-to-day processes at home, work and leisure; and since Web 2.0 applications have slowly found their place into all of these settings it seems only obvious to reflect upon their role in informal learning activities, of whose importance is largely underestimated, but who contribute to our pool of reliable facts and experiences much more than we even imagine. The acceptance of informal learning acknowledges that there is more to learning than the absorption of "explicit" knowledge codified in texts and delivered during formal courses. It also, crucially, consists of access to "tacit" or implicit knowledge, which is exactly what all sorts of social media have best to offer. Therefore, when considering the main benefits of user-generated-content fuelling the brought up "wisdom of crowds" phenomenon, one of the most obvious one would be the fact that users have a lot of tools at their disposal to join the global conversation and actively engage in the construction of their (learning) experience, rather than merely absorb content passively. And this content will be constantly refreshed by the users, it will not require expensive expert input, something which accentuates both its purely authentic character and its reliability, the democratic nature of the web making sure that every piece of information, data or statement out there can be reinforced or refuted by users with similar experiences/authorized opinions and various ways of expression at their disposal.

All in all, through the broad variety of versatile tools, social media or Web 2.0 in general allows the implementation of more effective learning strategies that can furthermore improve individual performance, actively foster the development of transversal competences, and nurture abilities to flexibly develop skills in a lifelong learning continuum. This is easily attainable because the Learning 2.0 spectrum offers accessible, flexible and dynamic learning environments that can complement and supplement initial training. Furthermore, the networking potential of social media, together with its power to overcome time and space barriers, supports interaction and collaboration among and between learners and teachers who are geographically dispersed and enables students to broaden their horizons, and collaborate across borders, language barriers, and institutional walls. Hence, team-work abilities are highly developed by collaborative work environments supported by most of the Web 2.0 tools like shared community spaces and inter-group communication platforms, which are also a massive part of what excites young people and therefore should contribute to users' persistence and motivation to learn. Last but not least, research results indicate that social media approaches to learning can mitigate existing inequalities and can be employed to successfully re-engage individuals who are at risk of exclusion from the knowledge society. Learning 2.0 strategies can thus effectively increase the accessibility and availability of learning opportunities for the hard to reach, and can significantly improve motivation and engagement in learning.

Challenges and Bottlenecks

While the potential of social media for enhancing learning opportunities is substantial, there are nevertheless a few obstacles to the smooth implementation of Learning 2.0 strategies. The first one we need to mention is the very basic premise for collaborative technologies becoming a part of any process: Internet access. Although the number of people going online has increased tremendously during the past few years, the Internet is still not a commodity everywhere, in some parts of the world being actually very far from that. So then we ask ourselves how can we talk about the blessings of Learning 2.0 in a democratic way when access to such practices is prohibited sometimes due to disparities in economic and technical development. Apart from the still nonunanimous use of Internet nowadays that will hopefully soon be overcome, we can identify further technical, organizational and pedagogical bottlenecks that hinder the fast spread and efficacy of Learning 2.0 practices. More than the lack of proper facilities allowing access to internet communication technologies in all educational institutions, access to basic digital skills constitute a major obstacle for the use of social media in education activities, and a key problem for inclusion and equality. In this sense both learners and teachers face a challenge – teachers in particular as they do not feel confident enough with their information and communication technology skills to experiment with Learning 2.0 strategies and further on they also need assistance sometimes, when their students don't have advanced digital competences, in supplying them with the necessary digital skills to safely use social media environments. Especially in this case, the mainstream deployment of Learning 2.0 approaches and strategies might be hindered by a lack of didactic methodologies, toolsets and training programmes for teachers which would also enable them to assume their new role as guides and mentors.

Another very important aspect when considering social media in educational institutions is the safety and privacy concern. Learning 2.0 strategies require the confident and critical use of these tools and an informed and critical attitude towards interactive media and digital information (Hulme, 2009). Constantly bearing this in mind is an extra responsibility that needs to be assumed by educators, who have to make sure that the identities of their learners are protected; that rules of conduct are implemented and adhered to; and that intellectual property rights are respected. Learning 2.0 brings requirements also on institutional change, as with their rooting in formal education processes comes also a re-evaluation of educational institutions' role in society as knowledge providers. This challenges rigid existing power structures, as resistance to change limits the development of new concrete ways to support teachers, learner and administrators and generally encumber these institutions when it comes to taking an active role in deploying promising Learning 2.0 strategies. And in order to offer a very objective depiction of this situation, it is sadly accentuated by the tumultuous character of social media landscape, which underlies continuous change and transformation and hence a lot of uncertainty concerning the future development and availability of current applications and services, the reliability of user-produced content, suitable assessment and certification strategies; and valid pedagogical concepts and methods for learning with social media.

Strongly related to this aspect appears the fact that, although it is easy to see the Web 2.0 environment as an extension or development of pre-existing tools and approaches for learning, there are however some critics of these tools and user-generated content in general that refer to a break-down in the traditional place of expertise, authority and scholarly input. They express concerns about trust, reliability and believability in relation to the move away from the printed word to the more ephemeral digital word. Furthermore, if content is created by users on different systems like podcasts, blogs, wikis, chat systems, and other social networking software, then it can be difficult to keep track of where everything is, and to access it with ease, both for those that use that content in formally structured learning frameworks and the casual visitor in search for informal learning fruits. This in turn calls for new tools to help users search and integrate across content that may be quite fragmented, a concern which is slowly but surely addressed through the proliferation of other innovative tools such as tagging, folksonomies and others. Last but not least, we must not forget that the great uses of Web 2.0 tools for learning are not guaranteed without the users' interest in such technologies and what they have to offer. And although there is a general consensus that at least the new generation of learners are all about collaborative technologies and social media, their attention and dedication to these tools might not always be constant. This can have serious consequences on the success of Web 2.0 applications, which is strongly dependent upon the users being regularly connected and contributing to the shared content on these platforms. Thus, there is a real need to understand the dynamics of the attention-grabbing effect of Web 2.0 and harness it for education purposes.

CONCLUSION

There is no doubt that new information and communication technologies become a more and more important part of our lives as we speak, reaching up to every layer of our existence. With the continuous globalization of information, learning independent from time, place, cost and other needs begins to make use of innovative Web 2.0 technologies, spreading an air of freshness and imminent transformations among old systems and learning patterns and determining a reassessment of their constitutive structures in order to better accommodate envisioned advantages of the new media. This chapter focused on the influence of such tools in the educational field as an emerging worldwide trend, endeavouring an objective depiction of pros and cons when considering the integration of social media within current conservative teaching and learning patterns. Departing from a historical approach upon the development of the internet into the socalled Web 2.0 social networking environment it has become nowadays, we are relating these innovative tools to educational practices and styles, trying to understand the emerging phenomenon of Learning 2.0 with the opportunities and challenges it brings for learner and education systems and structures worldwide.

Social media applications provide easy, fast and efficient ways to access a great diversity of information and situated knowledge. To quote Tiwana (2002), "knowledge is one of the few resources that demonstrates increasing returns to scale: the more you share it, the more it grows". Then it is only logical, if knowledge dissemination lays at the core of its thriving, that we should do everything standing in our power to stimulate and support the transfer of knowledge among as many individuals as possible even from our instruction years, offering ourselves the perfect tool for effectively building competences in collaboration with other learners, practitioners and stakeholders in a lifelong continuum. The technological development has brought us as far as being constant parts of an online, digital, parallel universe, with new, improved and easy to use applications, making the Internet maybe the most democratic space of all and the entire mankind a co-generating part of it. So why not use this "universe" to stimulate and support core learning processes, why not tap into all the advantages and opportunities Web 2.0 tools bring in the education field, why not let them facilitate for all of us the development of key competences for the 21st century?

Learning 2.0 encompasses after all the modern tools needed for appealing to a whole new generation of learners – the "digital natives" who absorb information quickly, in images and video as well as text, from multiple sources simultaneously, they operate at very fast speed, expecting instant responses and feedback, they prefer random "on-demand" access to media, expect to be in constant communication with their friends (who may be next door or around the world), and they are as likely to create their own media (or download someone else's) as to purchase a book or a CD (Tapscott, 2009). Using Web 2.0 applications in educational processes involving this new generation of learners is speaking their own language when preparing them for life and therefore becoming more efficient at it.

As we have shown throughout this chapter, Learning 2.0 represents also the development of e-learning applications, which begin to look much more like a blogging tool (viwed as a node in a web of content, connected to other nodes and content creation services used by other students), a personal learning center (where content is reused and remixed according to the student's own needs and interests) or like a personal portfolio tool. The idea here is that students will have their own personal place to create and showcase their own work. The portfolio can provide an opportunity to demonstrate one's ability to collect, organize, interpret and reflect on documents and sources of information. It is also a tool for continuing professional development, encouraging individuals to take responsibility for and demonstrate the results of their own learning. All of these new tools and opportunities for learning and developing young people have today constitute much more than a system of education – they shape an entire environment for flourishing learning. We say this because, in comparison to the very rigid demarcations of the classical education system before the smooth adoption of Web 2.0 tools, this new environment recognizes that the learning comes not from the design of learning content but from how it is used.

Slowly and surely more and more people among which learners, trainers, pedagogs and members of the academia begin to acknowledge these facts and dedicate research resources towards the better understanding of these intrinsic transformations in the education field, of their premises, consequences and influencing factors in order to harness the potential of Learning 2.0. In this sense, a great amount of work is being done, for example, in educational gaming and simulations. Although a rather new practice, several universities around the world have already a few years experience with such Web 2.0 enabled educational simulation programs, convinced by their promise to foster interaction and team-work abilities, increase active participation, assuming responsibility and gaining experience in a profesional simulated environment, as well as the opportunity to develop distance education and inter-institutional projects. Being actively involved in the development and derulation of a business simulation research project with participants from several Romanian universities, a personal appreciation of these type of programs would go directly to saying that the most important learning skills one sees children getting from such games and simulations are those that support the empowering sense of taking charge of their own learning. And the learner taking charge of learning is antithetical to the dominant ideology of a curriculum design, which is more than enough to understand why these developments are tremendously important in the field of education and why more and more efforts should be dedicated towards a more recurrent and efficient implementation of innovative tools of all kinds in various edicational contexts. One of such contexts would be also the realm of mobile learning, a rapidly rising domain, that offers not only new opportunities to create but also to connect, by defining new relationships and behaviours among learners, information, personal computing devices and the world at large (Wagner, 2005).

To sum up, the already undertaken research points out that there is not only a great potential of innovation at a technical, organizational and pedagogical level brought in by Learning 2.0 strategies, but that there are also several obstacles rising up in front of the social media efficacy in education institutions. There are indeed great arguments in favour of their adoption, like the fact that they allow learners to access a vast variety of (often freely available) learning content, which supports incessant learning and professional development even in informal settings, it enables distance education accentuating the interaction and motivation for learning, it contributes to equity and inclusion and puts pressure on education institutions to improve the quality and availability of their learning material. Moreover, since social media allow users to create digital content themselves and publish it online, it gives rise to a huge resource of user-generated content from which learners and teachers can mutually benefit, also encouraging more active and pro-active approaches to learning. Last but not least, it connects learners with one another, experts and teachers alike, allowing them to tap into the tacit knowledge of their peers and have access to highly specific and targeted knowledge in a given field of interest, at the same time supporting also the collaboration between them on a given project or a joint topic of interest, pooling resources, creating synergies and gathering the expertise and potential of a group of people committed to a common objective.

Although all these are great advantages picturing a bright future of the education system under the upcoming years of technical modernity we must not be naive and think that all these things can happen without a strong technological basis in form of access to proper facilities and advanced IT and social media instruction and assistance for learners and teachers; at the same, none of this is possible in the absence of institutional innovation and a fresh mindset that embraces the integration of social media with conservative learning techniques. Therefore we highly encourage the full acknowledgement of these impediments and further research into covering the gap of misperceptions and uncertainties regarding Learning 2.0 strategies and being concretely able to transform all of their opportunities and advantages into strong-stating facts.

REFERENCES

1. Alexander, B. (2006). Web 2.0: a new wave of innovation for teaching and learning?. Educause Review. Vol. 41, No. 2, 32-44, ISSN 1479-4403
2. Augar, N. et all (2004). Teaching and Learning Online with Wikis. Accessed 28/12/2009 http://ascilite.org.au/conferences/perth04/procs/augar.html
3. Ballantyne, N.; Quinn, K. (2006). Informal Learning and the Social Web. Accessed 12/12/2009 http://informallearning.pbwiki.com
4. Becta (2007). Emerging Technologies for Learning, Volume 2. British Educational Communications and Technology Agency. ISBN 1-853-79-467-8 Coventry, UK. Accesses 30/02/2010 http://www.becta.org.uk/research/emerging_technologies07.pdf
5. Bruns, A. (2008). Blogs, Wikipedia, Second Life and Beyond. From Production to Produsage, Peter Lang Publishing, ISBN 978-0-8204-8867-7, New York

6. Chang, C.K. et all (2008). Constructing a community of practice to improve coursework activity. Computers & Education. Vol. 50, No. 1, 235-247, ISSN 0360-1315
7. Cramer, K.M. et all (2007). The virtual lecture hall: utilisation, effectiveness and student perceptions. British Journal of Educational Technology. Vol. 38, No.1, 106-115, ISSN 0007-1013
8. Ellison, N.; Wu, Y. (2008). Blogging in the Classroom: A Preliminary Exploration of Student Attitudes and Impact on Comprehension. Journal of Educational Multimedia and Hypermedia. Vol. 17, 99-122, ISSN 1055-8896
9. Hulme, M. (2009). Life Support: Young people's needs in a digital age. Youth Net report. Accessed 18/10/2009 http://www.youthnet.org/mediaandcampaigns/ pressreleases/hybrid-lives
10. Konieczny, P. (2007). Wikis and Wikipedia as a Teaching Tool. International Journal of Instructional Technology and Distance Learning. Vol. 4, No. 1, 15-34, ISSN 1550-6908
11. Lee, M.J.W. et all (2008). Talk the talk: Learner-generated podcasts as catalysts for knowledge creation. British Journal of Educational Technology. Vol. 39, No. 3, 501-521, ISSN 0007-1013
12. Mason, R.; Rennie, F. (2007). Using Web 2.0 for learning in the community. Internet and Higher Education, Vol. 10, 196-203, ISSN 0360-1315
13. Mason, Robert M. and Tabitha Hart. (2007). Libraries for Global Networked World: Toward New Educational and Design Strategies. Paper presented at the World Library and Information Congress, 19-23 August. Durban, South Africa. Accessed 5/03/2010 http:// archive.ifla.org/IV/ifla73/papers/158-Mason_Hart-en.pdf
14. O'Reilly, T. (2005). What is Web 2.0? Design Patterns and Business Models for the Next Generation of Software. Accessed 01/06/2009 http://www.oreillynet.com/ pub/a/oreilly/tim/news/2005/09/30/what-is-web-20.html
15. Pascu, C. (2008). An Empirical Analysis of the Creation, Use and Adoption of Social Computing Applications. IPTS Exploratory research on Social Computing, JRC Scientific and Technical Reports. Accessed 22/05/2010 http://ftp.jrc.es/EURdoc/JRC46431.pdf
16. Redecker, C. et all (2009). Learning 2.0: The Impact of Web 2.0 Innovations on Education and Training in Europe. Final Report. JRC Scientific and Technical Reports. Accessed 19/04/2010 http://ipts.jrc.ec.europa.eu/publications/pub.cfm?id=2899

17. Rennie, F.; Mason, R. (2004). The Connection: Learning for the Connected Generation. Information Age Publishing, ISBN 1-59311-210-6, Greenwich, Connecticut
18. Tapscott, D. (2009). Grown Up Digital. How the net generation is changing your world, McGrawHill, ISBN 978-0-07-150863-6, New York
19. Tiwana, A. (2002). The Knowledge Management Toolkit. Orchestrating IT, Strategy and Knowledge Platforms, 2nd Edition, Prentice Hall PTR, ISBN 978-0-1300-9224-3, Upper Saddle River, NJ
20. Usluel, Y. K. ; Mazman, S.G. (2009). Adoption of Web 2.0 tools in distance education. Procedia Social and Behavioural Sciences, Vol. 1, 818-823, ISSN 0747-5632
21. Wagner, E.D. (2005). Enabling Mobile Learning. Educause Review. Vol. 40, No. 3, 40-53, ISSN 1303-6521

Chapter 9

COLLABORATIVE LANGUAGE LEARNING IN TELETANDEM: A RESOURCE FOR PRE-SERVICE TEACHER EDUCATION

Ana Cristina Biondo Salomão

São Paulo State University, Brazil

ABSTRACT

This article presents some of the results of a qualitative research project about the influences of the pedagogic strategies used by a mediator (graduate student in applied linguistics) in the supervision process of a Teletandem partner (undergraduate student in languages) on her pedagogical practice. It was done within the project "Teletandem Brazil: foreign language for all". Based on the reflective teaching paradigm and collaborative language learning, with special emphasis on tandem learning, we analyzed the contributions of the collaborative relationship established between the graduate student and the student-teacher in her first teaching experience. The results bring about implications for the field of language teacher education in a perspective of education within practice, evidencing the experience of collaborative learning in teletandem as an opportunity for reflective teacher education of pre-service teachers.

INTRODUCTION

Technological advances over the last few years, especially those related to the Internet, have brought to our language classroom a myriad of new resources for language teaching. In the field of Applied Linguistics, we now feel the necessity of understanding how this new scenario changes what happens inside our classrooms and teachers' and students' roles. Research has been conducted on these issues in an attempt to grasp the nuances of the new contexts shaped by technological changes, but we still have to take a closer look at how technology has assisted teacher education in preparing pre-service teachers to be reflective professionals and face the new challenges they might encounter in their classrooms.

The necessity of educating student-teachers to be constructors of knowledge increases the responsibilities of future teacher educators and it appears to us that the possibility of reflecting on theory and practice should be guided by reflection models and supervision strategies that may lead to autonomy. In this sense, we present here part of the results of a qualitative research study for a master's degree in Applied Linguistics (Salomão, 2008) conducted under the influences of a reflective supervision process during a student-teacher's pedagogical practicum within a technological environment, the Project "Teletandem Brazil: foreign languages for all" (www.teletandembrasil. org). This is a thematic research project from UNESP -São Paulo State University, Brazil-, in which professors, graduate and undergraduate students participate as researchers, mediators and Teletandem partners.

Teletandem is a collaborative learning model based on tandem learning. Foreign language learning in-tandem involves pairs of (native or competent) speakers whose aim is to learn each other's language by means of bilingual conversation sessions (Telles & Vassallo, 2006). Within this autonomous, reciprocal and collaborative learning context, each partner becomes both a learner of the foreign language and a tutor of his/her mother tongue (or language in which he/she feels proficient). Teletandem is an alternative proposal of tandem learning which makes use of technological tools available in the internet for videoconferencing, such as Skype, MSN, ooVoo, among others. The partners have an online tandem session which usually takes two hours a week (one for each language) in which they talk about a topic (which can be previously chosen), exchanging cultural information about their countries and giving each other feedback on language use, and reflect on their own learning (reflections may focus on content, culture, form, lexicon and the process of Teletandem interaction itself).

Teletandem procedures are carried out on bases of commonly agreed and shared principles of reciprocity and autonomy between the participants (Vassallo & Telles, 2006). They are autonomous in their learning but they may resort to a teacher's professional mediation or counseling if they wish.

In the first years of the Teletandem Brazil project at UNESP, mostly undergraduate students participated as Teletandem partners with undergraduate students from a number of different countries whose native languages were Spanish, French, English or Italian; and graduate students (Master and PhD candidates) took on the role of mediators (Vygotsky, 1994) of the tandem relationships.

Based on the reflective teacher paradigm, on supervision models and on collaborative language learning theories with special emphasis on tandem learning, we analyze in this article the influences of a mediator's supervision on a Teletandem partner's practice and its influences for her pedagogical practice. The text is organized as follows: first, an overview of the literature on the reflective teaching paradigm is presented, as well as supervision models for practicum work with student-teachers. Then, the methodology and context of the study are laid out. In the next session, the findings are outlined and discussed according to the influences noticed from the use of different supervision models. Finally, we put forth our final considerations.

THE REFLECTIVE TEACHING PARADIGM

Reflective practice theory originates from the works of Dewey (1933, in Schön, 1983; Zeichner & Liston, 1996), and provides teachers with a basis for analyzing their actions in the classroom as well as rationally justifying their decisions. Dewey (1933, in Zeichner & Liston, 1996) brought great contributions to education when he envisioned the teacher as a reflective professional who should play an important role in curriculum development and educational reform. Schön (1983) used Dewey's idea of reflective practice to elaborate two very important notions of how this could be realized in our pedagogical practice: reflection-in- and -on-action. As Schön puts it: The practitioner allows himself to experience surprise, puzzlement, orconfusion inasituationwhichhe finds uncertain orunique.Hereflectsonthephenomenon beforehim,andonthe prior understandings which have been implicit in his behaviour. He carries out an experiment which serves to generate both a new understanding of the phenomenon and a change in the situation. (1983, p. 68)

The work of the reflective practitioner in the language classroom, then, involves reflection before, during and after action e.g. he/she can firstly reflect on the planning and later on what actually happened in the classroom, but during the actual class there will also be reflection and decision-making.

Van Mannen (1977), cited in Williams (1999), differentiated between three levels of reflection: technical, practical and critical. These levels would imply that one should go from simple reflection to more complex ones, as in a scale, and the last level includes moral and ethical issues, deemed the most complex. Zeichner and Liston (1996) criticize such hierarchical treatment of the levels and prefer to understand them as reflection domains, which should be considered equally important in teachers' professional development. These authors claim that we have to recognize that teachers bring their own ideas, beliefs and theories, which are filters and contribute to their professional learning.

Although the reflective practitioner theory appears to be a good start for working with pre-service teachers, it seems to lack some practical notions of how the reflective process happens. Some authors have tried to suggest actions which might be taken in order to accomplish it. Zeichner and Liston (1996, p. 6) claim the actions are: examining, framing and trying to solve the dilemmas of classroom practice; being aware of and questioning assumptions and values brought to teaching; being attentive to the institutional and cultural contexts; taking part in curriculum development and being involved in school change efforts; and taking responsibility for one's own professional development. Bartlett (1990) created a model which suggests the following phases for the reflection process: mapping (collecting evidence about practice), informing (searching for meaning and intention in practice), contesting (contesting the ideas which underlie practice), appraisal (considering new ways to renovate practice) and acting (implementing the changes).

From these ideas, many proposals of models for supervision in teacher education were created in the 1990s, an era when the perspective of teacher training started to coexist with a new perspective of teacher development (Freeman, 2002).

MODELS OF SUPERVISION

Concerning the supervision of classroom activities and actions, Freeman (1990) brings the directive, alternative and nondirective models in a continuum which should take the student-teacher from training to development. The author indicates the supervisor as the one in charge for using the models and leading the student-teacher to effective and independent teaching.

Gebhard (1990) expands on Freeman's ideas by proposing models to be chosen according to the needs perceived. He criticizes the directive model, in which the supervisor directs, models and evaluates behaviors and actions, stating that this approach does not help student-teachers to make decisions, but to do what the supervisor wishes or tells them to do. Therefore, he proposes other models which aim at involving the student-teacher in reflection and may generate autonomy as a language teacher.

According to the author, in the *alternative supervision model*, the supervisor helps in the decision-making process by proposing alternatives to the student-teachers which will demand from them the analysis of their context in order to make such decisions. This would provide the opportunity for guidance with a window for reflection, especially interesting for inexperienced teachers.

In the *collaborative supervision model,* the supervisor's role would be to engage in a collaborative dialogue but not to overtly direct the studentteacher›s work. Gebhard (1990, p. 159) states that in this model «the supervisor actively participates with the teacher in any decisions that are made and attempts to establish a sharing relationship». The author notes here that cultural issues are involved in this kind of supervision since not all teachers may be willing to «share equally in a symmetrical, collaborative decision-making process».

In the *non-directive supervision model*, the supervisor does not provide answers, but an "understanding response", in an attempt to establish trust and freedom for the student-teacher to be able to express him or herself.In this model, the student-teacher has the power to guide the conference and make decisions without the supervisor's suggestions. Gebhard (1990, p. 161) cautions that some teachers report feeling anxious and alienated with this kind of supervision, especially inexperienced teachers.

The *creative supervision model* involves a combination of the former models according to student-teachers' needs, which may also involve the change of responsibility from the supervisor to other sources, or the use of ideas from different areas which do not appear in the models, such as peer supervision, use of metaphors, among others.

Self-help-explorative supervision involves both supervisor and student-teacher in self-observation and self-exploration. According to the author, "the goal to 'see teaching differently' is achieved not because the supervisor has helped the teacher to do so, but because the teacher has discovered a way to view his or her own teaching differently through self-exploration" (p. 163).

The bottom-line for a decision on the supervisory option seems to be the locus of power in each one of them.While in a directive supervision model the power rests completely at the supervisor›s hands, in the non-directive the student-teacher has power to choose and manage the conference and make independent decisions. The other models would be included in a continuum that provides opportunity for jointly negotiated discussion of topics and a decision-making process that requires more or less involvement of the supervisor (the collaborative and creative models seem to generate more involvement of the supervisor in decision-making while the alternative and self-help explorative seem to involve the student-teacher›s own gain of awareness of his or her context and teaching behaviors).

Korthagen and Kessels (1999) and Korthagen (2001) also focuses on the role of reflection, stating the teacher educator›s approach should be nondirective and related to the discovery of the student-teacher and of his or her own ways of learning and teaching, reminding one of the cores of Gebhard›s self-help explorative supervision. His model seems to operationalize the search for real life experiences that would help the student-teacher to gain awareness of his or her teaching behaviors by a set of steps, entitled ALACT, presented in Figure 1. It may be observed that the inner part of the circle contains the phases, whose initials create the name given to the model, whereas the outside presents the competences which are connected to each step.

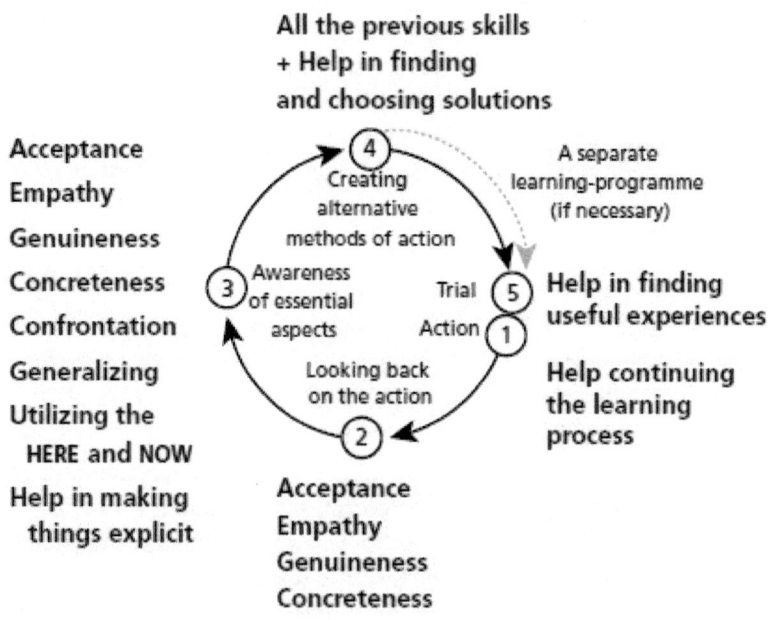

Figure 1. ALACT model (Korthagen & Vasalos, 2005, p. 49).

In this perspective, the teacher educator should start the reflection process by focusing on a practical experience of the student-teacher (Action). The next step (2) involves looking back at that practical experience in search of elements which could be discussed or questioned, and adopts some specific attitudes such as acceptance, empathy, genuineness and concreteness. The same attitudes should also be present in the next step (3), which involves bringing about awareness of the essential aspects to be discussed from practice. Other attitudes that might be added to further develop the problematization of the situations in this step are confrontation, generalizing, utilizing the here-and-now, and helping to make things explicit. The next step (4) involves creating alternative methods of action, which may involve a theoretical program to work as a bridge between practice and theory. The final step (5), named *Trial*, completes the circle by returning to the starting point and aims at giving continuity to the reflection process by a return to practice where new efforts will be made for achieving the objectives established during supervision. The new practical experience might work as fuel for new reflection development.

It seems to us that Gebhard's and Korthagen's models complement each other by bringing about the attitudes and power relations that might comprise the dynamics of a supervisory relationship which starts from practice (action) and goes back to it for a new trial after the reflective process.

Having overviewed the models of supervision in teacher education, we now present the context of the research and its methodology within the Project Teletandem Brazil.

METHODOLOGY AND CONTEXT OF THE STUDY

Teletandem Brazil is a research project from UNESP -São Paulo State University, Department of Education (UNESP -Assis), and the Graduate Program in Language Studies (UNESP -São José do Rio Preto), which aims at investigating computer assisted language learning as well as the development of language teachers within a technological context.

Its general objectives are: (1) describing the use students make of videoconferencing and instant messaging as tools and multimedia contexts for language learning in teletandem; (2) describing, from multiple perspectives, the features of the interaction and the learning process between teletandem partners; and (3) verifying pre- and in-service teacher education of the mediator in the context of Teletandem, with emphasis on his/her role and the processes of mediation.

The study presented in this article was one of the subprojects inserted in the third objective. It was a case study of one pair of Teletandem partners and their mediator and it specifically aimed at investigating the role of the mediator by analyzing the supervision strategies used and their influences on the pedagogical practice of the Teletandem partners (Salomão, 2008).

The data collection involved aspects of qualitative studies of an ethnographic basis (Bogdan, & Bilken, 1982; Erickson, 1986; Silverman, 2001), such as intense and long term participation of the researcher in the studied context, careful register of all facts and events by means of a number of different instruments (autobiographies, questionnaires, interviews, the recording of the Teletandem and mediation sessions) and analytical reflection over the material gathered.

The Teletandem partners were a Brazilian undergraduate student of languages (Portuguese and Spanish) in the second year of the course, named fictitiously[1] here Dani, with no prior experience in teaching; and an Argentinean undergraduate student of languages (Portuguese) with little experience in teaching.

The teacher educator, supervisor of the Brazilian Teletandem partner in the study, Andrea, had a major in languages and 6 years of experience as a language teacher, but no previous experience as a teacher educator. At the time of the study she was a future teacher educator who was working on an MA in Applied Linguistics.

The research involved the teaching and learning relationship established between the Brazilian Teletandem partner and the supervisor, student teacher and teacher educator respectively, as shown in Figure 2.

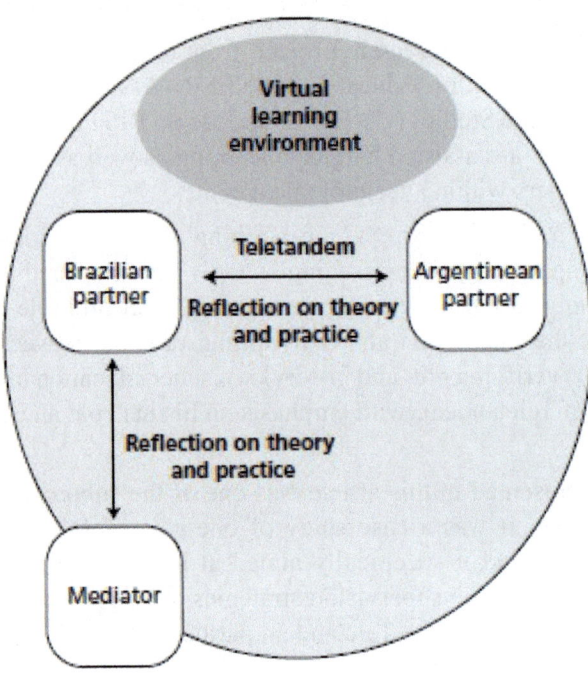

Figure 2. Context and participants.

The Brazilian and Argentinean Teletandem partners met regularly (usually twice a week) for 1-hour sessions of Teletandem, in which they taught each other their native languages (Portuguese and Spanish, respectively). The Brazilian Teletandem partner also met regularly with the mediator for supervision sessions. Both the Teletandem and the mediation session were seen as opportunities for reflection on theory and practice (Figure 2) for the Brazilian Teletandem partner as they provided her with a first practical experience as a teacher of her own language being supervised by the mediator (a practicum situation in a virtual learning environment).

During the 8 months of data collection (May to December, 2006), there were 22 Teletandem interactions and 9 mediation sessions scheduled according to necessity and negotiation between the Brazilian partner and the mediator, as graphically represented in Figure 3.

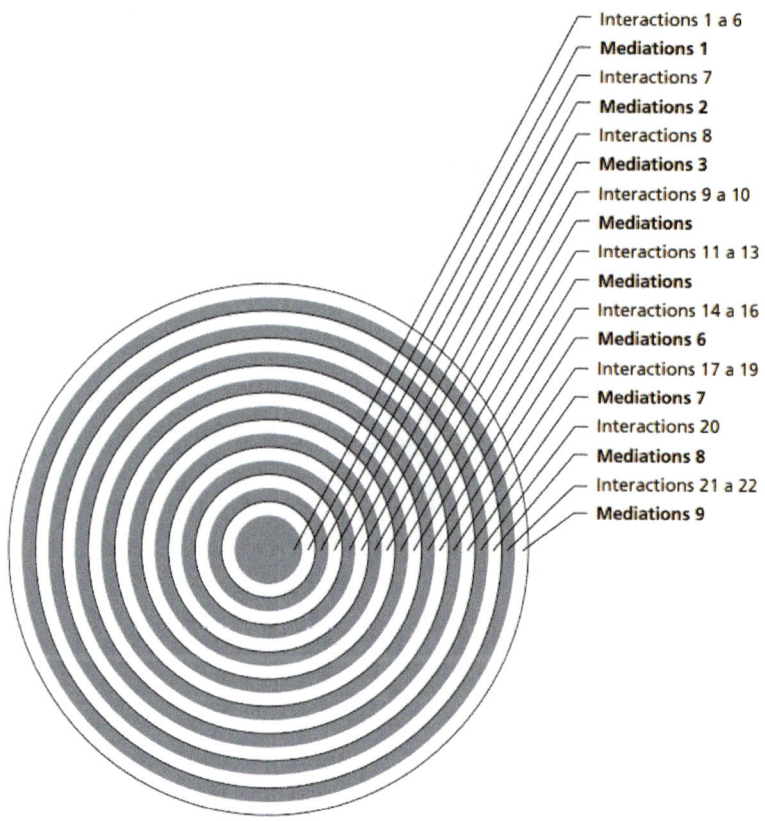

Figure 3. Interactions and mediations.

Figure 4 shows the dynamics used, which was based on Korthagen›s ALACT: both Dani and Andrea looked back on the Teletandem session (previously recorded) and separately took notes in their diaries on points to be discussed during the mediation session; after this process occurred in some interactions, they scheduled a mediation session in which they discussed the most important points that they had selected and then wrote new diary entries on their reflections. Dani restarted the cycle then by continuing to interact and trying to put in practice some of the decisions originated in the mediation session.

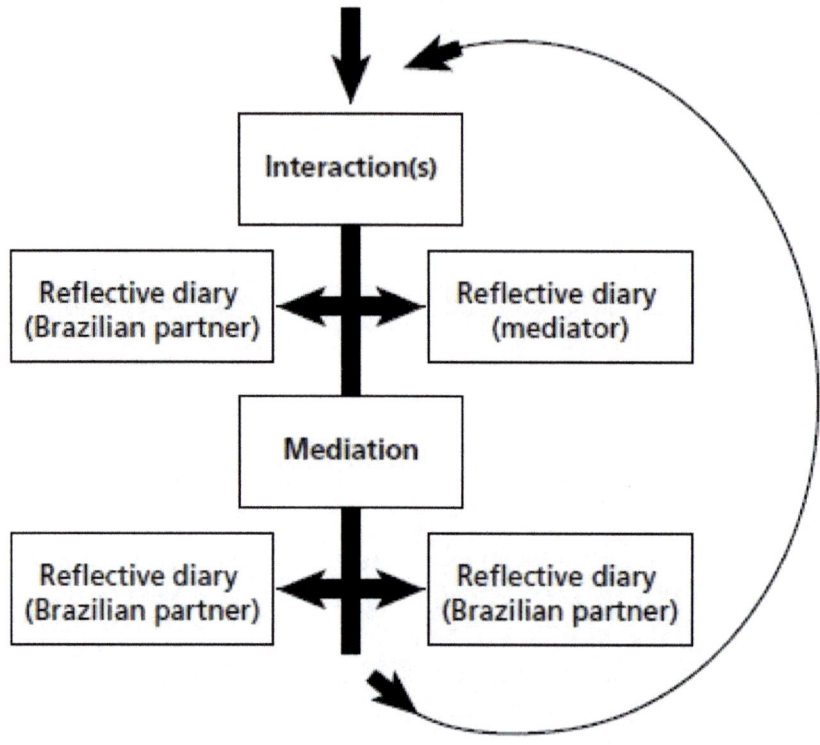

Figure 4. Dynamics of reflective work.

The data, which consisted of the interactions, mediations, diaries and questionnaires, were analyzed through an interpretative approach by reconstituting the participants' views of the events during the course of the 8 months of Teletandem sessions. The excerpts, which will be shown in the next secion, were translated into English.

FINDINGS

Since we guided our analysis by the reflective teaching paradigm, we attempted to find movements and traces of change in the pedagogical actions of the Brazilian partner (Dani) through her reflections in the diaries and questionnaires. It is not our intention to associate one specific mediation session or action to a specific change, as a direct cause and effect movement; thus, we divide them here according to the most salient characteristics in three moments: influences of alternative and non-directive supervision, influences of self-help explorative supervision, and influences of the use of theory and reflection brought by self-exploration.

Influences of alternative and non-directive supervision

Before the mediations began, all mediators were prepared through meetings with professors and coordinators of the research project to discuss guidelines which could direct their work, since most of them had never worked as teacher supervisors before. These meetings were guided by the reading of Korthagen (1999) and Sól (2004), and some directions for the mediation sessions were created collectively.

During the first four mediation sessions, Andrea's work seemed to be guided by the non-directive and alternative supervision models, since she did not pressure Dani or made any judgments. She did, however, offer some alternatives of action. Some of the topics addressed were error correction and feedback, negotiation of meaning and translation, preparation of themes, tandem principles (bilingualism and reciprocity), talking time of Argentinean partner, use of audio, use of visual resources, practice of the four skills, use of microphone and benefits of oral practice, linguistic transference, moments of silence, importance of pedagogical focus in tandem learning, principles and directions of Teletandem, and lack of institutional support from the Institute in Argentina.

Andrea tried to put forth concreteness by pointing out specific moments in Dani's practice to be discussed. Her strategies for being non-directive during supervision involved questioning Dani about her actions and showing empathy and acceptance for her answers and comments. She also appeared to assist Dani by offering scaffolding for reflection and not giving ready answers or directing her work, as well as led the conversation to moments of confrontation trying not to overwhelm the student-teacher. Table 1 contains an excerpt of mediation 1 where some of Andrea's attitudes are illustrated based on Korthagen›s ALACT.

Table 1. Excerpt from mediation 1

	Mediation session	Attitudes
Andrea	I saw that you ask her many questions and I think it is nice.	Concreteness/acceptance
Dani	Yes, hum-hum.	
Andrea	And I also saw that there are moments in which you correct her and there are moments that you don't. Why is that?	Questioning/utilizing the here and now
Dani	When we are speaking Portuguese you mean?	
Andrea	Yes. I just want to know what you think. There is no problem. It's because sometimes I notice that you correct her and sometimes you don't and sometimes you do it using the caps lock on.	Concreteness/acceptance
Dani	Well, yes, I noticed this too and then there was that day [in a meeting] when somebody mentioned the caps lock. Then I don't know if I should keep on doing that or just correct her normally.	
Andrea	Well, it is an option… Do you remember the meeting when we discussed the types of error correction and so? Which type of correction do you think you are making? Remember? There was the direct one, the one with reformulation, the one with questions… Which one do you think you use more?	Help in making things explicit
Dani	Hum, there are times when she puts something wrong and I reformulate it as an answer, you know?	
Andrea	Hum-hum.	Showing that she is listening and engaged in the conversation
Dani	Then I put the correct word thinking that in this way she will see how I am writing it…	
Andrea	Hum, ok.	Acceptance
Dani	Then she will realize that it was wrong, you see?	
Andrea	And do you think she can usually realize it?	Confrontation
Dani	Well, then I don't know.	

These first mediations were more centered on a procedural level of Dani's work as a teacher, since she complained about not knowing how to deal with error correction and the Teletandem session parts (interaction, feedback and evaluation of the session) and principles (autonomy and reciprocity). As Dani had little experience in teaching, the mediator offered some alternative in terms of suggestions so that Dani would have to think about what would suit her context better.

These kinds of supervision seemed to be understood by Dani as suggestions that might take her to reflect on possibilities and adapt them to her context. In the next extract, we can see how she expresses her view on the use of pre-prepared themes for the interactions after a mediation session:

The mediator and I reflected on the use of themes for the interactions. Many hypotheses appeared, but none excluded the other. (…) If we eliminate the use of themes there is the worry that by opting for spontaneous conversation the session could exclude the pedagogical intent and become a simple chat between two friends. Moreover, themes are productive for learning about the culture and ideological aspects of a people and in this sense we need our partner's collaboration and involvement (a situation addressed in the mediation since it sometimes does not happen). However, we run the risk of trying to force our partners to keep on themes they are not really involved with. (Diary of mediation 2)

The problematization generated by the discussion during the mediation session led Dani to think about the subject considering different perspectives which she had not contemplated before and understand that there was not one simple answer to the matter.

During this period of Teletandem interactions, Dani started to create new strategies for error correction and make them explicit in her diaries. She also tried to structure the session according to the Teletandem principles. In terms of procedures, Dani experimented with some of the suggestions of the mediator, as well as created her own, such as sending the correction through e-mail after the sessions.

Some of the first reflections Dani makes during this period are concerned with the difficulty she had in teaching her own language, as might be seen in this extract from her diary:

As incredible as it may seem I have been finding difficulty in teaching Portuguese, since there are things I do not know how to explain, and that is making me feel bad, because I know how it should be said, but I can't explain why it has to be that way. (Diary of interaction 7)

When Dani viewed the recordings of the Teletandem sessions in order to write her diaries, she also had some insights into the probable causes of the errors she had been spotting in her partners' output and related it to her own performance in the foreign language:

It is interesting how much we resort to our own language in order to express ourselves in a foreign one. (...) Doubtlessly, if my partner analyses my speech, she will find many of these resorts from my mother tongue. I believe our challenge is to try to separate our language from the foreign one, as much as possible. (Diary of interaction 10)

The mediation also seemed to have influenced this reflection above, since it was a topic of conversation during the sessions. The influences of self-help explorative supervision will be addressed next.

Influences of Self-Help Explorative Supervision

In the first mediations, as presented in the previous section, the discussions seemed to involve a more technical domain related to procedural issues and difficulties. In the mediations that followed (5 and 6), there were signs of a transition to reflection over the action implemented so far and to Dani's perception of her role as a language teacher. The main topics addressed were error correction, procedures, evaluation of the session, use of themes, parts of the session and pedagogical purposes, use of pedagogical resources, issues related to phonetics and pronunciation, communication strategies, technical and technological issues, context of interaction created by MSN, role as a teacher and a learner in the Teletandem interaction, tandem principles, and use of e-mail for scheduling and sending material. It is noticeable that some of the topics addressed are the same ones from the previous phase; however, during these mediation sessions Andrea attempted to help Dani explore the new actions she was trying to implement in her pedagogical practice by reflecting on her role as a teacher in the Teletandem partnership.

Andrea's strategies for self-help explorative supervision involved adopting a more questioning attitude that could lead Dani to analyze her pedagogical choices as a Portuguese tutor in the Teletandem session and understand and evaluate the efficacy of her procedures. Table 2 shows an excerpt of mediation 5 in which they were discussing different procedures used in two interactions.

It is noticeable that Dani during this stage feels freer to express her actions and analyze her insecurities. She also starts to consider the opinion and beliefs of her partner as an important factor for the success of her procedures. The influences of this kind of supervision were observed in Dani's attitudes during the Teletandem sessions, where she tried to establish some teaching procedures and reflect upon them, and also in the way she expressed her doubts and thoughts in her diaries on this first experience as a teacher (Schon's reflection on action):

Table 2. Excerpt from mediation 5

	Mediation session	Attitudes
Andrea	I would like to talk about something with you. There was an interaction when she read the material proposed, it was about the use of commas. And then there was this other one when you made a feedback right on the moment. Which one do you think was more productive?	Questioning/utilizing the here and now
Dani	The one she read and the one I explained, you mean?	
Andrea	Yes, for example this last interaction and the other. Which one do you fell [sic] was more positive?	Concreteness
Dani	Ah, well, I think it was this last one, because I think it was more natural, you know, when I explained.	

Andrea	Hum.	Showing that she is listening and engaged in the conversation
Dani	You see, it is a difficulty I have to explain because I don't know if I am 100% to explain things to her. But I try to explain and then I think I start to understand it even more and then I will know how to pass it to her in a better way. I think it is better, but now I don't know, maybe it would be interesting to ask her for her opinion on this too...	
Andrea	Yes.	Acceptance
Dani	If she prefers reading or me explaining.	

When we were speaking Portuguese, I tried to explain the use of commas, since it was something she'd asked for. It was a good experience, but I felt rather insecure and nervous, since it is a part of grammar that I do not cognize as I wish I could. If I had studied more or explained better, the interaction could have been better. I was insecure and afraid of confusing her. I don't know if I explained things well. (Diary of interaction 12)

She blames the lack of success of the activity proposed on her lack of knowledge of the topic and inability to explain it, which demonstrates concern with formal aspects of the language. This seems to be a first move in the direction of more complex reflections than the ones she was practicing before. Mostly, her reflections during this phase seemed to cover a practical level (Van Mannen, 1977), since she explored more and more in her diaries the new procedures she had been trying to incorporate into her practice according to the needs expressed by her partner and to the insights that the mediation and this practical pedagogical situation were giving her.

The changes in error correction during this phase can be mainly observed in relation to the fact that Dani could finally establish a moment to focus on this as she wanted, and in the attempts that she made in correcting and pointing out errors in different ways. While her preoccupation with error correction during the first phase seemed to be influenced by the mediator and by Dani's own beliefs on what teaching a language is, in this phase it also appeared to come from her perception on the gains of such practice for herself and her partner as learners.

Another peculiarity of this phase is that Dani seemed to incorporate the discourse of the mediator, noticed by her usage of academic terms in her reflections in the diaries, as shown in this excerpt:

We also addressed the difficulty of communicating when we do not know something or cannot express what we are thinking. These difficulties may be related to the knowledge of the lexicon of the language or to the lack of expressions. On the other hand, we may not be able to articulate our speech in

Portuguese and it could get worse, because nervousness can take place if we cannot maintain our turn once it is given us. (Diary of mediation 5)

When she writes about the "difficulties related to lexicon" and "turn taking", her words seem to come from the mediator's discourse in her questionings during the mediation sessions (the mediator's research focus is interlanguage and she often uses this kind of academic vocabulary in her speech).

Ultimately, this phase is mainly characterized by Dani's perception of her role as a teacher, a very important experience for her in the second year of her undergraduate course, as stated in her answer to the questionnaire:

Researcher: How did the Teletandem experience contribute to your education as a future language teacher?

Dani: Sincerely, I can say that after this experience I started to see in another way the "being a teacher", and this is probably due to the difficulties found in the interactions, which are doubtlessly a very important practice for us to act as teachers even before we graduate. Even so, dealing with the difficulties did not unmotivate [sic] me; on the contrary, it only made me reconsider some aspects of my education as a teacher. (Final questionnaire)

It is also interesting to note that Dani sees the mediation sessions as key to the insights she had been having on the interactions, as she states in her diary:

Mediation is certainly the moment of interaction (as I believe it is a continuation of the Teletandem interactions), which gives us clues so we can draw conclusions about our position as a Teletandem partner, and also as a student and teacher. With these reflections in every new interaction we become more able and more willing to improve. (Diary of mediation 5)

Through her words, it seems that this collaborative work between the teacher educator and the student-teacher creates a process through which the student-teacher can explore his or her beliefs in a practicum environment, in a reversion of the classical top-down theoretical approach for educating future teachers. In the next part of the article, the influences of the use of theory to bridge, understand and inform practice are discussed.

Influences of the Use of Theory

During the third phase of mediations, Andrea started to offer theoretical support which could help Dani with the difficulties she was having in the interactions. These mediations continued to present the self-help explorative supervision characteristics; however, it was observed that a collaborative atmosphere was also being constructed through the scaffolding provided by Andrea to help Dani relate theory and practice.

The main topics addressed were affective issues and their relation with interaction and culture; error correction (causes for recurrence of treated errors; elaboration of correction; the use of implicit signaling or explicit correction; differences of error correction in chats and oral interactions;motivation and correction; interference from L1), interruptions of other people during interaction; motivation for the preparation of materials (how they were used and partner's feedback); theory (looking back at practice, how it has helped reflection); technical and technological issues (the benefits of audio, comparisons with face to face tandem, pedagogical issues); influence of linguistic theories; knowledge acquired in undergraduate courses and observation of former teachers and professors on her practice in the interactions, perception of interactions with chat versus interactions with audio for language development, friendship (help or interference in communication and teaching).

Some of the topics addressed during these meditations continued to be the same ones already discussed in the previous phases, but the difference now is that Andrea was conjugating them with theory according to the needs perceived in the interactions, such as the relationship between error correction and motivation, or error correction and affective issues, and Dani was having the opportunity to explore her role as a teacher and the influences of her previous experiences as an undergraduate student. Table 3 shows how Andrea proposed a preactivity for Dani, for mediation 7, by conjugating theory about error correction and prompting her reflections through questions related to her practice during the Teletandem interactions.

Table 3. Use of theory for reflection in mediations

The next mediation involves as a pre-activity the reading of the following texts: http://www.lume.ufrgs.br/bitstream/handle/10183/1518/000300608.pdf?sequence=1 (pp. 17-28) http://www.ufsm.br/labler/publi/IIenpletrabs01.html	Recommendation of theoretical texts for reflection based on the difficulties Dani was having in the interactions with error correction.
Firstly, I would like to ratify the last message sent to you and your partner congratulating both for your linguistic development and for taking on responsibilities during this project. I believe your effort is substantial and, therefore, it was recognized by your partner, who has been dedicated to the interactions despite the problems she is facing.	
And, by the way, how do personal problems experienced and shared by you both in the interactions influence them? Do they help to understand more about the other's culture too? You and your partner are getting closer and closer. How does this assist communication between you two?	Showing empathy and acceptance
Since the first interaction, what do you think of the feedback given? Have you noticed that your partner produces errors which have already been commented or corrected?	Genuineness and helping making things explicit
How have you felt about it? What do you think could be lacking for a more thorough understanding?	
How do you evaluate yourself in a tandem session: as a friend or as a teacher? If both, explain in which moments you see yourself in each role. I have observed that are both trying to send files through e-mail. Why don't you try to send it through the MSN? Do you still find problems in using the technological tools? During the interactions, there are people who enter the room and disturb the conversation, how do you react to this?	Utilizing the here and now and questioning
I congratulate you again for your intense search for material and the cartoons sent to your partner. I believe they were important. That is why I would like to know what factor in the interaction motivated you to send them. Have you tried to search for other materials to help your teaching? How did you partner react to that and how did you use them in your practice?	Concreteness, empathy and confrontation
In relation to the texts read, do you believe they helped you in your reflections? How? Thanks for your attention! *Your mediator*	Bridging theory and practice

The influences are mainly felt in the way Dani expresses the importance of linking theory to practice. She finds it very interesting that the theory is related to the problems she is facing in her practice.

I found the text on feedback and the one on interaction in chats very productive. It's a way to incorporate the theory more productively. (Diary of mediation 7)

During this phase, Dani's diary entries show that she is now reflecting on her own choices and actions as a teacher and on the probable effects of those on the learner:

In the interactions in Portuguese, I am always careful not to miss any mistakes so that I can tell my partner later, since that is what I would like to happen when I speak Spanish, but I think the corrections are making my partner a bit daunting or it is even being a little boring. In this situation I do not know if I should let some little mistakes pass and correct only the most visible ones or if I should go on doing what I do. I'm also wondering if I am correcting her well or if there is a better way to do it. If it was her who was correcting me this way, I would like it, but I understand that people are different and that it is perhaps being a bit "heavy". (Diary of interaction 20)

One noticeable change in Dani's posture in this extract is that she states a problem that she herself noticed in relation to her partner's motivation and her possible solutions for it, which seems to be a clear step forward from her previous attitude. During the mediation session, Andrea addresses this topic and recommends that Dani read a text on motivation in order to be able to think about how to deal with the problem. Here is how she describes the experience:

Another important aspect of this mediation was the discussion of personal issues influencing the development of interaction. Obviously personal problems interfere with our work and in this case with our studies. My partner has been through some personal problems recently and I think it may have affected a little her motivation during the interactions. In this sense it would and will be necessary for me through the preparation of interaction materials to be able to motivate her to continue our interactions and get good results. After reading the second chapter of the book "Psychology for Language Teachers", suggested by my mediator, I could pay attention to this aspect of motivation and how it is closely related to learning. I think I've got to be more attentive to the problems of my partner and know how to adapt the interaction in those moments, since if she is psychologically shaken, a session of corrections will be a little discouraging. (Diary of mediation 8)

It is interesting to observe that Dani's concern with error correction before aimed only at establishing a moment for it to occur, and then on different ways of doing it. But now it also included aspects related to motivation or lack of motivation generated by correction. She also started to reflect more on the strategies she had been using for error correction and described them in her diary. But this time, instead of only outlining the corrections made, she commented on the moments she decided to interfere, which shows that she was considering other aspects besides accuracy during interaction (reflection in action), as can be seen in this excerpt:

We began our interaction with the Portuguese language and I believe it was a good interaction. On the issue of corrections, which I've been concerned with, everything went well. I tried to make indirect corrections when I realized that my partner was confused with how to write something in order to provide the vocabulary she was looking for at one point. I interfered at times I thought it would be appropriate to show the way a certain word should be written, and the rest which demanded further explanation I left for the final moments of our interaction. (Diary of interaction 22)

One of the reasons we believe may explain the fact that Dani started expressing her corrective choices this way now is because she is more aware of them, and the mediation was key to directing her attention to the different levels of reflection she should have as a teacher concerning error correction.

This first experience as a teacher may have helped Dani to start constructing an identity as a language teacher and to make a link between practice and theory, reflecting on teaching and learning from a practical perspective. She herself states that this experience brought her into contact with Applied Linguistics, an unknown subject for her at the time (she would have this subject in her undergraduate course only in the following year), and helped her to reflect on her role as a teacher and learner in the Teletandem experience she had been through:

The readings provided the opportunity to know theories of language teaching and even about Applied Linguistics itself, totally unknown to me before. After each reading, I reflected on the learning process of my partner, trying to apply what I thought was relevant and would assist in her learning process. I also tried to draw from the readings points that I thought would help me learn and develop my skills on the foreign language (Spanish). (Final questionnaire)

For Dani, this contact with theory contributed to her incorporating in her discourse academic terms related to language teaching. This first contact with Applied Linguistics through the needs originating in her practice appeared to be extremely favorable in terms of her motivation and interest in theory which could inform her pedagogical practice as a language teacher (and even as a language learner as she states). This resonates with what Brazilian authors and researchers, such as Gimenez (2005), Paiva (2005), Vieira-Abrahão (2006; 2007), claim about the early conjugation of theory and practice in pre-service education.

In general, the supervision strategies used by the mediator seemed to generate a growing motivation for Dani to build her identity as a language teacher by looking for different ways to improve her practice as well as to better understand the reasons for her choices in the practical teaching situation she was experiencing.

As she was an inexperienced student-teacher, the offering of alternatives in the beginning of the mediation sessions seemed to bring concreteness in terms of procedures that were fundamental for her to establish pedagogical objectives to the interactions and, at the same time, the non-directive stance of the mediator made her feel free to customize the changes implemented. Then, the use of self-exploration helped her to reflect on these changes and to take a more active role in the interactions, increasingly seeing herself as a teacher. Finally, the conjugation of theory, chosen according to the needs arising from practice, brought her opportunity to bridge theory and practice based on the situations experienced and aroused her interest for theories of language teaching, with which she had not yet had contact during her undergraduate course.

FINAL CONSIDERATIONS

Our results showed that Teletandem seems to be not only an environment aimed at teaching and learning foreign languages in a virtual and collaborative way, but also an environment that may help pre-service teacher education, due to the possibility of making mediation a collaborative and knowledge-building work between teacher educator (mediator) and student-teacher (Teletandem partner).

The opportunity of combining teaching and learning within this context seems to bring to the Teletandem partners the opportunity for a first teaching practice, within which they can look at their own language through the contact with a foreign one. The exchange of roles also appears to help the student-teacher to make a more critical observation of practice since, in our study, the Brazilian Teletandem partner began to observe not only her own pedagogical methods and motivations, but also her partner's. This opportunity to observe the practice of another teacher is configured differently in Teletandem from regular practices: the Teletandem partners observed each other and swapped roles as student and teacher, which appeared in the data as something very positive. In addition, the opportunity created by the partnership between two student-teachers also seemed to enable the discussion of issues related to their undergraduate courses, as well as the comparison of curricula.

Furthermore, having a first teaching experience supervised by a more experienced person, the mediator, in the role of a teacher educator who offers scaffolds for knowledge building, contributed to enable a bridging between theory and practice that starts in practice and relates it meaningfully to theory. The supervision models used by the mediator seemed to provide support for the Brazilian Teletandem partner as a student-teacher, to find elements in her practice that could lead her to see herself as a teacher and establish pedagogical objectives to her teaching in-teletandem. They also provided the opportunity for her to gain confidence and explore her pedagogical practice on different levels: in practical terms, by paying more attention to techniques and procedures used, changing or substituting the ones that she found to be ineffective; and, in more reflective terms, by exploring her decisions and actions pedagogically and relating them to the theory she had been reading.

We can conclude that the mediator's supervision in this relationship provided scaffold for learning by means of resolving procedural, technical, pedagogical and organizational problems that arose from an authentic teaching situation, without being directive or having a pre-established syllabus in mind. The importance of such findings lies in the fact that much of the theory on supervision has been grounded on a theoretical basis with short instances of practical examples. The experience reported here shows that the establishment of partnerships between undergraduate and graduate students for collaborative work may be useful for pre-service education in a reflective teaching paradigm and that the complexity of the relationship between the supervisor and the student-teacher is a fertile ground which still needs further mapping and investigation.

REFERENCES

1. Bartlett, L. (1990). Teacher development through reflective teaching: In J.C Richards, D. Nunan (Eds.), *Second Language Teacher Education* (pp. 202-214). Cambridge: Cambridge University Press.
2. Bogdan, R. D., & Bilken, S. K. (1982). *Qualitative research for education*. Boston: Allyn and Bacon.
3. Erickson, F. (1986). Qualitative methods in research on teaching. In M. C.Wittrock (Ed.), *Handbook of research on teaching* (pp. 119-161). 3rd ed. New York: MacMillan.
4. Freeman, D. (1990). Intervening in practice teaching. In J. C Richards, D. Nunan (Eds.), *Second language teacher education* (pp. 103-117). United Kingdom: Cambridge University Press.
5. Freeman, D. (2002). The hidden side of the work: Teacher knowledge and learning to teach. *Language Teaching, 35*, 1-23.
6. Gebhard, J. G. (1990) Models of supervision. In J. C Richards; D. Nunan (Eds.), *Second language teacher education* (pp. 156-166). UK: Cambridge University Press.

7. Gimenez, T. (2005). Desafios contemporâneos na formação de professores de línguas: contribuições da lingüística aplicada. In M. M. Freire; M. H. Vieira-Abrahão; A. M. F. Barcelos (Orgs.), *Lingüística Aplicada e contemporaneidade* (pp. 183-201). Campinas: ALAB/Pontes.
8. Korthagen, F.A. J.(1982). Helping student teachers to become reflective: The supervision process. In Korthagen, F. A. J. Leren reflecteren als basis van de lerarenopleiding [Learning to reflect as a basis for teacher education]. ‹s-Graven-hage:SVO.
9. Korthagen, F. A. J., & Kessels, J. P. A. M. (1999). Linking theory and practice: Changing the pedagogy of teacher education.*Educational Researcher, 28*(4), 4-17.
10. Korthagen, F. A. J. (2001). *Linking practice and theory: the pedagogy of realistic teacher education*. Paper presented at the Annual Meeting of the American Educational Research Association, Seattle.
11. Korthagen, F., Korthagen, F., & Vasalos, A. (2005). Levels in reflection: Core reflection as a means to enhance professional growth. *Teachers and Teaching: theory and practice, 11*(1), 47-71.
12. Paiva, V. M. O. P. (2005). O novo perfil dos cursos de licenciatura em Letras. In L. M. B Tomich; M. H. Vieira-Abrahão; C. Daghlin; D. I. Ristoff (Orgs.), *A interculturalidade no Ensino de Inglês* (pp. 345-363). Florianópolis: UFSC.
13. Salomão, A. C. B. (2008). *Gerenciamento e estratégias pedagógicas na mediação dos pares no Teletandem e seus reflexos para as práticas pedagógicas dos interagentes*. 2008. 316 f. Dissertação (Mestrado em Estudos Lingüísticos) - Instituto de Biociências, Letras e Ciências Exatas, Universidade Estadual Paulista - UNESP, S. J. do Rio Preto.
14. Schön, D. (1983). The reflective practitioner: How professionals think in action. London: Temple Smith.
15. Silverman, D. (2001). *Doing qualitative research*. Londres: Sage.
16. Sól, V. S. A. (2004). *A natureza da prática reflexiva de uma formadora de professores e duas professoras em formação*. 2004. Dissertação (Mestrado em Lingüística Aplicada). Faculdade de Letras, Universidade Federal de Minas Gerais, Belo Horizonte.
17. Telles, J. A., & Vassallo, M. L. (2006). Foreign language learning in-tandem: Teletandem as an alternative proposal in CALLT.*The ESPecialist*, 27(2), 189-212.
18. Vassallo, M. L., & Telles, J. A. (2006). Foreign language learning in-tandem: Theoretical principles and research perspectives. The ESPecialist, 27(1), 83-118.

19. Vieira-Abrahão, M. H. (2006). A formação inicial e o desenvolvimento profissional do professor de línguas estrangeiras: práticas e pesquisas. Horizontes, 5(2), 3-23.
20. Vieira-Abrahão, M. H. (2007). A formação inicial do professor de língua estrangeira: Parceria universidade e escola pública. In M. L. O. Alvarez; K. A. Silva (Orgs.), Lingüística Aplicada: múltiplos olhares (pp. 155-166). Brasília, DF: UnB/Finatec; Campinas, SP: Pontes Editores.
21. Vygotsky, L. S. (1994). *A formação social da mente*. São Paulo: Martins Fontes.
22. Williams, M. (1999). Learning teaching: A social constructivist approach - Theory and Practice or Theory with practice? In H. Trappes-Lomax; I. Mcgrath, *Theory in language teacher education* (pp. 11-20). England: Longman.
23. Zeichner, K. M., & Liston, D. P. (1996). *Reflective teaching: An introduction*. New Jersey: Lawrence Erlbaum Associates Publishers.

Chapter 10

ENGLISH LANGUAGE AND LITERACY LEARNING: RESEARCH TO PRACTICE

INTRODUCTION

The English Language Learning Progressions (ELLP) explain what ESOL specialists and mainstream teachers need to know about English language learners. They will help teachers to choose content, vocabulary, and tasks that are appropriate to each learner's age, stage, and language-learning needs. This may include learners for whom English is a first language but who would benefit from additional language support.

Carolyn is not alone. She is among many teachers instructing English language learners (ELLs), who are found in every state in growing numbers. ELLs come from families with a wide range of education, from the highly educated to those with very limited or no formal education. They are represented in every socioeconomic level and speak more than 470 different languages, although Spanish is the home language for at least 75 % of these students. Despite these differences, researchers have identified effective instructional and assessment practices for beginning readers who are ELLs.

As with all reading instruction, the ultimate goals are reading for understanding, learning, and interest. In the early grades, with most students, the focus is on moving to meaning after assuring that students have foundational skills such as phonemic awareness, phonics, fluency, and vocabulary. How do these goals differ for English language learners? The broad goals of reading are the same for all students. An additional goal with ELLs is to simultaneously build oral language skills. While building oral language skills is important with all students, it is even more essential for English language learners. Although we do not include a chapter dedicated exclusively to oral language, ways of building oral language are referred to in each chapter and are integrated into the activities.

Many ELLs are learning a new language as they acquire and develop literacy skills, especially vocabulary, in English. The integration of practices for English as a second language (ESL) with effective reading instructional practices can provide students the support they need to develop both language and literacy skills in a cohesive manner. The most effective teachers integrate instructional objectives seamlessly in teaching the elements of reading and use language- and meaning-based approaches.

Fortunately, the similarities in the cognitive processes involved in learning to read different alphabetic languages have been documented. These similarities provide researchers and educators a starting point in identifying effective instructional practices in the teaching of reading.

WHAT DOES THE RESEARCH SAY ABOUT SECOND LANGUAGE ACQUISITION?

Studies of second language acquisition (SLA) focus primarily on the learning of oral language. They provide valuable information about how second languages are learned and the factors that influence the language learning process. Little research has been conducted on second language acquisition with English language learners in adult education contexts, and no controlled intervention studies have been done. The complexities of adult English as a second language (ESL) instruction make research in this field challenging. Investigating issues of culture, language, and education as well as tracking learner progress over time are not easy when working with diverse and mobile learner populations in varied learning contexts (e.g., workplace classes, general ESL classes, family literacy classes). However, the SLA literature gives important insights into the language acquisition process that can guide adult ESL instruction.

SLA researchers examine the development of communicative competence in a language— the ability to interpret the underlying meaning of a message, understand cultural references, use strategies to keep communication from breaking down, and apply the rules of grammar of the language (Savignon, 1997). They also study nonlinguistic influences on SLA such as age, anxiety, and motivation. (See Ellis, 1997; Gass & Selinker, 2001; & Pica, 2003 for extensive discussions of SLA theory and research.)

The following sections summarize the three major areas that are covered in the second language acquisition literature and that are critical to acquiring a second language: learner motivation, opportunities for interaction, and vocabulary knowledge.

Motivation

Defines motivation as "why people decide to do something, how long they are willing to sustain the activity, [and] how hard they are going to pursue it."

Studies indicate that *integrative motivation* (wanting to learn a language in order to identify with the community that speaks it) promotes SLA regardless of the age of the learner or whether the language is being learned as a second or a foreign language (Gardner, 1985; Masgoret & Gardner, 2003). Learners may have *instrumental motivation*, the desire to learn the language to meet their needs and goals, such as getting a job or talking to their children's teachers (Morris, 2001; Oxford & Shearin, 1994). Whether learners' motivation is integrative or instrumental, research indicates that teachers should learn about and respond to learners' needs and goals when planning instruction (Dörnyei & Csizer, 1998; Weddel & Van Duzer, 1997).

Teachers can help learners identify their motivations for learning English and their short-term goals and reflect on their progress and achievements. One way to do this is by using tools like those described below:

- Self-evaluation tools such as checklists to identify their skills, strengths, and weaknesses;
- Weekly checklists to track their progress towards meeting a learning goal; and
- Reflection tools such as learning diaries to help them build autonomy and take charge of their learning (Marshall, 2002).

Recent research looks at how instructional contexts affect motivation. A learner's motivation may vary from day to day and even from task to task, and social factors (e.g., group dynamics, learning environment, and a learning partner's motivation) may affect a learner's attitude, effort, classroom behavior, and achievement (Dörnyei, 2002b). Therefore, teachers should create an environment that is conducive to learning by encouraging group cohesion in the classroom and by using varied and challenging instructional activities to help learners stay focused and engaged with instructional content (Dörnyei & Csizer, 1998). Activities that are done in pairs and small groups can provide learners with opportunities to share information and build a sense of community (Florez & Burt, 2001).

Research also suggests that teachers should create opportunities for learners to continue their language learning outside of class (Clement, Dörnyei, & Noels, 1994). Projects that are started in class and continued outside class are one way to do this. For example, a class might work together to create a book of information about community services for new families. In class they might brainstorm ideas and develop the outline for the book. Outside class, individual learners might collect information about different community agencies, write it up, and bring it to class to be compiled in the book. Projects like this one give learners opportunities to work with others to accomplish tasks and to use English in real-life situations.

New research on motivation and second language acquisition is examining specific factors that influence motivation and learning, such as personal goals, levels of self-confidence, and features of the learning environment (Dörnyei, 2003; Noels, Clement, & Pelletier, 2003).

Opportunities for Interaction

Interaction refers to communication between individuals, particularly when they are negotiating meaning or working to prevent a breakdown in communication (Ellis, 1999). Interaction provides learners with opportunities to receive language input (through hearing the language) and feedback (when the conversational partner responds, corrects, or asks for clarification). It also allows them to make changes to their language as the conversation proceeds (Gass, 1997; Long, 1996; Pica, 1994; Swain, 1995). This allows learners to "notice the gap" between their use of the language and correct, native speaker use (Schmidt & Frota, 1986, p. 311).

Empirical research with second language learners indicates that participating in language interactions facilitates second language development. For example, a study of conversational interaction and learners' acquisition of question formation found that interaction increased their rate of acquisition (Mackey, 1999).

Research on interaction includes studies of task-based language learning and focus on form.

Task-based learning

- The goal of an interactive task is for learners to focus together on a topic or activity and exchange meaning about it (Ellis, 1999). Most tasks are done in pairs or small groups. SLA researchers have found that carefully designed tasks give learners opportunities to use the language (in this case English) in authentic situations and in meaningful ways. They have also found that learners tend to produce longer sentences and negotiate meaning more often in interactive tasks than they do in teacher-fronted instruction, where the teacher stands at the front of the room and leads the discussion (Doughty & Pica, 1986). When designing tasks, teachers should consider the learners' language proficiency, the goals of the lesson, the language to be practiced, the skills to be learned and content areas to be covered, opportunities to give feedback to learners, and classroom logistics.

- Interactive tasks seem to be most successful when they:

- o Center on a problem that is new or unfamiliar to the participants;
  - o Require learners to exchange information;
  - o Have a specific outcome;
  - o Involve discussion of details; and
  - o Involve the use of naturally occurring conversation and narratives (Ellis, 2000).

- In *problem-solving tasks*, learners have opportunities to share ideas, build consensus, and explain decisions about real-life issues that are important to them. For example, group might have a hypothetical amount of money to spend and figure out a monthly budget for a family of four. (See Van Duzer & Burt, 1999, for discussion and examples of problem-solving tasks.)

- *Information gap tasks*, in which two people share information to complete the task, may be more structured than problem solving tasks and give learners opportunities to ask and answer questions. In *one-way information gap tasks*, one learner has all of the information (e.g., one learner describes a picture while the other draws it). In *two-way information gap tasks*, both learners have information that they must share with the other to complete the task (e.g., both have some information about directions to a location, but they have to share the information that they have to complete the directions).

Focus on form

Instruction focused on grammatical forms and correct grammatical usage does not need to take place in isolation. Rather, learners' attention can be drawn to grammatical forms in the context of meaningful activities. The teacher's focus on the forms to be taught can be informed by the problems that learners are having with comprehension or production (Long, 2000). Research studies suggest that instruction that uses a focus-on-form approach and that incorporates form with meaning is as effective as more traditional approaches in which grammar is taught in isolation (Norris & Ortega, 2001). When lessons are based on authentic communication and there is a focus on form within that context, learners incorporate new and correct structures into their language use (Ellis, Basturkmen, & Loewen, 2001).

When teaching about the forms of language, teachers need to consider learners' needs and goals and their readiness to understand the instruction. Teachers then need to decide how to draw learners' attention to a specific form and give them opportunities to practice it in meaningful activities (Doughty & Williams, 1998). For example, in a workplace class with intermediate- or advanced-level learners, the class might read and discuss a memo from an employer to an employee and focus on the use of the passive voice in the memo (e.g., "This report *must be finished* by 3:00 today).

Vocabulary Knowledge

Word knowledge is an essential component of communicative competence, and it is important for production and comprehension of a second language (Coady & Huckin, 1997). What does it mean to know a word? Vocabulary knowledge includes both the number of words one knows and the depth of knowledge about those words. Depth of knowledge refers to the pronunciation, spelling, and various meanings of the word; the contexts in which it can be used; the frequency with which it is used; its various parts of speech and forms; and how it combines (or collocates) with other words (e.g., vocabulary item "squander" is often combined with "time," "money," or "resources," as in "squander resources") (Folse, 2004; Qian, 1999).

Recent research has focused on *incidental vocabulary*, new words that are learned when one is focused on a meaningful task, such as hearing or reading a story, rather than specifically on learning new words. Learners figure out the meanings of words by paying attention to "clues" in the context; for example, learning that "picnic" means a meal outside when hearing about a family that has a picnic at the beach. (See Gass, 1999, for a summary of research on incidental vocabulary acquisition.) However, researchers argue that learners need to understand about 3,000 word families in order to pick up word meaning from context (Laufer, 1997). (For example, the family of "think" includes think, thinks, thought, thoughtful, thoughtfully.) Teachers then need to help learners build their vocabulary. One way to approach vocabulary instruction is to organize the words to be learned into thematically related units (e.g., vocabulary related to eating out with friends or taking a trip to the mall) (Folse, 2004).

Research also suggests that learners gain vocabulary knowledge through extensive reading, especially when reading is accompanied by vocabulary building activities (Paribakht & Wesche, 1997; Wesche & Paribakht, 2000). Teachers should include opportunities for reading to be done in class and assist learners in selecting texts that are of high interest to and at the appropriate level for them. Teachers should preview the important vocabulary in a reading passage before learners read it and teach words that are key to the meaning and that occur frequently. They also should show learners how to use dictionaries effectively.

Negotiation of meaning seems to have a positive effect on vocabulary acquisition (de la Fuente, 2002; Ellis & He, 1999; Ellis, Tanaka, & Yamazaki, 1994). Teachers can provide learners with multiple opportunities to use new vocabulary in interactive situations in the following ways:

- Tasks requiring information sharing and information-gap activities
- Games such as Bingo, Password, and Concentration;
- Projects and tasks that learners carry out outside of class, such as keeping vocabulary journals with new words they encounter and the strategies they use to learn them).

Giving learner's opportunities to interact with the teacher and with each other, planning instruction to include tasks that promote these opportunities, and teaching language forms and vocabulary in the context of meaningful learning activities are all ways in which second language acquisition research may be applied in the classroom.

WHAT DOES THE RESEARCH SAY ABOUT LEARNING TO READ IN ENGLISH?

The National Adult Literacy Survey (NALS) found that more than half of the U. S. population studied had low literacy skills and that compared to native English speakers, a higher percentage of non-native English speakers read English at the lowest levels (Kirsch, Jungeblut, Jenkins, & Kolstad, 1993; Greenburg, Macías, Rhodes, & Chan, 2001). Adults performing at the lowest levels had difficulty with basic literacy tasks in English, such as reading documents (e.g., time tables, forms, and maps), reading prose (e.g., newspaper articles, instructions on medicine bottles), and performing numeracy tasks (e.g., computing hours, calculating interest rates). These outcomes have caused concern that many adults, both native and non-native English speakers, lack the reading, writing, and functional skills necessary for living in a literate society. However, there is very little research on the reading development of adults who are non-native English speakers.

The National Center for ESL Literacy Education (NCLE) synthesized the limited research on adults learning English that was published between 1980 and 2002 (Burt, Peyton, & Adams, 2003). This synthesis focused on the reading development of adults in adult education and college-based intensive English programs (IEPs). The adults in these studies were ages 16 years and older and not enrolled in secondary schools. The research reviewed was published in refereed (peer-reviewed) journals, dissertations, the ERIC database, the Modern Language Association database, the Linguistics and Language Behavior Abstracts database, and books. Studies were included if they reported (1) outcomes related to reading (and, where applicable, general literacy) development, (2) descriptions of the adults participating, (3) details on the intervention or study situation, and (4) information on the procedures and outcome measures. The studies included used experimental or quasi-experimental methodologies based on comparisons between groups (with statistical tests for significance), non-experimental methods, and qualitative methods (descriptive and practitioner research). Theoretical discussions of reading development also were included. Descriptions of the articles reviewed, along with an annotated bibliography of the research

In addition, Kruidenier (2002) has reviewed the research on reading instruction with native English speakers in adult basic education (ABE) programs.

This discussion draws from the resources above to give a brief overview of the following questions and suggest implications for instruction:

- What factors influence the literacy development of adults learning English, and what challenges do they face when learning to read?

- What reading skills do adult English language learners need?

- What are the overall benefits of reading in a second language?

WHAT FACTORS INFLUENCE THE LITERACY DEVELOPMENT OF ADULTS LEARNING ENGLISH, AND WHAT CHALLENGES DO THEY FACE?

The factors discussed most frequently in the literature on learning to read in English as a second language are summarized here—learners' first-language literacy, educational background, second-language proficiency, and goals for learning English. Additional factors include learners' ages; motivations to read; instructional, living, and working environments; socio-cultural backgrounds; and learning abilities or disabilities.

First Language Literacy

Researchers have identified six different types of literacy learners according to their first-language literacy background: pre-literate, non-literate, semi-literate, non-alphabet literate, non-Roman alphabet literate, and Roman alphabet literate.

Pre-literate learners come from cultures where literacy is not common in everyday life. They might include those whose native language is not written or is being developed (e.g., the Bantu of Somalia and the Dinka of Sudan). They often have had little or no exposure to written text and may not be aware of the purposes of literacy in everyday life. They need to be taught how written language works. They generally progress slowly in literacy and other language instruction and may need frequent re-teaching of skills.

Non-literate learners come from cultures where literacy is more common, but they have not had sufficient access to literacy, often because of their socio-economic or political status. (For instance, adults from Central America may not know how to read or write in their native Spanish because of disrupted schooling due to war and poverty.) Although they have not learned to read, they have probably been exposed to written language and may have greater awareness of the value and uses of literacy than pre-literate learners. These adults may be reluctant to disclose their limited literacy background in class, and instruction with them may proceed slowly.

Semi-literate learners usually have had access to literacy in their native culture, but because of their socio-economic status or political or educational situation, they have not achieved a high level of literacy in their native language. These adults may have left school at a young age for economic or political reasons (e.g., as did many Southeast Asian refugees and Central American immigrants in the 1970s and 1980s), or they may have lived in the United States and developed oral English proficiency but not literacy.

Written materials used in teaching may be of limited use with pre-literate, non-literate, and semi-literate learners, and their retention of class material may be limited because they cannot use educational texts or take notes for later review. Because of their limited educational experiences, they may feel intimidated about learning English. At the same time, they are often highly motivated to learn. They need opportunities to increase their self-confidence in educational situations and to develop positive images of themselves as readers and writers (Goldberg, 1997; Strucker, 1997). They also may have learning disabilities that have not been diagnosed or addressed (Schwarz & Terrill, 2000). Programs should have procedures to identify and meet the needs of English language learners with learning disabilities.

The following groups of learners are literate in their first language, have already developed reading skills, have formed reading behaviors, and know that written language can represent speech. Described below are characteristics and implications for teaching reading to individuals from these groups.

- Learners who are *literate in a language with a non-alphabetic script* (e.g., Chinese or Japanese) may focus on entire words rather than on letters or other word parts (as English readers do when using phonological decoding to identify words). This is because the symbols in non-alphabetic scripts often represent syllables or entire words. The written symbols in these languages do not represent sounds, as letters do in alphabetic languages. Therefore, like young readers, as described in the report of the National Reading Panel (2000), they must develop an "alphabetic strategy" (Birch, 2002, p. 33) to be able to read and write in an alphabetic script (Adams, 1990).

- Learners who are *literate in a language with a non-Roman alphabetic script* (e.g., Arabic, Greek, Korean, Russian, or Thai) know how to read with an alphabet, but they may struggle to find English words in the dictionary, and they need time to process written materials presented in class, because the writing system of their first language is different from that of English, both in the letters and, in some cases the directionality of the writing (e.g., Arabic, which is written from right to left).

- Learners who are *literate in a language with a Roman-alphabetic script (*e.g., French, German, or Spanish) know about sound/symbol correspondences. With regard to vocabulary, they may find many linguistic similarities between their native languages and English. They can study ESL texts and take notes in class to learn new vocabulary or structures, and they can read outside of class. They still need to learn the sound-symbol correspondences of English before they are able to read well (Hilferty, 1996; Strucker & Davidson, 2003).

For a more detailed discussion of the role of the first-language in reading development see Burt & Peyton (2003) at www.cal.org/caela/digests/reading.htm. For more discussion of the types of first language backgrounds described here, see Birch (2002); Hilferty (1996); Huntley (1992); and Strucker & Davidson (2003).

In many adult ESL programs, decisions about learner placement and instructional approaches are based solely on learners' oral proficiency in English. However, learners' first-language literacy should be taken into consideration as well, because it can strongly influence the types of instruction they need and the rates of progress they are likely to make (Robson, 1982; Strucker & Davidson, 2003). First-language literacy is an important factor in the following decisions:

- *Assigning learners to classes.* Pre-literate, non-literate, and semi-literate learners may have difficulty using writing to reinforce what they learn orally and may learn less rapidly than other learners. They may benefit from being placed in both oral ESL *and* English literacy classes and in different classes from literate learners. This is not always easy to do, but it is sometimes possible in larger programs.

- *Designing and teaching ESL lessons.* Lessons that involve conveying a lot of information through writing (e.g., on the board or in written exercises) will be harder for pre-, non-, and semi-literate learners to understand. They may need much more conversational and visual support for content and skills covered than do literate learners.

- *Teaching literacy skills.* Non- and low-literate learners need to be taught basic literacy skills such as sound/symbol correspondence, the relationship between written symbols and oral speech, and the directionality of writing. Those who are literate in their first language need a different focus. According to some researchers, literate learners need to know 3,000 to 5,000 words in English before they can transfer their literacy skills from their first language to English (Laufer, 1997). This is a fairly high level of English; as a result, even literate learners probably need a heavy emphasis on vocabulary building. Furthermore, the transfer of reading skills from the native language to English will not be automatic. Learners need to be shown how to use the reading skills they have in their first language to help them read in English. They will also need direct instruction in English sound/symbol correspondences and other reading strategies.

Educational Background

Learners' language proficiency and literacy are often linked with their educational experiences in the following ways:

- *Learners with limited or no literacy in their first language* have probably had little or no experience with formal education. They may not be accustomed to sitting at desks for long periods of time, listening to a teacher, interacting with other adults as fellow learners, getting information from print, and studying outside of class. Their educational experience may have involved watching and learning from others. Therefore, their learning will be different from that of learners who have had more experience with formal education. Literacy instruction with these learners is more likely to be successful when they believe it is relevant to their lives and they feel comfortable in the instructional setting (Hardman, 1999; Klassen & Burnaby, 1993).

- *Learners who are highly literate in their first language* are more likely to have had formal education in that language, but their prior educational experiences may differ from those they have in the United States (Constantino, 1995; Tse, 1996a, 1996b). They may come to classes in the United States expecting a great deal of direct teaching and traditional approaches to learning, such as memorizing vocabulary lists and doing mechanical exercises. They may also tend to focus more on reading accuracy than on fluency. To improve their reading fluency and increase their exposure to English vocabulary, they may benefit from pleasure reading of texts appropriate to their reading proficiency level (texts in which they can read approximately 95 percent of the words) (Cho & Krashen, 1994; Coady, 1997; Laufer, 1997; Sökmen, 1997; Tse, 1996a, 1996b).

Second-Language Proficiency

Adult English language learners have varying levels of proficiency in English, which may influence their reading speed and comprehension (Tan, Moore, Dixon, & Nicholson, 1994). Studies suggest that learners need some level of proficiency in the second language to read effectively in the language (Alderson, 1984; Carrell, 1991; Tan, et al., 1994). It is as yet unclear how much of a grammar and discourse foundation is needed before one can read effectively. It seems, however, that the amount of foundation needed will vary, depending on the students themselves (Grabe & Stoller, 2002).

Goals for Learning English

Adults learning English have different needs for literacy. Some of the most common are to be successful at work, participate in their children's education, achieve U.S. citizenship, participate in community activities in English, and pursue further education (Marshall, 2002).

Some learners may focus on improving their functional literacy for *advancement in the workplace* (Mikulecky, 1992). Many cannot advance in their jobs or receive the job training they need until they have achieved a functional level of English literacy. In many cases, a General Educational

Development (GED) certificate may be required for job promotion (Mikulecky, 1992; Strucker, 1997).

Others may want to improve their literacy skills to *help their children in school* (Shanahan, Mulhern, & Rodriguez-Brown, 1995). The belief that parents' literacy influences children's eventual literacy attainment is one of the reasons behind the support for family literacy in the U.S. Department of Education (National Center for ESL Literacy Education, 2002). Since much of school-related communication is conducted in written English, limited English literacy may limit parents' involvement in their children's education and their communication with teachers, administrators, and counselors. Furthermore, adults who are not literate in English will have difficulty reading in English with their children and helping them learn English vocabulary.

A common literacy goal of adult ESL students focuses on *community participation*. Effective community participation includes having the skills to handle financial transactions and keep informed about developments in the community (Klassen & Burnaby, 1993; Strucker, 1997). In addition to integrating into the English-speaking community, adults who speak languages other than English and also are literate in English can be valuable resources for other community members. Opportunities for involvement in community activities are usually announced in writing and in English, and most advocacy activities that reach decision makers are conducted in English.

Adult ESL students also may wish to *gain U. S. citizenship*. To do this, they need to pass a written test on U.S. government and history, and at every step in the residency and citizenship process, they need to have the literacy skills to fill out immigration and citizenship forms.

Finally, many learners want to improve their literacy skills to *increase their opportunities to continue their education*. Some need to obtain a high school equivalency degree. Others are seeking English certification of degrees and skills they have in their native language or their home country. Still others need English reading skills to pass tests such as the Test of English as a Foreign Language (TOEFL) in order to enroll in institutions of higher education.

Curricula and materials used in instruction (commercial textbooks and teacher-produced materials) should match the goals of the learners. That is, school-related instruction and materials should be used with parents in family literacy programs, workplace instruction and materials should be used with workers, and civics-focused instruction and materials should be used in citizenship classes. It is a challenge, of course, to address learners' interests when a variety of goals for developing literacy are represented in one class or program.

WHAT READING SKILLS DO ADULT ENGLISH LANGUAGE LEARNERS NEED?

Researchers working with native English speakers have focused on the following component skills of reading development: alphabetics, fluency, vocabulary, and reading comprehension. (See Kruidenier, 2002, for discussion of these reading component skills with adult native English speakers.) Researchers working with adults learning English as a second language have focused on similar skills, but they are labeled and grouped somewhat differently— phonological processing, vocabulary knowledge, syntactic processing, and background knowledge. Figure IV–1 shows the terms used in reading research and instruction with native English speakers and gives implications for instruction with these two groups. Following the figure is a discussion of findings from research on English reading with adults learning English and their implications for instruction.

Alphabetics. "Alphabetics includes both phonemic awareness, or knowledge of the sounds of spoken language; and word analysis, or knowledge of the connection between written letters and sounds (letter-sound correspondence)" (Kruidenier, 2002, p. 35).

> *Phonological awareness* is the "broad term that includes phonemic awareness. In addition to identifying and manipulating larger parts of spoken language, such as words, syllables, and onsets and rimes, phonological awareness encompasses an awareness of other aspects of sound, such as rhyming, alliteration, and intonation" (Armbruster, Lehr, & Osborn, 2001, p. 3).
>
> *Phonemic awareness.* One type of phonological awareness, "phonemic awareness, is the ability to hear, identify, and manipulate the individual sounds—phonemes—in spoken words" (Armbruster, Lehr, & Osborn, 2001, p. 4).
>
> *Phonics* "is the understanding that there is a predictable relationship between phonemes (the sounds of *spoken* language) and graphemes (the letters and spellings that represent those sounds in *written* language)" (Armbruster, Lehr, & Osborn, 2001, p. 4).
>
> *Word analysis* involves decoding words, sight word recognition, dictionary use, and structural analysis of words (e.g., knowledge of prefixes and suffixes) (Kruidenier, 2002).

- *Application to native English speakers:* Instruction in word analysis with native English speakers is usually done by having learners pronounce letters, word parts, or whole words. Nonsense words are often used to push learners to decode and not rely on sight words. The ability to read sight words is often assessed by having learners read lists of regularly and irregularly spelled words.

- *Application to non-native English speakers:* Alphabetics instruction often assumes high oral language skills and vocabulary knowledge, which adults learning English may not have. Using nonsense words is a questionable activity with these learners, who do not necessarily have proficiency in oral English.

Fluency is the ability to read easily and accurately with appropriate rhythm, intonation, and expression.

- *Application to native English speakers:* Instruction focuses on the accuracy and speed of oral or silent reading.

> - *Application to non-native English speakers:* Oral reading accuracy and speed may be complicated by interference from the native language and may not indicate actual reading skill in the native language or in English.
>
> **Vocabulary** refers to the words that a person understands and knows the meaning. Vocabulary knowledge is critical to the comprehension processes of a skilled reader.
>
> - *Application to native English speakers:* Vocabulary building activities often build on themes such as family, the community, or the workplace. Learners are encouraged to determine the meanings of words from context. Learners often define words or choose the correct meanings of words among several choices.
> - *Application to non-native English speakers:* Adults learning English may not have the background knowledge they need to work effectively with the themes usually used in U. S. classes. Teachers need to use themes that learners are familiar with or give them the background information they need. Learners need to have multiple exposures to specific words in different contexts and know how to use English and bilingual dictionaries (Folse, 2004). They need explicit instruction in defining words and doing multiple choice exercises
>
> **Reading comprehension** is the ability to derive meaning from a written text. Skilled readers are purposeful and active in applying comprehension strategies to texts.
>
> - *Application to native English speakers:* Native English speakers have oral English and culture-specific knowledge that guides their understanding of reading texts used in U. S. classes, and they can often describe orally the strategies they use to comprehend what they read.
> - *Application to non-native English speakers:* English language skill and cultural knowledge may impede English language learners' comprehension and ability to talk about texts. Some researchers argue that readers need to understand more than 95 percent of the words in a passage before they can effectively determine meaning from context (e.g., Qian, 1999). Non-native English speakers may use comprehension strategies in their native language that they need to be taught to use when reading English, and they may not be able to talk about the strategies that they use. Teachers need to tie readings to learners' native languages and cultures whenever possible and teach specific strategies for comprehending a passage. Teachers should preview unfamiliar ideas, vocabulary, and formats (titles, pictures, graphics, and text structure) of texts before learners read them.

Figure IV–1: Reading Terms and Their Application

Research on Adults Learning to Read in English

The following discussion is organized around the categories that researchers studying English language learners typically focus on phonological processing, vocabulary knowledge, syntactic processing, and background knowledge.

Phonological Processing

Phonological processing (or decoding) involves interpreting written letters as sounds (*phonological awareness*) and combining letters into syllables and words (*word analysis*) (Adams, 1990; Kruidenier, 2002; Snow, Burns, & Griffin, 1998). Some researchers argue that phonological processing skills are among the primary reading skill components that differentiate native and non-native English speakers learning to read (Koda, 1999). Researchers also argue that teaching adult ESL literacy students the letter-sound correspondences in the English writing system through phonics instruction will improve their reading (Jones, 1996; Koda, 1999; Strucker & Davidson, 2003). Even advanced English learners whose native language is written with the Roman alphabet need instruction in decoding and in matching letters to sounds in English (Hilferty, 1996; Strucker & Davidson, 2003).

Some ways that teachers can develop students' phonological processing skills are to provide opportunities for them to do the following:

- Match letters to sounds (*phonics*).

- Listen to words related to a specific topic that begin with similar sounds (e.g., food – cheese, chicken, cherries) (*phonemic awareness*).

- Attach morphemes to words (e.g., past tense markers on verbs, plural and possessive markers on nouns) and observe pronunciation changes (*word analysis*).

- Participate in oral readings and choral readings (*phonemic awareness*).

***Note*:** Beginning literacy learners may need structured, systematic instruction in decoding (Armbruster, Lehr, & Osborn, 2001). Kruidenier (2002) cites research on children that may apply to adult learners. This research shows that systematic phonics instruction is more effective with beginning readers than incidental instruction. Although the research cited was not done on English language learners, teachers working with groups of very low readers may find a structured program useful. "A program of systematic phonics instruction clearly identifies a carefully selected and useful set of letter-sound relationships and then organizes the introduction of these relationships into a logical instructional sequence" (Armbruster, Lehr, & Osborn, 2001, p. 16). Some examples of systematic language programs include *The Wilson Reading System, Lindamood-Bell,* and *Orton-Gillingham.*

Vocabulary knowledge

Vocabulary knowledge has been found to have a strong effect on reading comprehension (Brown, 1993; Sökmen, 1997; Coady, 1997; Coady, Mgoto, Hubbard, Graney, & Mokhtari, 1994; Folse, 2004; Zimmerman, 1997). Reading specialists argue that readers need to know 3,000- 5000 words in the language they are reading in order to read independently (Grabe & Stoller, 2002; Laufer, 1997). Vocabulary knowledge includes both breadth (the number of words a reader knows or the number of content areas in which a reader is familiar with the vocabulary) and depth (the amount of knowledge a reader knows about individual words including their pronunciation, spelling, the parts of speech they may be used for, prefixes and suffixes that can be used with them and how those change word meaning and use, how the words are used in sentences, and various meanings of the words).

The following strategies to increase learners' vocabulary knowledge have been suggested in the literature:

- Teach vocabulary that learners will need to use often (high-frequency vocabulary).
- Teach key sight words that learners will need, such as *emergency, 911, last name, first name*, especially when learners are at beginning literacy levels. (Sight word knowledge is the ability to recognize words without having to sound them out.)
- Provide multiple opportunities for learners to read and use specific words in different texts and activities that are thematically related, such as the following:
    o Brainstorm vocabulary on a specific topic, such as food shopping.
    o Practice food vocabulary with flash cards.
    o Practice dialogues in which food vocabulary is used (e.g. "I am going shopping." "What do you need?" "I need bread, beans, and chicken.").
    o Complete cloze exercises (worksheets with sentences or paragraphs about food; key vocabulary words related to food are left out, with a blank for the learners to fill in).
    o Make a shopping list of items they need to buy.
    o For homework, copy food words from packages.
- Preview key vocabulary that will be used in a text or activity.
- Give the meanings of vocabulary words that may be difficult.
- Have learners write their own sentences with words they have read in a text.
- Teach learners how to use dictionaries.

- Use computer programs to provide more interactive vocabulary learning opportunities.

Syntactic processing

Syntactic processing (related to reading comprehension in the literature on native English speakers) involves understanding the structures of the language and making connections among words in a sentence or among sentences and paragraphs in a text. For example, learners should be taught language forms that change the meanings of words, such as prefixes and suffixes. Learners should know common prefixes, such as non-, in-, <u>im</u>-, and un- that make words negative (as in *possible/impossible, happy/unhappy*), and suffixes, such as the -ed verb ending used to form the past tense and the passive voice. They should also understand words that bring cohesion to a text (e.g., *however, therefore, nevertheless*).

Grammar instruction should be integrated with reading instruction, with learners' attention directed to syntactic structures in reading texts. Teachers can point out certain grammatical structures in a passage (e.g., all of the past tense verbs), choose reading passages that highlight the grammatical structures that students are learning, and have students find and mark specific grammatical structures.

Teachers also can help build learners' knowledge of grammar and syntax by having them do the following:

- Learners complete a cloze exercise, in which specific words left out of a text with blanks that they fill in. Some exercises might focus on nouns, others on verbs or adjectives, and so on. To provide support for students, these exercises may be done initially as a whole class, then in small groups, and then individually.

- Learners identify the parts of speech of certain words in a text (nouns, verbs, adjectives, prepositions, etc.).

- Learners write their own sentences or longer texts, using specific grammatical forms (e.g., past tense verbs) and cohesion words (e.g., *however, therefore*).

Background knowledge

Background knowledge is also related to reading comprehension in the literature on native English speakers. Readers generally understand texts more easily if they are familiar with and have information about the topics covered and the genres and text structures involved (Adams & Collins, 1985; Carrell, 1991; Goldberg, 1997; Hudson, 1982). If learners have low reading proficiency, readings about culturally familiar topics should be selected (Eskey, 1997). Even if readers are more advanced, the topics and structures of reading texts should be reviewed before learners begin reading, so that they are familiar (Goldberg, 1997).

To build on learners' background knowledge, teachers can do the following:

- Relate reading texts to ideas, concepts, and events from learners' cultures and personal experiences whenever possible.

- Use visual aids and physical objects to support understanding of unfamiliar ideas and themes.

- Preview unfamiliar ideas, actions, and settings.

- Preview titles, pictures, graphics, grammatical structures, and cohesion words used.

- Create language experience texts. In the language experience approach, learners have an experience together or share knowledge about an experience, such as taking a class trip, shopping for food, or coming to the United States. They discuss or answer questions about the experience and the teacher writes a text. They then copy the text and read it themselves. (See Holt, 1995, and *Activities to Promote Reading Development,* page II–57, for details about developing language experience stories.)

WHAT ARE THE BENEFITS OF READING IN A SECOND LANGUAGE?

We have described above how second language proficiency facilitates reading development, but reading in English also can help develop language proficiency. The act of reading itself exposes us to language that we process as we seek to gain information that is important and meaningful. Therefore, at the same time that students learn from their reading about gardening, parenting in the United States, U.S. citizenship, or workplace benefits, they also are learning English.

Some of the benefits of reading for language development are the following:

- Reading texts provides one source of language input.

- Extensive or sustained reading can promote knowledge of the vocabulary and structures of English.

- Learners engaged in extensive reading tend to be more likely to enjoy reading and feel comfortable reading new texts.

- Extensive reading seems to develop writing ability in some learners, especially those with greater English proficiency and literacy skills.

In summary, reading can build second language vocabulary, conversational proficiency, and writing ability as well as reading proficiency. Teachers need to carefully select texts for learners or assist them in choosing their own texts at appropriate levels of reading difficulty. They need to focus on the level of decoding, vocabulary knowledge, and cultural or background knowledge needed to handle the texts. They also need to create classroom activities that will help learners understand and work with the texts and develop the key reading component skills.

REFERENCES

1. Adams, M. J. (1990). *Beginning to read: Thinking and learning about print.* Cambridge, MA: MIT Press.
2. Adams, M. J. & Collins, A. (1985). A schema-theoretic view of reading. In H. Singer & R. B. Ruddell (Eds.). *Theoretical models and processes of reading,* pp. 404-425. Newark, DL: International Reading Association.
3. Adams, R., & Burt, M. (2002). *Research on the reading development of adult English language learners: An annotated bibliography.* Retrieved December 14, 2004, from http://www.cal.org/caela/esl_resources/bibliographies/readingbib.html
4. Alderson, J. C. (1984). Reading in a foreign language: A reading problem or a language problem? In J. C. Alderson & A. H. Urquhart (Eds.). *Reading in a foreign language* (pp. 1-27). New York: Longman.
5. Armbruster, B. B., Lehr, F., & Osborn, J. (2001). *Put reading first: The research building blocks for teaching children to read.* Washington, DC: Center for the Improvement of Early Reading Achievement.
6. Artiles, A. J., & Ortiz, A. A. (2002). *English language learners with special education needs: Identification, assessment, and instruction.* Available from http://calstore.cal.org/store
7. Birch, B. M. (2002). *English L2 reading: Getting to the bottom.* Mahwah, NJ: Erlbaum.
8. Brown, C. (1993) . Factors affecting the acquisition of vocabulary: Frequency and saliency of words. In T. Huckin, M. Haynes, & J. Coady (Eds.), *Second language reading and vocabulary learning* (pp. 263-86). Norwood, NJ: Ablex.

9. Burt, M., & Peyton, J. K. (2003). *Reading and adult English language learners: The role of the first language.* Retrieved December 14, 2004, from http://www.cal.org/caela/esl_resources/ digests/reading.html
10. Burt, M., Peyton, J. K., & Adams, R. (2003). *Reading and adult English language learners: A review of the research.* Washington, DC: Center for Applied Linguistics. Retrieved March 8, 2008, from www.cal.org/caela/research/raell.pdf
11. Carrell, P. L. (1991). Second language reading: Reading ability or language proficiency. *Applied Linguistics, 12*, 159-79.
12. Carson, J. E., Carrell, P. L., Silberstein, S., & Kuehn, P. (1990). Reading-writing relationships in first and second language. *TESOL Quarterly 24*, 245-66.
13. Cho, K. S., & Krashen, S. D. (1994). Acquisition of vocabulary from the Sweet Valley Kids series: Adult ESL acquisition. *Journal of Reading, 37*, 662-7.
14. Clement, R., Dörnyei, Z., & Noels, K. A. (1994). Motivation, self-confidence, and group cohesion in the foreign language classroom. *Language Learning, 44*, 417-448.
15. Coady, J. (1997). L2 vocabulary acquisition through extensive reading. In J. Coady & T. Huckin (Eds.), *Second language vocabulary acquisition* (pp. 225-37). Cambridge: Cambridge University Press.
16. Coady, J., & Huckin, T. (Eds.). (1997). *Second language vocabulary acquisition: A rationale for pedagogy.* United Kingdom: Cambridge University Press.
17. Coady, J., Mgoto, J., Hubbard, P., Graney, J. & Mokhtari, K. (1994). High frequency vocabulary and reading proficiency in ESL readers. In T. Huckin, M. Haynes, & J. Coady (Eds.), *Second language reading and vocabulary learning* (pp. 217-28). Norwood, NJ: Ablex.
18. Constantino, R. (1995). Reading in a second language doesn't have to hurt: The effect of pleasure reading. *Journal of Adolescent and Adult Reading, 39*, 68-9.
19. de la Fuente, M. J. (2002). Negotiation and oral acquisition of L2 vocabulary: The roles of input and output in the receptive and productive acquisition of words. *Studies in Second Language Acquisition, 24*, 81-112.
20. Dörnyei, Z. (2002a). *Teaching and researching motivation.* Essex, England: Pearson Education Limited.
21. Dörnyei, Z. (2002b). The motivational basis of language learning tasks.

In P. Robinson (Ed.), *Individual differences and instructed language learning* (pp. 137-158). Amsterdam: John Benjamins.

22. Dörnyei, Z. (2003). Attitudes, orientations, and motivations in language learning: Advances in theory, research, and applications. *Language Learning, 53* (Suppl. 1), 3-32.

23. Dörnyei, Z., & Csizer, K. (1998). Ten commandments for motivating language learners: Results of an empirical study. *Language Teaching Research, 4,* 203-229.

24. Dörnyei, Z., & Kormos, J. (2000). The role of individual and social variables in oral task performance. *Language Teaching Research, 4,* 275-300.

25. Doughty, C., & Pica, T. (1986). "Information gap" tasks: Do they facilitate second language acquisition? *TESOL Quarterly, 20,* 305-325.

26. Doughty, C., & Williams, J. (Eds.). (1998). *Focus on form in classroom second language acquisition.* New York: Cambridge University Press.

27. Ellis, R. (1997). *Second language acquisition.* New York: Oxford University Press.

28. Ellis, R. (1999). *Learning a second language through interaction.* Philadelphia: John Benjamins.

29. Ellis, R. (2000). Task-based research and language pedagogy. *Language Teaching Research, 4,* 193-220.

30. Ellis, R., Basturkmen, H., & Loewen, S. (2001). Learner uptake in communicative ESL lessons. *Language Learning, 51,* 281-318.

31. Ellis, R., & He, X. (1999). The roles of modified input and output in incidental acquisition of word meanings. *Studies in Second Language Acquisition, 21,* 285-301.

32. Ellis, R., Tanaka, Y., & Yamazaki, A. (1994). Classroom interaction, comprehension, and the acquisition of L2 word meanings. *Language Learning, 44,* 449-491.

33. Eskey, D. E. (1997). Models of reading and the ESOL student: Implications and limitations. *Focus on Basics, 1*(B), 9-11.

34. Florez, M. C., & Burt, M. (2001). *Beginning to work with adult English language learners: Some considerations.* Retrieved December 14, 2004, from http://www.cal.org/caela/esl_resources/ digests/beginQA.html

35. Folse, K. S. (2004). *Vocabulary myths: Applying second language research to classroom teaching.* Ann Arbor, MI: The University of Michigan Press.

36. Gardner, R. C. (1985). *Social psychology and second language learning: The role of attitude and motivation.* London: Edward Arnold.
37. Gass, S. M. (1997). *Input, interaction, and the second language learner.* Mahwah, NJ: Lawrence Erlbaum Associates.
38. Gass, S. M. (1999). Discussion: Incidental vocabulary learning. *Studies in Second Language Acquisition, 21,* 319-333.
39. Gass, S. M. & Selinker, L. (2001). *Second language acquisition: An introductory course.* Mahwah, NJ: Lawrence Erlbaum Associates.
40. Goldberg, R. (1997). Deconstructing the great wall of print. *Connections: A Journal of Adult Literacy, 1,* 8-13.
41. Grabe, W., & Stoller, F. L. (2002). Comparing L1 and L2 reading. In *Teaching and researching reading* (pp. 40–63). Harlow, England: Longman.
42. Greenberg, E., Macías, R. F., Rhodes, D., & Chan, T. (2001). *English literacy and language minorities in the United States.* Washington, DC: U.S. Department of Education, Office of Education Research and Improvement.
43. Hardman, J. C. (1999). A community of learners: Cambodians in an adult ESL classroom. *Language Teaching Research, 3,*145-66.
44. Hilferty, A. G. (1996). *Coding decoding: Predicting the reading comprehension of Latino adults learning English.* Unpublished doctoral dissertation, Harvard University, Cambridge.
45. Holt, G. M. (1995). *Teaching low-level adult ESL learners.* Retrieved December 14, 2004, from http://www.cal.org/caela/esl_resources/digests/holt.html
46. Hudson, T. (1982). The effects of induced schemata on the "short circuit" in L2 reading: Non-decoding factors in L2 reading performance. *Language Learning, 32,* 3-31.
47. Huntley, H. S. (1992). *The new illiteracy: A study of the pedagogic principles of teaching English as a second language to non-literate adults.* (ERIC Document No. ED356685)
48. Jones, M. L. (1996). *Phonics in ESL literacy instruction: Functional or not?* Philadelphia: World Conference on Literacy. (ERIC Document No. ED436104)
49. Kirsch, I. S., Jungeblut, A., Jenkins, L., & Kolstad, A. (1993). *Adult literacy in America: A first look at the findings of the National Adult Literacy Survey.* Princeton, NJ: Educational Testing Service.
50. Klassen, C., & Burnaby, B. (1993). Those who know: Views on literacy

among adult immigrants in Canada. *TESOL Quarterly, 27*, 377-97.
51. Koda, K. (1999). Development of L2 intraword orthographic sensitivity and decoding skills. *Modern Language Journal, 83*, 51-64.
52. Kruidenier, J. (2002). *Research-based principles for adult basic education reading instruction.* Retrieved May 24, 2004, from http://www.nifl.gov/partnershipforreading
53. Laufer, B. (1997). The lexical plight in second language reading: Words you don't know, words you think you know, and words you can't guess. In J. Coady & T. Huckin (Eds.), *Second language vocabulary acquisition: A rationale for pedagogy* (pp. 20-34). United Kingdom: Cambridge University Press.
54. Long, M. H. (2000). Focus on form in task-based language teaching. In R. D. Lambert & E. Shohamy (Eds.), *Language policy and pedagogy: Essays in honor of A. Ronald Walton* (pp. 179-192). Philadelphia: John Benjamins.
55. Long, M. H. (1996) . The role of the linguistic environment in second language acquisition. In W. C. Ritchie & T. K. Bhatia (Eds.), *Handbook of research on language acquisition: Vol. 2. Second language acquisition* (pp. 413-468). New York: Academic Press.
56. McKay H., & Tom, A. (1999). *Teaching adult second language learners.* New York: Cambridge University Press.
57. Mackey, A. (1999). Input, interaction, and second language development: An empirical study of question formation in ESL. *Studies in Second Language Acquisition, 21*, 557-587.
58. Marshall, B. (2002). *Preparing for success: A guide for teaching adult English language learners.*
59. Washington, DC, & McHenry, IL: Center for Applied Linguistics & Delta Systems. Available from http://calstore.cal.org/store
60. Masgoret, A. M., & Gardner, R. C. (2003). Attitudes, motivation, and second language learning: A meta-analysis of studies conducted by Gardner and associates. *Language Learning, 53* (Suppl. 1), 167-210.
61. Mikulecky, L. (1992). *Workplace literacy programs: Variations of approach and limits of impact.*
62. San Antonio, TX: National Reading Conference. (ERIC Document No. ED353461)
63. Morris, F. (2001). Language learning motivation for the class of 2002: Why first year Puerto Rican high school students learn English. *Language and Education, 15*, 269-278.

64. Moss, D., & Ross-Feldman, L. (2003). *Second language acquisition in adults: From research to practice.* Washington, DC: National Center for ESL Literacy Education. Retrieved December 14, 2004, from http://www.cal.org/caela/esl_resources/digests/SLA.html
65. Moss, D., & Van Duzer, C. (1998). *Project-based learning for adult English language learners.*
66. Washington, DC: National Center for ESL Literacy Education. Retrieved December 14, 2004, from http://www.cal.org/caela/esl_resources/digests/ProjBase.html
67. National Center for ESL Literacy Education. (2002). *Family literacy and adult English language learners.* NCLE Fact Sheet. Retrieved December 14, 2004, from http://www.cal.org/caela/ esl_resources/collections/factsheets.html#fam
68. National Reading Panel. (2000). *Report of the National Reading Panel: Teaching children to read: An evidence-based assessment of the scientific research literature on reading and its implications for reading instruction: Reports of the subgroups.* Washington, DC: National Institute of Child Health and Human Development.
69. Noels, K. A., Clement, R., & Pelletier, L. G. (2003) . Perceptions of teachers' communicative style and students' intrinsic and extrinsic motivation. *Modern Language Journal, 83*, 23-34.
70. Norris, J. M., & Ortega, L. (2001). Does type of instruction make a difference? Substantive findings from a meta-analytic review. *Language Learning, 51* (Suppl. 1), 157-213.
71. Oxford, R., & Shearin, J. (1994). Language learning motivation: Expanding the theoretical framework. *Modern Language Journal, 78*, 12-28.
72. Paribakht, T. S., & Wesche, M. (1997). Vocabulary enhancement activities and reading for meaning in second language vocabulary acquisition. In J. Coady & T. Huckin (Eds.), *Second language vocabulary acquisition: A rationale for pedagogy* (pp. 174-200). United Kingdom: Cambridge University Press.
73. Pica, T. (1994). Research on negotiation: What does it reveal about second-language learning conditions, processes, and outcomes? *Language Learning, 44*, 493-527.
74. Pica, T. (2003). Second language acquisition research and applied linguistics. *Working Papers in Educational Linguistics, 18.*
75. Qian, D. D. (1999). Assessing the roles of depth and breadth of vocabulary

knowledge in reading comprehension. *Canadian Modern Language Journal, 56*, 262-305.

76. Robson, B. (1982) . Hmong literacy, formal education, and their effects on performance in an ESL class. In B. T. Downing & D. P. Olney, (Eds.). *The Hmong in the west: Observations and reports* (pp. 201- 225). Minneapolis, MN: University of Minnesota.

77. Savignon, S. (1997). *Communicative competence: Theory and classroom practice.* New York: McGraw-Hill.

78. Schmidt, R., & Frota, S. (1986). Developing basic conversational ability in a second language: A case study of an adult learner of Portuguese. In R. Day (Ed.), *Talking to learn: Conversation in second language acquisition* (pp. 237-326). Rowley, MA: Newbury.

79. Schwarz, R. & Terrill, L. (2000). *ESL instruction and adults with learning disabilities.* Retrieved December 14, 2004, from http://www.cal.org/caela/esl_resources/digests/LD2.html

80. Shanahan, T., Mulhern, M., & Rodriguez-Brown, F. (1995). Project FLAME: Lessons learned from a family literacy program for linguistic minority families. *The Reading Teacher, 48,* 586-93.

81. Snow, C. E., Burns, S. M., & Griffin, P. (Eds.) (1998). *Preventing reading difficulties in young children.* Washington, DC: National Academy Press.

82. Sökmen, A. J. (1997). Current trends in teaching second language vocabulary. In N. Schmitt & M. McCarthy, *Vocabulary: Description, acquisition, and pedagogy* (pp. 237-257). Cambridge: Cambridge University Press.

83. Strucker, J. (1997). What silent reading tests alone can't tell you: Two case studies in adult reading differences. *Focus on Basics, 1*(B), 13-17.

84. Strucker, J., & Davidson, R. (2003). *Adult reading components study (ARCS): A NCSALL research brief.* Boston, MA: National Center for the Study of Adult Learning and Literacy.

85. Swain, M. (1995). Three functions of output in second language learning. In G. Cook & B. Seidlhofer (Eds.), *Principle and practice in applied linguistics: Studies in honour of H. G. Widdowson* (pp. 125-144). Oxford, England: Oxford University Press.

86. Tan, A., Moore, D. W., Dixon, R. S., & Nicholson, T. (1994). Effects of training in rapid decoding on the reading comprehension of adult ESL learners. *Journal of Behavioral Education, 4,*177-89.

87. Tse, L. (1996a). When an ESL adult becomes a reader. *Reading Horizons, 37,* 16-29.

88. Tse, L. (1996b). If you lead horses to water they will drink: Introducing second language adults to books in English. *California Reader, 29* (2), 14-7.
89. Van Duzer, C., & Burt, M. (1999). *A day in the life of the González family.* Washington DC & McHenry, IL: Center for Applied Linguistics & Delta Systems. Available from http://calstore.cal.org/store
90. Weddel, K., & Van Duzer, C. (1997). *Needs assessment for adult ESL learners.* Washington, DC: National Center for ESL Literacy Education. Retrieved December 14, 2004, from http://www.cal.org/caela/esl_resources/digests/Needas.html
91. Wesche, M. B., & Paribakht, T. S. (2000). Reading-based exercises in second language learning: An introspective study. *Modern Language Journal, 84,* 196-213.
92. Zimmerman, C. B. (1997). Do reading and interactive vocabulary instruction make a difference? An empirical study. *TESOL Quarterly, 3*(1), p. 121-140.

Chapter 11

DESIGNING FOR LANGUAGE LEARNING: AGENCY AND LANGUAGING IN HYBRID ENVIRONMENTS

Françoise Blin[1] and Juha Jalkanen[2] ISSN: 1457-9863

[1]Dublin City University
[2]University of Jyväskylä

ABSTRACT

Since the beginning of the 21st Century, we have witnessed a remarkable shift in the ways learning takes place across networks, multiple sites and timescales. As the world changes, language teaching is facing growing pressures to rethink and redesign language learning environments to respond to the demands of the 'knowledge society'. While new digitally enhanced learning spaces offer new affordances to language teachers and learners, they also increase the complexity of language teaching and learning. Furthermore, it has become evident that the affordances of new tools and spaces for learning are not always realised in formal education. Language teachers, who are willing to embrace new technologies and transform their teaching practice, need to reconceptualize their approach to language, language learning, and language teaching. In this paper, we argue that a renewed focus on design is needed. Following a brief discussion on languaging and agency, we present three educational design models and approaches, namely learning design, designed based research and activity theoretical designs, which are being used to assist course designers and teachers with the design of technology - rich learning environments and activities. We argue that design models rooted in cultural historical activity theory (CHAT) in particular can help us address the challenges briefly outlined above. Drawing on CHAT principles and their applications to design for language teaching and learning, we revisit the design of a Finnish literacy skills course offered to international students at the University of Jyväskylä (Jalkanen & Vaarala 2012a, 2012b, 2013) and its enactment, with a particular focus on the development agency and languaging episodes.

INTRODUCTION

Since the beginning of the 21st Century, rapid societal changes have been emerging as a result of globalization and technologization. We have witnessed a remarkable shift in ways people access, process and produce information and in how learning takes place across networks, multiple sites and timescales (Castells 1996; Bliss 1999; Ludvigsen et al. 2011). Both learning and technologies have become ubiquitous (Cope & Kalantzis 2009). One example of the technologization of society is the ever increasing adoption of social media applications in personal, professional and educational contexts, along with the emergence of new social learning spaces such as those making use of augmented reality, gaming technologies or 3D-graphical immersive environments (e.g., Second Life). However, while technologies, and more specifically social media applications, offer new affordances to language teachers and learners, they also increase the complexity of language teaching and learning and present new educational challenges. In particular, the emergence of informal technological spaces requires from the students and teachers an ability to make use of the tools and resources available to them and to combine them to construct and shape their own personal learning environments (Laakkonen 2011). Yet, as McLoughlin and Lee (2008) remark:

"Student-centred" and "constructivist" learning has become somewhat of a mantra in higher education, yet there continue to be significant gaps between the espoused and enacted pedagogies of teachers, both in face-to-face and online environments. (McLoughlin and Lee 2008: 641)

Furthermore, teachers often replicate, at least initially, their face-to-face teaching practice in new digital spaces as stated by Conole (2008):

A disappointing aspect of current practice when using new technologies is that it often seems to offer more of the same, replicating, mirroring existing practice in the new medium rather than exploiting the opportunities of creating a truly new learning environment and associated experience. (Conole 2008: 188)

It has indeed become evident in many studies that the affordances of new tools and spaces for learning are not realised in formal education (Taalas 2005; Luukka et al. 2008; Kankaanranta & Puhakka 2008; Blin & Munro 2008; Jalkanen et al. 2012). As the world changes, language teaching is facing growing pressures to rethink and redesign language learning environments that respond to the demands of the 'knowledge society', in other words, that "match the needs of our learners to a world that is changing with great rapidity" (Jacobs 2010: 7).

Among many others, Wiggins and McTighe (2005: 15) argue that "too many teachers focus on the *teaching* and not the *learning*". Teachers "spend most of their time thinking, first, about what they will do, what materials they will use, and what they will ask students to do rather than first considering what the learner will need in order to accomplish the learning goals" (*ibid*). We suggest that a renewed focus on *design* might provide some new prospects for this educational dilemma. Pre-service and in-service language teachers, who are willing to embrace new technologies and transform their teaching practice, need to reconceptualise their approach to language, language learning, and language teaching. This reconceptualisation is likely to lead to profound focus shifts, such as:

- a shift from language viewed simply as a code to *languaging*;
- a shift from a focus on learner autonomy to *learner agency*;
- a shift from teaching to *designing for learning*.

Following a brief discussion on languaging and agency, we present three educational design models and approaches, namely *learning design*, *design-based research* and *activity theoretical designs,* which are being used to assist course designers and teachers with the design of technology-rich learning environments and activities. We argue that design models rooted in cultural historical activity theory (CHAT) in particular can help us address the challenges briefly outlined above. Drawing on CHAT principles and their applications to design for language teaching and learning, we revisit the design of a Finnish literacy skills course offered to international students at the University of Jyväskylä (Jalkanen & Vaarala 2012a, 2012b, 2013) and its enactment, with a particular focus on the development agency and languaging episodes.

RETHINKING LANGUAGE AND LANGUAGE LEARNING IN DIGITALLY ENHANCED ENVIRONMENTS

The concept of *languaging* is frequently used in the literature to capture and explain the dynamic and multidimensional nature of language (Swain 2006, Swain et al. 2009, Pietikäinen et al. 2008, Dufva et al. 2011, Zheng & Newgarden 2012). By using a verb instead of a noun, the focus shifts from language as an object of study to language as an action or process. According to Swain (2006:98), languaging is "the process of making meaning and shaping knowledge and experience through language". In particular, languaging about language is an integral part of the language learning process itself:

Languaging about language is one of the ways we learn language. This means that the language (the dialogue or private speech) about language that learners engage in takes on new significance. In it, we can observe learners operating on linguistic data and coming to an understanding of previously less well understood material. In languaging, we see learning taking place. (Swain 2006: 98.)

Although primarily concerned with 'languaging about language', Swain's notion of languaging is in line with ecological perspectives on language and learning.

From an ecological perspective, van Lier (2000: 246) argues that "the learner is immersed in an environment full of potential meanings [... that] become available gradually as the learner acts and interacts within and with this environment". He further argues that, in terms of language learning, "language emerges out of semiotic activity" (van Lier 2000: 252). The environment "provides a 'semiotic budget' (analogous to the energy budget of an ecosystem) within which the active learner engages in meaning-making activities together with others, who may be more, equally, or less competent in linguistic terms" (*ibid*).

The notion of *emergence* is also discussed by Pennycook (2010):

[G]rammars and structures of language [...] are always emergent rather than predefined. Once we accept that language is a social practice, it becomes clear that it is not language form that governs the speakers of the language but rather the speakers that negotiate what possible language forms they want to use for what purpose.' (Pennycook 2010: 129).

Pennycook (2010) further argues that the concept of *competence* needs to be revisited in light of the above. Drawing on Canagarajah (2008), he suggests that 'if we want to retain a notion such as competence, it refers not so much to the mastery of a grammar or sociolinguistic system, as to the strategic capacity to use diverse semiotic items across integrated media and modalities' (Pennycook 2010: 129). Indeed, the ubiquity of technology in everyday life as well as the many digital environments that we inhabit for work, play or socialisation, provides us with an ever expanding 'semiotic budget'. They thus provide us with increased opportunities for languaging about the world and about language as we engage in diverse activities (as in the case of online games requiring the use of a specific lexicon, register or genre in order to complete a mission or quest), and consequently for developing a capacity to use various semiotic items when the situation we find ourselves requires it (as in the case of having to use a car voice-activated command in a foreign language when abroad).

According to Holland and Lachicotte (2007), "semiotic mediation provides the means for humans to control, organize, and resignify their own behavior" (Holland & Lachicotte 2007: 115). The development of a capacity to use various semiotic resources as required in a given context or local situation can thus be seen as intrinsic to what has been traditionally referred to as the development of learner autonomy and more particularly of autonomous language use (see for example Blin 2004, 2005; Benson 2007).

However, "without ownership, agency and self-determination, autonomy cannot develop" (van Lier 2007: 48). The notion of *agency* is also particularly relevant to approaches to language teaching and learning that see languaging and emergence as constituents of the language learning process. According to Ahearn (2001: 112), agency is the "socioculturally mediated capacity to act". More specifically, it is the "capability to transcend a present situated activity context and create a new one" (Holland and Lachicotte 2007: 116), thus, as proposed by Engeström (2007: 363), enabling teachers and students to become "masters of their own lives". Such capability is in turn "made possible by the human capacity for semiotic regulation of one another and of oneself" (Valsiner 1998: 388; cited in Holland & Lachicotte ibid.), in particular with the help of tools made by oneself (Engeström 2007: 363).

Constructing and developing language pedagogies based on the above principles remain a challenge. In any given institutional context, a number of factors are likely to both afford and constrain the design activity. In the next section, we will review prevalent design models and argue for the instantiation of models that seek to bring together the concepts of languaging and agency within a systemic and ecological approach to second language development.

EDUCATIONAL DESIGN MODELS

Lund and Hauge (2011) remark that "[w]hen the complexity of learning environments and, thus, learning trajectories increases it becomes difficult for teachers to plan or predict how learning activities will be enacted in class" (p. 259). They use design "as a term that affords the unexpected but is enacted without resorting to mere improvisation or rigid planning" (*ibid*). In recent times, many researchers have pointed to the need for conceptual models that would structure the educational design process and support the analysis of the resulting learning activity for further enhancements (see for example Barab 2006; Laurillard 2012; Conole 2012). This interest in educational designs has led to the development of new design methodologies as well as frameworks to evaluate designs with a view to enhance them. We briefly review two of these conceptual models below, *learning design (LD)* and *design-based research (DBR)*.

Learning Design

Conole (2012) describes learning design (LD) as [a] methodology for enabling teachers/designers to make more informed decisions in how they go about designing learning activities and interventions, which is pedagogically informed and makes effective use of appropriate resources and technologies. This includes the design of resources and individual learning activities right up to curriculum -level design. A key principle is to help make the design process more explicit and shareable. (Conole 2012: 7-8)

According to Conole (2010), "[t]he learning design research work has developed in response to a perceived gap between the potential of technologies in terms of their use to support learning and their actual use in practice" (p. 10). The primary motive behind the approach is thus to promote the use of technologies in teaching and learning in ways that are innovative and 'pedagogically sound'.

The main focus of the learning design methodology is to produce representations of teachers' designs with a view to make them explicit and shareable (Conole 2010: 10).

Different representations of learning designs have been advocated by proponents of this approach. Koper and Oliver (2004) focus on the technical description of a learning design, which they define as "an application of a pedagogical model for a specific learning objective, target group and a specific context or knowledge domain" (p. 98). Together with their colleagues at the Open University of the Netherlands (OUNL), they developed what is commonly known as the IMS LD specification, which is a metalanguage represented in XML that describes teaching strategies and educational objectives. According to Sitthisak and Gilbert (2009), "the IMS LD specification was developed to support pedagogical diversity and innovation, as well as to promote the exchange and interoperability of E-learning materials" (p. 3). However, its high level of abstraction and generality makes it difficult for teachers and designers to apply it in their everyday practice (Sitthisak and Gilbert 2009). Although the IMS LD specification continues to be refined and expanded, in particular through the development of tools that can run IMS LD specifications, Conole (2010) argues that "the work has not had a fundamental impact on changing teacher practice, focusing more on the technical description and running of the designs" (p. 11). Other learning design approaches are more practice -oriented and aim to capture actual practice while providing teachers and designers with guidelines and tools to help them implement a wide range of pedagogical models in their own context. One such approach has been developed by the Open University in the UK.

The Open University Learning Design Initiative (OULDI) centres around three areas:

- Conceptualisation – the development of a range of conceptual tools to help guide the design decision-making process and to provide a shared language to enable comparisons to be made between different designs.
- Visualisation – use of a range of tools to help visualise and represent designs.
- Collaboration – mechanisms to encourage the sharing and discussing of learning and teaching ideas. (Conole 2010: 15)

The visualisation aspect is particularly interesting to us. It makes use of diagrams and icons to represent the key features of a learning activity. The connections between these key features thus give "an indication of structure and a sense of flow or movement" (Conole 2008: 192), which allow teachers and designers to focus on possible sequences of mediated actions. As an example, we adapted Conole's (2010) "task swimlane", and created a visual representation (Figure 1) outlining the intended trajectory that we imagined as we were designing an online language learning task according to the following scenario [1]:

A charity dealing with homelessness has approached your group to help raise money for them. Your group is tasked with coming up with a completely new event that would raise awareness on the issue, raise funds for the organisation and also would be fun and enjoyable for participants. It must be a completely new concept, traditional events such as auctions or race-nights are not acceptable!

Intended Learning Outcomes:

After completion of the task, and using the target language to communicate and to produce semiotic artefacts, learners will be able to:

- Plan for a small project work
- Negotiate a joint outcome for a project work
- Create a project proposal and introduce it orally

Starting from the left, the first column (orange dots) outlines the pedagogical reasoning (or goals) for the task and each of the sub-tasks. The second column (blue dots) defines the activities that learners are expected to carry out using the tools and resources specified in the third column (green dots). Finally, the last column (red dots) represents anticipated teaching interventions.

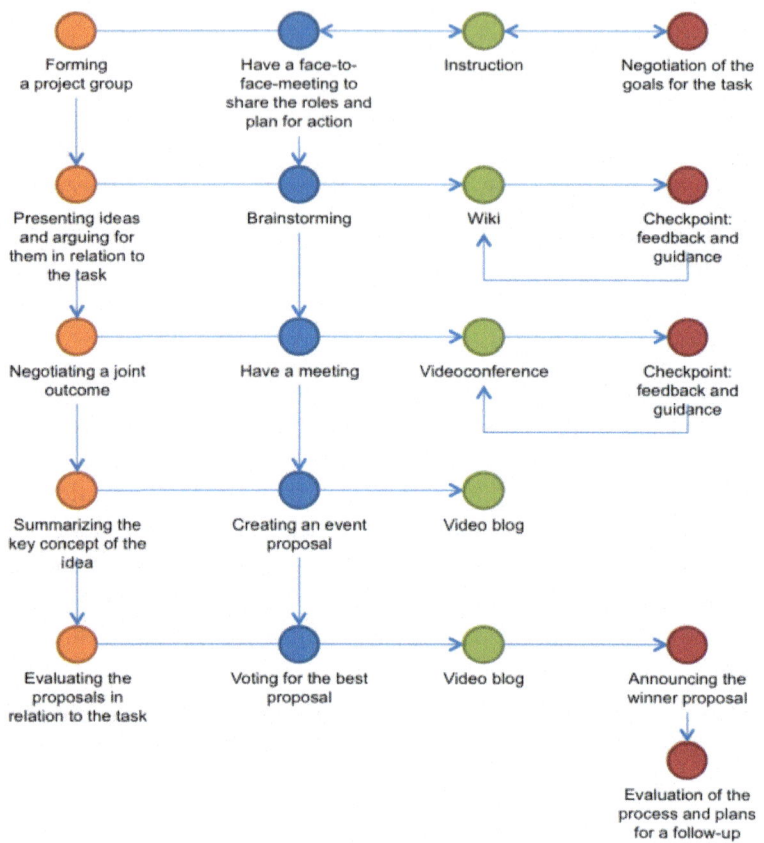

Figure 1: Visualisation of a learning design (Scenario 1)

As an alternative to textually constructed lesson plans, visual representations such as Figure 1 above enable teachers to represent, share and discuss their design ideas, among each other or with their students (Conole 2012). They function as a pedagogical blueprint, which can then be used to track the actual trajectory produced by students and teachers when the design is enacted. However, the learning design methodology as it has been described thus far does not offer conceptual tools nor does it suggest methods to critically assess the designs produced by teachers as they are enacted in real settings. Nor does it provide means to understand deviations from the intended trajectory or to deal with the unexpected. For this, the learning design methodology needs to be complemented with other approaches that strive to address theoretical as well as practice-oriented questions that are likely to emerge in complex learning environments.

Design-based research

Methods originating in the design-based research (DBR) tradition may complement the above learning design methodology by enabling researchers, designers, and teachers to "bridge the gap between educational research and practical educational innovation" (Engeström 2007: 368). According to the Design-Based Research Collective (2003), "design-based research [...] is an emerging paradigm for the study of learning in context through the systematic design and study of instructional strategies and tools" (p. 5). In practical terms, design-based research involves the setting up of design experiments. The latter are iterative and involve "putting a first version of a design into the world to see how it works" (Collins *et al.* 2004: 18) and refining it constantly "until all the bugs are worked out" (*ibid*).

Design experiments are both pragmatic and theoretical in orientation: they "are conducted to develop theories, not merely to empirically tune what works" (Cobb *et al.* 2003: 9). Bergroth-Koskinen and Seppälä (2012) provide a detailed example of the instantiation of DBR in the context of language teaching and learning in higher education. Drawing on Conole (2012) as well as Lund and Hauge (2011), they adopt a design-based research approach to investigate learning designs that are enacted in real settings and seek to promote the development of learner's agency and communication expertise in the context of higher education language teaching. Taking on the role of teacher-researchers, they examine the development of learner agency as it emerged as the result of the enactment of their initial designs. Their analysis enables them to refine the latter while providing them with new insights into the affordances that potentially enable learners to shape their own learning paths, thus contributing to theory development.

Cobb *et al.* (2003) also emphasise the complexity of educational settings, which consists of interacting complex systems "rather than [...] a collection of activities or a list of separate factors that influence learning" (p. 9). According to them, a key aim of design experiments is to provide a better understanding of a learning ecology "by designing its elements and by anticipating how these elements function together to support learning" (Cobb *et al.* 2003: 9). Typical elements of a learning ecology include "the tasks or problems that students are asked to solve, the kinds of discourse that are encouraged, the norms of participation that are established, the tools and related material means provided, and the practical means by which classroom teachers can orchestrate relations among these elements " (*ibid*).

Activity theoretical perspectives on design

Despite its focus on learning ecologies and its methodology consisting of iterative cycles of enactment, reflexion, and refinement of the design, DBR remains nevertheless a linear process, with a beginning (the initial design) and an end (a 'refined' design), suggesting an "emphasis on completeness, finality, and closure" (Engeström 2007: 369). Engeström further argues that the notion of refinement implies that "researchers have somehow come up with a pretty good model which needs to be perfected in the field" (*ibid*) and summarises his main criticism of DBR as follows:

To sum up, in discourse on "design experiments", scholars do not usually ask: Who does the design and why? It is tacitly assumed that researchers make the grand design, teachers implement it (and contribute to its modification), and students learn better as a result. This linear view ignores what sociologists teach us about interventions as contested terrains that are full of resistance, reinterpretation, and surprise from the actors in the design experiment. (Engeström 2007 : 369)

Even when they are combined together, the learning design methodology and DBR fall short of enabling, among all stakeholders, the formation of *critical design agency*, which includes "the will and courage to say "no" – to challenge the designs offered previously" (Engeström 2007: 370):

Students form specific cognitive "endpoints" in complex learning ecologies and actively make sense of and reconfigure tasks and the contexts of the tasks among the participants. In other words, what is initially presented as the problem or the task is interpreted and turned into a meaningful challenge several times over in the process of the intervention. (Engeström 2007: 370).

Bergroth-Koskinen's and Seppälä' (2012) aforementioned study is indeed a rare example of a DBR project where the initial design is produced and implemented by teachers, and where learner agency is a central feature of the design aims and process. The formation of critical design agency in formal education requires a new approach to design for complex and technology-rich learning environments.

Lund and Hauge (2011) argue for a reconceptualisation of 'didactics', which they define as "the design of social practices in which learners, teachers and (social and material) resources are configured and re-configured in activities that make knowledge domains and knowledge advancement visible, and that continuously create opportunities for reflective participation in such activities" (Lund and Hauge 2011: 263). Linking design to didactics, their approach "gives priority to agency, dynamics, and object over content (what) and method (how)" and acknowledges the "vital role of artifacts in 21st century education" (Lund and

Hauge 2011: 264). It seeks to reconcile the tension between teaching and learning, which they see as "as a unified and dialectic entity" (Lund and Hauge 2011: 262).

According to them, *design for teaching* and *design for learning* are two distinct, yet mutually constitutive aspects of design:

Design for teaching is basically the teacher's responsibility and emerges through interpreting curricula and competence aims, but may well involve learners in the process. However, the intentionality behind this aspect of the design is primarily that of the teacher and the larger educational policies. Thus, there is an institutional dimension to designs for teaching. *Design for learning* refers to the enacted design; what actually happens when teachers and learners engage in joint construction of the (learning) object. While designs for teaching delimit the activities, designs for learning are context sensitive and respond to, for example, immediate opportunities, learner initiatives and serendipity. Also, designs for learning open up for using learners' out-of-school social and cultural experiences, their life worlds (Cope & Kalantzis, 2000). (Lund and Hauge 2011: 262)

The key design challenge for researchers, designers, and teachers is thus to achieve the delicate balance between design for teaching and design for learning. Lund and Hauge (2011) argues that cultural historical activity theory (CHAT) provides conceptual tools to guide educational designs that will address this challenge.

In line with Lund and Hauge (2011), we believe that "for educators CHAT is not only an analytical lens for examining (and explaining) phenomena, but can also be used as a framework for interventions that can effect change in learning and teaching" (Lund and Hauge 2011: 259). Following an overview of the main tenets of CHAT, we outline a CHAT inspired design model (Blin 2010), which was initially developed to facilitate the development and exercise of learner autonomy.

Cultural historical activity theory: an overview

CHAT has its origins in Marxist philosophy and in Vygotsky's cultural historical psychology (Chaiklin *et al.* 1999). It draws upon two related but distinct traditions: Vygotsky's (1978) concept of mediated action and A.N. Leontiev's (1978) *first generation* activity theory (Engeström 2001). Leontiev proposed a hierarchical structure of human activity, defined in terms of three constituents (*subject, object*, and mediating *tools and artefacts*) operating on three different interacting levels (collective *activity*, individual or group *actions*, and routinised *operations*). Activities are collective, oriented toward one or more objects, which can be both ideal and material, and motivated by the need to transform these objects into desired outcomes. This motive gives sense and direction to the goal - oriented actions that are carried out by the subjects (individuals or teams) of the activity. These actions are intentional, mediated by tools or artefacts, and carried out through a series of automated operations that are contingent on material conditions.

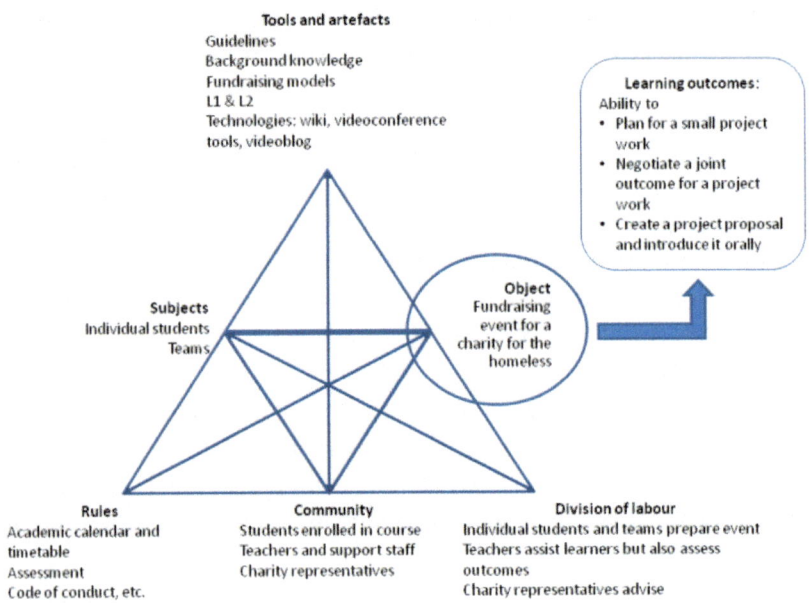

Figure 2: Representation of the mediational structure of the 'fundraising event' activity system (based on Engeström 1987)

First generation activity theory mainly focused on the activity, actions and operations of an individual. Engeström's (1987, 2001) *second generation activity theory* takes a whole activity system as the unit of analysis. Engeström (2008) defines activities as object-oriented collective systems that have a complex mediational structure (Engeström 2008: 26), which includes not only Leontiev's tool-mediated relationship between subject and object but also 'social mediators' (Engeström 2008: 27). *Third generation activity theory* seeks 'to understand dialogue, multiple perspectives, and networks of interacting activity systems (Engeström 2001: 135). For example, individual learners involved in the co - production of a digital artefact are likely to bring to the activity different ideas or representations of what this artefact may be or look like (Roth 2004). They are also likely to participate in other related activities, within or outside formal education.

The mediational structure of an activity system is normally represented by a triangle (Engeström 1987) highlighting the relationships between its constitutive elements. In order to clarify the above concepts, we use our previous example and translate the earlier learning design visualisation (Figure 1) into activity theoretical terms (see Figure 2 below).

The language learning activity relating to our example is shaped by its object, in this case the collective creation of a fundraising event. The top of the triangle diagram above (Subjects – Tools & Artifacts – Object) depicts the "visible curriculum" or "tip of the iceberg" (Engeström 2008: 90), as embedded in the tools and resources (e.g. CMC technologies, language, fundraising and project management methods, authentic materials and guidelines) used by students carrying out actions or chains of actions, including languaging about the object of their activity, in response to the given task. The bottom part of the figure represents what Engeström calls the "hidden curriculum" (2008, p. 86), mediated by the "deep social structure of the activity" (p. 90). In our example, social mediators include the implicit or explicit rules governing the actions carried out by the subjects of the activity (schedule of events, required assignments, expected mode of interaction, expected online behaviour, etc.), the community to which they belong and with whom they share the object of the activity (members of the class or group, teachers and support staff, charity representatives, etc.), and finally, the division of labour (students organise the fundraising event, teachers guide students, charity representatives advise students and teachers, etc.) and the associated distribution of power between the different actors (teachers not only carry out pedagogical interventions but they also assess students' learning, students take on different roles within their team, etc.).

Contrary to frequent misconceptions (Roth 2004), activity systems are inherently dynamic and constitute unstable and multivoiced entities (Engeström 2001). They interact with other activity systems and evolve over time in response to internal and external contradictions (Engeström 2001), which emerge within and between interacting activity systems. Contradictions 'manifest themselves as problems, ruptures, breakdowns, clashes' (Kuutti 1996: 34), or as disturbances, which Engeström (2008) defines as 'actions that deviate from the expected course of normal procedure' (2008: 27).

Contradictions are source of change and development. As they respond to emerging contradictions, activity systems move through cycles of transformations, which can be *expansive*, leading to new forms of activity that are shaped by expanded objects and characterised by a new mediational structure (Engeström 2001). Expansive learning is normally triggered when 'individuals begin to question the existing order and logic of their activity' (Engeström & Sannino 2010: 5).

A CHAT Inspired Design Model

Building on the concepts briefly introduced above, Blin's (2010) design model was initially developed to promote the development of learner autonomy, which is defined as the individual and collective capacity to resolve contradictions (Blin 2005). The model sought to provide teachers with practical means to both address the institutional and societal demands regarding education for the 21st Century while enabling the co-configuration and re-configuration of the learning context, together with learners. Consequently, the model is underpinned by the four principles below (Blin 2010: 186-187), which were derived from an earlier study (Blin 2005):

Principle 1: Language learning activities should be object-centred. Objects that are particularly suitable for the development of learner autonomy include the creation of multimodal artefacts whose purpose and life-cycle will go beyond those of the language course and that can be re-used or re-mixed by self or others (e.g., wikis, blogs, podcasts and video clips, electronic glossaries, interactive web-based exercises, etc.). The mediating components of the language learning activity should provide students with opportunities to construct and expand the given objects in different, yet converging, ways (i.e., to be agents of their own learning).

Principle 2: The language learning activity should be mediated by a rich horizontal division of labour. In other words, the construction of the object should require students to collaborate, and it should not be possible for the object to be constructed by students working independently of each other.

Principle 3: Carefully thought-out focus shifts should be built into the syllabus to avoid prolonged and unwelcome disruptions by providing students with basic digital literacies. Unforeseen focus shifts can then provide opportunities for further learning.

Principle 4: Internal and external contradictions are fundamental to the development and exercise of learner autonomy. Rather than being systematically eliminated, they should be identified and built upon through, for example, careful pedagogical scaffolding taking place at the macro, meso and micro levels (van Lier, 2007: 60) and helping students to question the established practice and to create new forms of activity. Contradictions that cannot be resolved by the participants during the period allocated to the course, module or task should constitute the basis for future design initiatives.

The model can be used at the level of a whole programme of studies, a full course or a lesson, a project, or a discrete task. In line with Coughlan and Duff (1994) and Roebuck (2000), we propose that a language learning task is what designers and teachers *want* learners to do. Tasks thus act as a stimulus and provide students with an initial structure as well as boundaries and constraints for their actions. By contrast, a language learning activity is the "behavior that is actually produced when an individual (or group) performs a task. It is the process, as well as the outcome of the task, examined in its sociocultural context" (Coughlan & Duff 1994: 175).

The model comprises five distinct, yet interconnected steps (Blin 2010, 2012), and prompts teachers to reflect on different aspects of the learning activity they are about to design. In other words, the model helps teachers make *design for teaching* decisions that are cognizant of the broader educational context in which they operate and relevant to their target audience. The guiding questions in Table 1 below also serve as a guide to monitor and analyse the enacted design. The model thus also serves as a benchmark enabling teachers to assess to what extent "the enacted design for learning deviates from the intentions embedded in the design for teaching" (Lund & Hauge 2001: 269) and whether "the delicate teaching|learning balance is disrupted" (*ibid*).

Table 1: A five-step activity theoretical design model (Blin 2010: 190)

Step 1	Identify expected and desired *learning outcomes* • What knowledge, skills and competencies will learners exhibit upon completion of the task? How can these be assessed?
Step 2	Define the *object* of the activity • What kind of *object* can be transformed into the *desired outcomes*? What will learners attend to or construct during the realization of the task? • What *goal-oriented actions* or *chains of actions* are likely to facilitate the transformation of the *object* into the *desired learning outcomes*?
Step 3	Identify and describe the *actors* of the activity • Who will be the *subjects* of the activity? What histories are they bringing to the language learning activity? What cultural tools do they bring to the activity, including their native language, communicative and literacy practices? Which other communities (networked or otherwise) do they belong to? • What motivates their participation in the language learning activity? • What are the characteristics of the *community* being shaped by the object of the activity (i.e., real vs. imaginary, local vs. geographically dispersed, networked, etc.)?

Step 4	Specify the *mediators* of the activity
	• What *tools and artefacts* will be available to learners (e.g., technologies, concepts and methods, texts, etc.)? How will communication and interaction be mediated (e.g., face-to-face, Web 2.0 technologies, synchronous or asynchronous CMC technologies, social networks, Virtual Worlds, etc.)? Which language will be the main mediator of the activity?
	• Are there *explicit and implicit rules and conventions* imposed from the outside (e.g., academic calendar and timetables, assessment schedules and methods, typical student workload, etc.)? What other rules and conventions will govern the realization of the task (e.g., directives, instructions, guidelines, etc.)? What implicit rules are embedded in the technologies deployed by the institution?
	• How will the *division of labour* be organized? Will learners work independently or in teams? What level of agency, power and control will be allocated to learners? To teachers?
Step 5	Outline potential *internal and external contradictions*
	• What are the potential sources of conflict, breakdowns or disruptions? Are they likely to be resolved by the community?
	• What focus shifts are likely to occur? What level of teacher intervention may be required? At the design stage? During the activity? What are the competencies required from learners?

In the next section, we use the above model to revisit the design for teaching of a Finnish literacy course offered to international students at the University of Jyväskylä. Drawing on data collected during two consecutive enactments of the design (Jalkanen & Vaarala 2012a, 2012b, 2013), we propose a preliminary analysis of the designs for learning that emerged, with a particular focus on agency and languaging.

Design for Teaching

Upon completion of the course, students are expected to be able to engage and participate in diverse activities (e.g. read, produce, and discuss) around different types of texts and media, and to gradually construct their identity as a 'competent' user of the Finnish language, able to function successfully in a variety of Finnish discourse communities (e.g., academic, social, etc.). To attain the intended learning outcomes, students are expected to carry out various tasks, individually and collaboratively, in and out of class, requiring them to read, listen, write and speak in a variety of registers and genres.

Recognizing that technology enables social processes that can foster the emergence of meaningful communities (Wenger, White & Smith 2009: 191), the tasks proposed as part of the *Tekstejä suomeksi 2* course are to be carried out across multiple spaces. Face-to-face sessions are led by the teacher and function as an arena for collaborative work in diverse group combinations and on different types of texts. Between these sessions, students have access to the institutional virtual learning environment, *Moodi*, which provides them with a shared space for analysing prescribed texts on multiple levels and from multiple perspectives, both individually and collaboratively. Finally, students were encouraged to use Twitter for media sharing and for one-to-one or whole group communication, using the course specific hashtag.

Recalling Pennycook's (2010) definition of competence given earlier, th e object of the overall language learning activity is thus primarily ideal and is motivated by the need to help foreign students develop their "strategic capacity to use diverse semiotic items across integrated media and modalities" in the Finnish language. The object is also material in so far that students will be producing language in the form of spoken and written texts. In particular, they are required to prepare a group presentation to be delivered to the whole class at the end of the course. Working in small groups, students are required to select one of the course themes, which mostly relate to an aspect of Finnish culture and social or professional practice. Eight themes are prescribed by the course curriculum: Finnish music, education in Finland, Finnish design, traveling in Finland, climate change, social media (with a particular focus on blogs), information literacy, and working life and recruiting in Finland. Students are encouraged to support their presentation with creative artefacts that are to be collaboratively produced. Examples of possible artefacts include PowerPoint shows, posters, music mashups, images, etc.

Students participating in the course are international university students, some of whom are following a Masters or doctoral programme. Others are exchange students, only spending a relatively short period of time in Finland. All students are advanced learners in their own specialism, with good Finnish language skills (B1-B2), and based on the same campus (the University of Jyväskylä).

A range of tools and artefacts is made available to students. In addition to the tools and technologies offered by the institutional VLE, students are provided with personal tablets for the duration of the course in order to support literacy practices in and beyond the language classroom. The teaching and learning resources available within *Moodi* are to be supplemented by artefacts selected by students (e.g. newspaper articles, radio programmes, websites and other documents as relevant to a given task). In terms of rules and conventions, students are expected to attend and actively participate in scheduled face-to-face sessions, to complete at least 80% of the tasks associated to each theme, and to actively prepare and present the group project, which are all elements of the course continuous assessment. Finally, the division of labour is primarily horizontal: students work independently between classes (although they may be interacting with members of the wider community), and in small groups during the face-to-face sessions, which are facilitated and managed by the teacher. The latter also assesses student participation, task realisation, and the final group presentation.

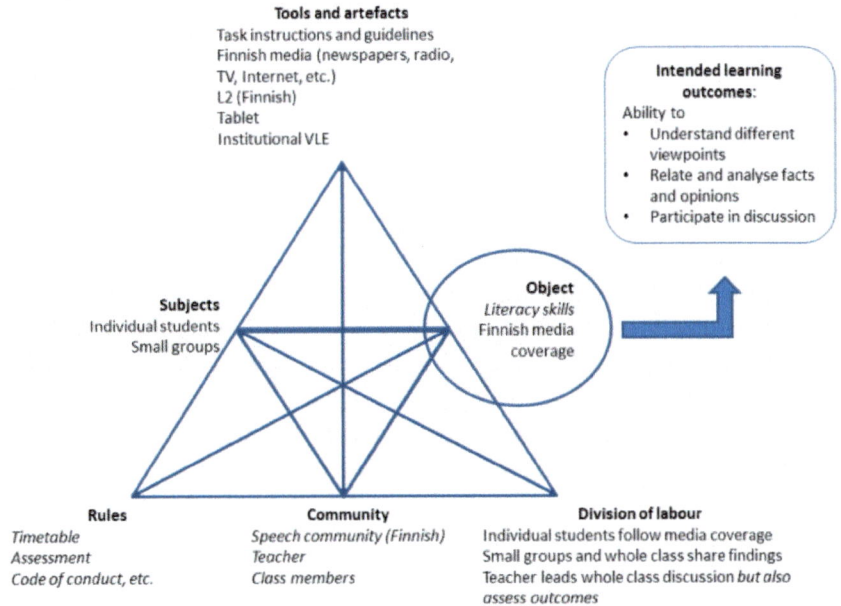

Figure 3: *Design for teaching* of the 'Finnish media coverage' activity system

The following is an example of a design for teaching, illustrated in Figure 3 below, produced by a teacher for one particular task to be carried over a full week. From a *design for teaching* perspective, the task was motivated by the need to help students identify different perspectives related to the topic of their group presentation and to incorporate these in their discussion and arguments. Task specific intended learning outcomes include the ability to understand different viewpoints, to relate and analyse facts and opinions, and to participate in a whole class discussion. The task required that students follow media coverage of news items (e.g. economy, sport, entertainment, etc.) during the week, prior to the face-to-face session. In class, students were to share and discuss their findings, first in small groups, then as a whole class.

Most of the planned mediators are shared with the parent activity (in italics in Figure 3 below). The whole class discussion was to be led by the teacher, and throughout the face-to-face small group and whole class discussions, students had their tablets at their disposal.

Enacted designs for learning

The enactment of any educational design is likely to be characterised by unpredictability and varying degrees of student agency and languaging, which will both arise from and give rise to the emergence of internal and external contradictions (Engeström 2001, Blin 2010, Blin & Appel 2011). The enactment of the *design for teaching* of *Tekstejä suomeksi 2* is no exception. Throughout the two instantiations of the course (in 2012 and 2013 respectively), different contradictions within the enacted design activity system emerged, which manifested themselves through focus shifts, misunderstandings or conflicts. For example, in the second instantiation of the course, it soon became apparent that students had very little experience, if any, of Twitter and tablets, especially in a learning context. Similarly, the tools available through Moodi were configured in such a way that students encountered difficulties in using them. Intensive technical assistance was thus required to help students exploit the opportunities for learning that the various tools potentially offered. Finally, rules that were imposed from the outside, such as assessment regulations and standards, were not completely aligned to the course object and intended learning outcomes.

Most of the above contradictions can be addressed in future designs for teaching. For example, additional technical support or learner training in the use of tools can be embedded in the design, assessment regulations and standards can be better aligned to the intended learning outcomes. Others may however be unpredictable, contingent on a particular context at a particular time. Similarly, unpredicted opportunities for learning are likely to emerge as the result of "learner initiatives and serendipity" (Lund and Hauge 2011: 62, *op. cit.*). As a result, different *designs for learning* are likely to emerge, arising from, as well as providing opportunities for the formation of critical design agency and languaging.

Design for learning and the formation of 'critical design agency'

In both instantiations, most students were new to the culture of sharing via digital means and using the work of others as a resource for learning. Some wholeheartedly embraced a new digital social practice for learning, others resisted and initially refused to question the social practice they were accustomed to.

In the first instantiation of the course (2012), most students appropriated the initial *design for teaching* and developed it further by contributing to the evolution of the learning community as well as repurposing tools and environments in line with their personal learning contexts and objectives (Jalkanen & Vaarala 2012a, 2012b). For instance, some students began to share life events in Twitter, thus creating a temporary space for the development of interpersonal relationships beyond the context of the course. Another student used her tablet to record a discussion at the doctor's to be able to listen to it again at home. These examples illustrate the blurring of boundaries between in and out-of-school "social and cultural experiences" that is often characteristic of *designs for learning* (see Lund's & Hauge's (2011) definition of design for learning discussed earlier).

By contrast, in the next instantiation of the course (2013), some students initially rejected the *design for teaching* by resisting the use of Twitter and tablets, as they did not perceive the connection between the object of the learning activity and the tools available to them. However, feedback discussions at the end of the course provided evidence of a transformation in the attitudes of those students who were most critical towards the use of Twitter and the tablets. Students indicated that their understanding of literacy practices had widened during the course and that they now perceived Twitter and the tablets as valuable tools for learning. This transformation of students' attitudes and practices can be attributed to the sustained negotiation, co-construction, and re-construction of the learning object by both teachers and students. Teachers had to redefine their design for teaching to make the pedagogical reasoning behind it more visible to and shared by students. Students progressively developed some critical design agency, eventually accepting to challenge their old designs for learning, thus embracing a "radically wider horizon of possibilities " (Engeström 2001: 137). This however required "teachers to participate with a persistent presence in learners' trajectories" (Lund & Hauge 2011: 269) so that the enacted *design for learning* could be brought in line with the "intentions embedded in the design for teaching" (*op. cit.*).

Designs for learning and languaging

Designs for learning can also be seen as sites for languaging . As students performed different tasks around texts, several instances of 'making meaning and shaping knowledge and experience through language' (Swain 2006: 98) emerged. By examining some of these instances, and recalling Lund's and Hauge's (2011) definition of *design for learning,* we can identify episodes where teachers and learners respond to immediate opportunities and serendipity, or where learners take initiatives. In such instances, languaging directly contribute the development of the design for learning.

For example, in the context of the media coverage task performed in the first instantiation of the design (2012), some students had focused on sport news, and more specifically on rallying, a very popular motorsport in Finland. As three students discuss the media coverage of sporting events during the week, the name of a Finnish rally driver, Tommi Mäkinen, comes up in the discussion (Excerpt 1). S1 asks the other members of the group whether they know him. S2 confirms that he knows who the person is and provides additional information: "a motor sport man", which is further explicated by S1 ("rally driver"). However, S1 produces the wrong phoneme (S instead of R), and S3 and S2 do not understand the word. S3, using his tablet, types the driver's name in Google, finds the right form, and says it out loud. A shared understanding is then reached and the discussion can proceed.

Excerpt 2

S1: Tiedätkö Tommi Mäkinen	(Do you know Tommi Mäkinen)
S2: Tiedän joo mutta - - autourheilija	(I know yeah but - - a motor sport man)
S1: Lalliajaja	(*Sally driver)
S3: Mitä se - -	(What it - -)
S2: Lalli aa	(Sally aa)
S1: Lalli	(Sally)
S3: Tommi Mäkinen (käyttää googlea iPadilla) odota - - aa ralli niin	(Tommi Mäkinen [using Google on iPad] wait - - aa rally yes.)

In the above example, S3 operates on linguistic data unknown to him, accesses the rich semiotic budget afforded by the technology (i.e., the Internet accessible through the tablet), and turns a communication breakdown into a learning opportunity for his peers. As a result, S1 is made aware of her pronunciation error and comes to "an understanding of previously less well understood material" (Swain 2000: 98). The misunderstanding was resolved without teacher intervention, which is an indication of S3's "strategic capacity to use diverse semiotic items across integrated media and modalities" (Pennycook 2010: 129) to overcome comprehension problems.

Later on in the same session, the teacher (T1) leads a whole class discussion. As the discussion moves to the topic of Tommi Mäkinen and his birthplace, Puuppola, the teacher asks where the latter is located (Excerpt 2).

S6 replies that Puuppola is in Jyväskylä. T1 corrects the information provided by S6 and clarifies that the place is actually some kilometres up north from the town. However, she is not sure of the exact distance between Jyväskylä and Puuppola. Before she can provide an estimate, S6 comes up with the right answer, which he had looked up on the Internet. At first surprised, the teacher soon realizes that the student had access to Wikipedia.

Excerpt 2

T1: Vielä kysymys, missä on Puuppola?	(One more question, where is Puuppola?)
S6: Jyväskylässä	(In Jyväskylä)
T1: Puuppola on Jyväskylästä vähän matkaa pohjoiseen. Kuinkas monta kilometriä, oisko se tuota - -	Puuppola is some kilometres up north from Jyväskylä. How many kilometres, I wonder if it's er - -)
(S6 kirjoittaa Puuppolan hakusanaksi Googleen)	(S6 types Puuppola on Google on her iPad)
S6: Kaksitoista	(Twelve)
T1: Kaksitoista. Mistäs te sen tiedätte? Aa, Wikipediakin tietää Puuppolan.	(Twelve. How do you know that? Ah, Wikipedia knows Puuppola as well.)

The above example is an instance of learners taking the initiative, in this case, configuring and reconfiguring roles through languaging and technologymediated actions. The fact that the teacher is no longer the primary information provider encourages learner active participation. In this example, S6 contributes to the collective re-configuration of social and material resources in the classroom while solving an unpredicted information gap through the use of language and technology (Lund & Hauge 2011).

CONCLUSION

Throughout this paper, we have looked at the notion of educational design in the context of language teaching and learning in increasingly technology -rich environments. We have claimed that a renewed focus on design, which needs to be cognizant of the rapid societal and technological changes that characterize 21st Century knowledge creation and social practices, was necessary to address the increased complexity and unpredictability of language teaching and learning. Following a brief overview of agency and languaging as emerging approaches to language use and learning, we have discussed some recent developments in the field of educational design, namely learning design and design -based research, that are particularly interesting to the educational technology and Computer Assisted Language Learning communities. While we believe that these approaches provide robust methods and tools to develop strong designs for teaching, they however fall short of providing conceptual tools to describe and analyse the corresponding enacted designs for learning. In particular, they do not easily enable course designers and teachers to understand deviations from the intentions embedded in the design for teaching. Nor do they leave much room for unpredictability.

Drawing on Lund's and Hauge's (2011) definition of didactics, and in line with their focus on the dialectical relationship between design for teaching and design for learning, we have argued that designs rooted in cultural historical activity theory address these challenges. They do so by giving priority to the construction and re-construction of the object of the learning activity, and to the configuration and co-configuration of the mediational structure of the learning activity over pre-defined content, skills and methods.

The examples discussed in this paper have illustrated how activity-theoretical designs can be used for better understanding the relationship between *design for teaching* and *design for learning* in complex language learning environments. They also provided examples of languaging and of the formation of critical design agency in context. In particular, it was shown that students negotiated and co - constructed new 'horizons of possibilities', even though they may have initially rejected a new form of activity.

Maintaining the balance between teaching and learning called for by Lund and Hauge (2011) remains however difficult. Knowing when and how to intervene in enacted designs for learning is a teaching skill that increasingly requires the ability to reconcile societal and institutional demands, the will to challenge existing designs and their associated social practice, and the ability to seize opportunities arising from unexpected events. Most of all, it requires teachers to fully participate in the joint construction of the object of learning with their students and to facilitate the formation of their critical design agency.

ENDNOTES

[1]This scenario and the associated task are part of the resources created under the auspices of the SpeakApps Project, funded by the EU Lifelong Learning Programme, Project N° 511552-LLP-1-2010-1-ES-KA2-KA2MP, http://speakapps.eu

[2]The authors want to thank M.A. Kristiina Litola for her indispensable help with the transcription of the video data.

REFERENCES

1. Ahearn, L. M. 2001. Language and agency. *Annual Review of Anthropology,* 30, 109–137. Barab, S. 2006. Design-based research: A methodological toolkit for the learning
2. scientist. In R. K. Sawyer (ed.), Cambridge Handbook of the Learning Sciences. New York: Cambridge University Press.
3. Benson, P. 2007. Autonomy in language teaching and learning. State of the art article. *Language Teaching,* 40 (1), 21-40.
4. Bergroth-Koskinen, U-M. & R. Seppälä 2012. Teacher-researchers Exploring Design-based Research to Develop Learning Designs in Higher Education Language Teaching. *Apples – Journal of Applied Language Studies,* 6(2), 95-112. Available from http://apples.jyu.fi/
5. Blin, F., 2004. CALL and the Development of Learner Autonomy: Towards an Activity - Theoretical Perspective. *ReCALL,* 16(02), 377–395.
6. Blin, F., 2005. *CALL and the development of learner autonomy - an activity theoretical study.* Unpublished doctoral thesis. The Open University, UK. Available from: http://webpages.dcu.ie/~blinf/BlinThesis.pdf.
7. Blin, F., 2010. Designing cybertasks for learner autonomy: towards an activity theoretical pedagogical model. In M. J. Luzón, M. N. Ruiz-Madrid, & M. L. Villanueva, (eds.). *Digital Genres, New Literacies and Autonomy in Language Learning* . Newcastle upon Tyne: Cambridge Scholars Publishing, 175 –196.
8. Blin, F., 2012. Bologna and the 21st century language learner: in tegrating technology for learner autonomy. In J. Burston, D. Tsagari, & F. Doa, eds. *Foreign Language Instructional Technology: Theory & Practice* . Nicosia: University of Nicosia Press, 60 –77.
9. Blin, F. & C. Appel 2011. Computer supported collaborative writing in practice: an activity theoretical study. *CALICO Journal,* 28(2), 473–497.
10. Blin, F. & M. Munro 2008. Why hasn't technology disrupted academics' teaching practices? Understanding resistance to change through the le ns of activity theory. Computers and Education, 50, 475-490.
11. Bliss, J., R. Säljö & P. Light (eds.) 1999. Learning Sites: Social and. technological resources for learning. Oxford: Pergamon.
12. Canagarajah, S. 2008. Foreword in A. Clemente & M. Higgins, Perform ing English with a post-colonial accent: Ethnographic narratives from Mexico. London: The Tufnell Press, ix-xiii.
13. Castells, M. 1996. The Rise of the Network Society. Oxford: Blackwell.

14. Chaiklin, S., M. Hedegaard & U. J. Jensen (eds.) 1999. *Activity theory and social practice: cultural-historical approaches*. Aarhus: Aarhus University Press.
15. Cobb, P., J. Confrey, A. diSessa, R. Lehrer & L. Schauble 2003. Design Experiments in Educational Research. *Educational Researcher*, 32(1), 9–13.
16. Collins, A., D. Joseph & K. Bielaczyc 2004. Design Research: Theoretical and methodological issues. Journal of the Learning Sciences, 13 (1), 15-42.
17. Conole, G. 2008. The role of mediating artefacts in learning design. In L. Lockyer, S. Bennett, S. Agostinho & B. Harper (eds.), *Handbook of Research on Learning Design and Learning Objects: Issues, Applications and Technologies* . Hershey, PA: IGI Global, 187 – 207.
18. Conole, G., 2010. Learning design –Making practice explicit. In *ConnectEd 2010: 2nd International conference on Design Education*. Sydney, Australia. Available from: http://oro.open.ac.uk/21864/ (Accessed August 31, 2013).
19. Conole, G. 2012. *Designing for learning in an open world* . New York: Springer.
20. Cope, B. & M. Kalantzis (eds.) 2009. *Ubiquitous learning*. Chigaco: University of Illinois Press.
21. Coughlan, P. & P. Duff 1994. Same task, different activities: analysis of a SLA task from an activity theory perspective. In J.P. Lantolf & G.Appel (eds.), *Vygotskian Approaches to Second Language Research*. Norwood, NJ: Ablex, 173–193.
22. Design-Based Research Collective 2003. Design-Based Research: An Emerging Paradigm for Educational Inquiry. *Educational Researcher*, 32 (1), 5-8.
23. Dufva, H., M. Suni, M. Aro & O.-P. Salo 2011. Languages as objects of learning: language learning as a case of multilingualism. *Apples – Journal of Applied Language Studies*, 5 (1), 109–124.
24. Engeström, Y. 1987. *Learning by expanding: An activity -theoretical approach to developmental research*. Helsinki: Orienta-Konsultit.
25. Engeström, Y. 2001. Expansive learning at work: Toward an activity theoretical reconceptualization. *Journal of Education and Work,* 14(1), 133-156.
26. Engeström, Y. 2007. Putting Vygotsky to work: The Change Laboratory as an application of double stimulation. In H. Daniels, M. Cole & J. V.

Wertsch (eds.), *The Cambridge companion to Vygotsky.* Cambridge: Cambridge University Press, 363 -383.

27. Engeström, Y. 2008. *From Teams to Knots: Activity-theoretical Studies of Collaboration and Learning at Work.* Cambridge: Cambridge University Press.

28. Engeström Y. 2011. From design experiments to formative interventions. *Theory & Psychology,* 21, 598–628.

29. Engeström, Y. & A. Sannino 2010. Studies of expansive learning: Foundations, findings and future challenges. *Educational Research Review,* 5, 1–24.

30. Holland, D. & W. Lachicotte Jr. 2007. Vygotsky, Mead, and the new sociocultural studies of identity. In H. Daniels, M. Cole, J.W. Wertsch (eds.), *The Cambridge Companion to Vygotsky.* Cambridge: Cambridge University Press, 101-135.

31. Jacobs, H. H. 2010. *Curriculum 21: essential education for a changing world.* Alexandria, VA: Association for Supervision & Curriculum Development.

32. Jalkanen, J. & H. Vaarala 2012a. Opettamisesta oppimiseen – oppimateriaaleista toimintaan [From teaching to learning - from learning material to activities]. *Kieli, koulutus ja yhteiskunta* 3 (2).

33. Jalkanen, J. & H.Vaarala 2012b. From teaching to learning: hybrid spaces and emerging practices in a second language learning course. Paper presented at EuroCALL 2012 conference, Gothenburg, Sweden.

34. Jalkanen, J., A. Pitkänen-Huhta & P. Taalas 2012. Changing society – changing language learning and teaching practices? In M. Bendtsen, M. Björklund, L. Forsman, & K. Sjöholm (eds.), *Global Trends Meet Local Needs.* Vaasa: Åbo Akademi Press, 219-241.

35. Jalkanen, J. & H. Vaarala 2013. Opiskelijat sisällöntuottajina: tavoitteet, työkalut ja toiminta [Students as content producers: goals, tools and activity]. Unpublished keynote presentation in Suomen kielen ja kulttuurin opettajien opintopäivät [seminar for teachers in Finnish language and culture], Vaasa, Finland.

36. Kankaanranta, M. & E. Puhakka 2008. *Kohti innovatiivista tietotekniikan opetuskäyttöä. Kansainvälisen SITES 2006 -tutkimuksen tuloksia.* [Towards innovative uses of learning technologies. Results from the international SITES 2006 study.] Jyväskylän yliopisto: Koulutuksen tutkimuslaitos.

37. Koper, R. & B. Olivier 2004. Representing the learning design of units of learning. *Educational Technology & Society*, 7(3), 97–111.
38. Kuutti, K. 1996. Activity theory as a potential framework for human-computer interaction research. In B.A. Nardi (ed.), *Context and Consciousness: Activity Theory and Human-computer Interaction*. Cambridge, MA: The MIT Press, 17 –44.
39. Laakkonen, I. 2011. Personal learning environments in higher education language courses: an informal and learner-centred approach. In S. Thouësny & L. Bradley (eds.), *Second language teaching and learning with technology: views of emergent researchers*. Dublin: Research-publishing.net.
40. Laurillard, D. 2012. *Teaching as a design science. Building Pedagogical Patterns for Learning and Technology.* New York: Routledge.
41. Leontiev, A.N. 1978. *Activity, Consciousness and Personality* . Englewood Cliffs, NJ: Prentice Hall.
42. Ludvigsen, S., A. Lund, I. Rasmussen & R. Säljö (eds.) 2011. *Learning across sites: New tools, infrastructures and practices*. Abingdon: Routledge.
43. Luukka, M-R., S. Pöyhönen, A. Huhta, Taalas, M. Tarnanen & A. Keränen 2008. *Maailma muuttuu - mitä tekee koulu?* Äidinkielen *ja vieraiden kielten tekstikäytänteet koulussa ja vapaa-ajalla*. [The world changes – how does the school respond? Mother tongue and foreign language literacy practices in school and in free -time.] Jyväskylän yliopisto: Soveltavan kielentutkimuksen keskus.
44. Lund, A. & T. E. Hauge 2011. Designs for teaching and learning in technology-rich learning environments. *Nordic Journal of Digital Literacy,* 6 (4), 258-272.
45. McLoughlin, C. & M. Lee 2008. Mapping the digital terrain: New media and social software as catalysts for pedagogical change. In R. Atkinson & C. McBeath (eds.),
46. *Hello! Where are you in the landscape of educational technology? Proceedings ascilite Melbourne 2008.* Geelong, Vic. : Deakin University, 641-652. Available from http://www.ascilite.org.au/conferences/melbourne08/procs/mcloughlin.html
47. Pennycook, A. 2010. *Language as a local practice*. New York: Routledge.
48. Pietikäinen, S., R. Alanen, H. Dufva, P. Kalaja, S. Leppänen & A. Pitkänen-Huhta 2008. Languaging in Ultima Thule: Multilingualism in the life of a Sami boy. *International Journal of Multilingualism*, 5 (2), 79–99.

49. Roebuck, R. 2000. Subjects speak out: How learners position themselves in a psycholinguistic task. In J. P. Lantolf (ed.), *Sociocultural Theory and Second Language Learning*. Oxford: Oxford University Press, 79 –95.

50. Roth, W.-M. 2004. Introduction: "Activity Theory and Education: An Introduction".*Mind, Culture, and Activity*, 11(1), 1–8.

51. Sitthisak, O. & L. Gilbert 2009. Improving the pedagogical expressiv eness of IMS LD. Paper presented at the TELearn 2009 Conference, 6 -8 October 2009, Taipei, Taiwan. Available from: http://eprints.soton.ac.uk/268228/ (Accessed 1 September 2013).

52. Swain, M., S. Lapkin, I. Knouzi, W. Suzuki & L. Brooks 2009. Languaging: Univ ersity students learn the grammatical concept of voice in French. *The Modern Language Journal*, 93(1), 5–29.

53. Swain, M. 2006. Languaging, agency and collaboration in advanced second language proficiency. In H. Byrnes (ed.), *Advanced Language Learning: The contribution of Halliday and Vygotsky*. London: Continuum, 95-108.

54. Taalas, P. 2005. *Change in the making: Strategic and pedagogical challenges of technology integration in language teaching*. Centre for Applied Language Studies. Jyväskylä: University of Jyväskylä.

55. van Lier, L. 2007. Action-based teaching, autonomy and identity. Innovation in *Language Learning and Teaching*, 1(1), 46-65.

56. van Lier, L. 2000. From input to affordance: social -interactive learning from an ecological perspective. In J. P. Lantolf (ed.) *Sociocultural theory and second language learning*. Oxford: Oxford University Press.

57. Vygotsky, L. S. 1978. *Mind in society*. Cambridge: Harvard University Press.

58. Wenger, E., N. White & J. D. Smith 2009. *Digital habitats: Stewarding technology for communities*. Portland: CPsquare

59. Wiggins, G. & J. McTighe 2005. *Understanding by design*. Alexandria, VA: Association for Supervision and Curriculum Development.

60. Zheng, D. & K. Newgarden 2012. Rethinking language learning: virtual worlds as a catalyst for change. *International Journal of Learning and Media*, 3(2), 13-36.

Chapter 12

CONTENT DOMAIN AND LANGUAGE COMPETENCE IN COMPUTER-MEDIATED CONVERSATION FOR LEARNING

Paola Leone

University of Salento

ABSTRACT

This study addresses the issue of interactional dominance in Teletandem conversations, in which two speakers communicate via video calls and chat and alternatively use their L2, the latter being the native language of the interlocutor. In particular, the research focuses on the impact of language competence (native/non-native) and content expertise (minus/plus familiarity with the topic at hand) on the role assumed by each interlocutor in structuring conversation. The data consists of 3 hours of computer -mediated recorded and transcribed conversations during 3 meetings: meeting comprises free discussion for mutual introduction; meeting 2 is a discussion in English of a topic chosen by the Italian native speaker; meeting 3 is a discussion in Italian of a topic chosen by the English native speaker. The participants' language proficiency in L2 ranged from upper-intermediate to advanced. The following indicators were considered: sequential dominance, determined by identifying and counting topic moves; interaction dominance, defined in terms of average turn length; interruptions. The research design considers behaviours that are potentially salient for language learning (e.g. clarification requests). Results show no tendency by the native speaker to control conversation flow: neither the English nor the Italian speaker is dominant during events in which her own native language is used. As regards content familiarity, this seems to have an effect when topic knowledge becomes expertise like during meeting 3, when the English native speaker produces more topic moves and longer turns in L2 than her partner.

INTRODUCTION

The study investigates the impact of content choice and language competence on conversation structure in order to gain a better understanding of the influence of context variables on those activities salient for language acquisition (e.g. making clarification requests, starting negotiation of meaning, etc., see also Kasper 2004). The focus is conversational dominance during multimodal computer communications, an emerging learning context that is increasingly being employed in various institutions (e.g. Brazilian and Italian universities) for effective L2 use and learning.

Data have been collected during Teletandem sessions, in which pairs of native speakers of two different languages converse alternately in their L1 and L2 as a component of their study of each other's native language. The communication is multimodal that is, conducted via Internet using voice, video and instant messaging software applications (e.g. Skype). Dominance will be intended as the communicative behaviour of an interlocutor who controls the conversation flow (Zhou et al. 2004) in both oral and written communicative modes.

Teletandem (www.teletandembrazil.org) communicative exchanges present similar characteristics to face-to-face tandem conversations (Brammerts 2003). They can be regarded as a variety of "conversation for learning"(Kasper 2004) since in both learning contexts, speakers talk having a "dual-focus" in mind (Apfelbaum 1993; Bange 1992). One is the language used for communication; for instance, the discourse includes pedagogical turns in which participants correct/repair interlocutors' language misuse, negotiate meanings, explain a rule related to their first language, etc. The other focus is the topic under discussion: the interaction process is characterized, for instance, by the presence of appraisal/agreement sequences. This latter quality makes Teletandem conversation close to natural peer communication (Apfelbaum 1993; Anderson & Banelli 2005; Leone 2009a, 2009b).

In particular, among sequences of focus on form, negotiation of meaning and repairs play an especially important role, since both of them allow the development of L2 communication ability. Negotiation of meaning is prompted by non-comprehension and aims at resolving communication problems (Gass 1997; Leone 2009a, 2009b). As regards Teletandem communication, written chat is employed as a strategy to facilitate communication: by writing the new word, and sometimes its translation, interlocutors use a semiotic code that makes the message permanent and accessible over time (Leone 2009b). Repairs arise because appropriate target language vocabulary or expression is missing or because the non-native speaker is not sure whether certain forms are correct or understandable. Repairs are often self-initiated, that is, the learner either attempts to resolve communicative problems alone, testing out a hypothesis on the target word or explicitly asking the interlocutor for help (e.g. *how do you say...?*), or using the expression in another language, thus showing indirectly his/her need to be assisted (e.g. in our data: ENGL1: *sì ho lezioni e poi a:hm ho molti compiti ancora di fare per adesso devo fare i compiti per morfol[ogia] e poi la notte abbiamo entrenamento allena- e:hm training;* ITL1: *[u:hm u:hm] allenamento sì*; see also Apfelbaum 1993; Rost-Roth 1995, 1999; Kasper 2004; Anderson & Banelli 2005).

Code-switching is another common characteristic of Tandem and Teletandem. It is employed not only for facilitating communication, as mentioned above, but also for evoking a context in which, for example, an event takes place (e.g. in England + I don't know - people of my AGE don't really sort of read the newspaper or watch the news. *And here it's like if you have people around for dinner or something you can and they like – oh telegiornale uh!;* Anderson & Banelli 2005: 94).

Like in face-to-face tandem, also in Teletandem conversations speakers integrate gestures and body movements into their communication process. During Teletandem, for instance, one of the partner's movement towards the webcam is interpreted by the primary speaker as a signal of non -understanding and a request for repetition. In Teletandem communication, interlocutors use written chat in different moments and for different functions: for instance, at the beginning of a Teletandem session to check if the interlocutor is listening (e.g . *can you hear me?*) or to facilitate communication by writing the new word and sometimes its translation (Leone 2009b).

Tandem and Teletandem conversation is a form of exolingual communication, during which participants do not share their mother tongue and talk alternatively in their second language and in the first language of the interlocutor. During (Tele)tandem conversations imbalance in expertise can be related either to language competence or to contents under discussion. The two dimensions are separate from each other. Language proficiency ranges from novice (e.g. the non-native speaker) to expert (the native speaker). Along the continuum there are different levels of non-native speaker competence, reaching the very advanced level of the L2 locutor for whom the only obviously non - native aspect of target language use is accent. Conversely, the level of expertise relative to the contents under discussion can vary from complete lack of familiarity to advanced knowledge of a specific discipline. Teletandem conversation can be shaped by different forms of expertise in the two dimensions mentioned. In particular, those discussed in the present study are: upper intermediate language competence and native competence in language use for communication and familiarity with a topic, which emerges when one of the interlocutors selects the subject for discussion. In order to compensate for the gap between native and non-native speaker in the target language competence, for the purposes of this study, the low-proficiency L2 user has been asked to choose a topic for discussion.

Background to the study

In interactional studies, dominance and asymmetry describe different aspects of interaction. The distinction between these two concepts can be explained by referring to speakers' behaviour in ordinary and institutional conversation. In ordinary conversations, although contribution to conversation development may be unbalanced, equality in participation can be easily brought about. In fact, if one speaker controls the conversation flow more for any reason (i.e. a speaker's familiarity with the topic at hand, a temporary lapse of one interlocutor's attention), his/her interlocutor may modify "participant structure" (Philips 1972, 1983) and "establish the conversational order" (Orletti 2000: 13–14). Conversely, in institutional conversations (e.g. doctor-patient) the "global management" of the interaction cannot be changed (e.g. Linell & Luckmann 1991; Orletti 2000). For example, during a doctor-patient conversation, to the doctor's question "how are you?" the latter does not reply "Fine, thank you and how are you?" since the imbalance in participant knowledge and status is manifested in the different rights of each interlocutor in managing interaction. The former type of "inequity" will be referred to as *dominance*, and the latter *asymmetry* (Linell 1990; Orletti 2000).

Dominance is a general term which is used in different fields of study (e.g. biology). Particularly, in psychology and sociology it refers to the position of power and authority of one group or individual over others in both human and animal behaviour and it is intended as the opposite of submission. On the other hand, in applied linguistics, specifically in interaction studies, dominance is defined as "temporary lack of reciprocity" in conversation (Hakulinen 2009: 61). An interactional dominant behaviour is verified when one of the speakers takes a number of initiatives during conversation (e.g. introducing topics) to which one or more interlocutors reply.

Research in applied linguistics has analysed the relationship between macro-social variables (e.g. gender differences, status differences) and the way dialogues are structured, aiming to highlight the relation between social power and speakers' linguistic and communicative behaviour (Orletti 2000: 9) and to use observation of these dialogues and discourse as a basis for generalizations about asymmetries in other contexts.

Conversely, this study focuses on the effects of situational variables and individual factors (e.g. language competence, topic familiarity) on interaction structure. For a proper understanding of the significance of its results, it is important to point out that there is no logical and necessary relationship between social or psychological forms of authoritarianism and the way a dialogue unfolds. The features of discourse practices captured by the analysis will not be considered to be signs of social and psychological power of one interlocutor over the other. In other words, an individual communicative choice cannot be a predicting behaviour of either authoritarianism or submission. Silence, for instance, is not a dominant interactional action but can manifest either social or psychological dominance over the interlocutor. As underlined by Linell and Luckmann, "…the analyst must always keep the distinction in mind; it is one thing to identify dominant actions, another thing to determine what they mean or what they are signs of…a person who possesses power need not be, or at least not always be, dominant in interaction" (1991: 11).

Dominance and language learning in tandem

The concept of interactional dominance is linked to the principles of *reciprocity*, *autonomy* and *collaboration*, on which tandem and Teletandem are based (Brammerts 2003; Telles 2009). Indeed, joining one of these educational programs implies that:

- there must be mutual recognition by each partner of the same rights and privileges in relation to participation in the activity (reciprocity);
- activity planning must be free from external control (autonomy). For instance, the instructor is a consultant and collaborates to find solutions when requested (Telles & Vassallo 2006);
- partners must work in conjunction in order to achieve results (collaboration).

In particular, investigating interactional dominance means analysing whether or not one partner more actively controls the conversation flow, thus actually affecting the degree of reciprocity and autonomy in using conversational patterns, and imposing a definite form of collaboration. That is to say, if one partner asks many more questions, thus taking a dominant role, s/he puts the interlocutor in the position of having to reply or of having to request to "restore order", by recognizing his/her right to intervene actively (e.g. by saying *please, let me ask you some questions*). This situation is limiting for the submissive partner who sees his/her freedom to manage the flow of conversation jeopardized. This also has an effect on the forms of cooperation established between interlocutors, since each participant might feel engaged to a differing degree in the general communicative task (see Linell 2009: 178), thus creating the conditions for a form of collaboration, based on static roles and not on dynamics as it is when speakers share the equal right to introduce new material into the discourse (Linell 2009: 179).

Therefore, the definition of reciprocity, of autonomy and of collaboration we are aiming at is determined by the situation and by the way participants interpret their roles during Teletandem sessions. These roles emerge during the conversation flow and reflect *external conditions*, such as the kind of task to be accomplished, and *internal conditions* such as individual factors (e.g. personality). In fact, the focus of the present study is to determine whether modifying certain external conditions, that is, topic choice made by the non - native speaker, leads to possible alternation in conversation management, giving both interlocutors the opportunity to use particular language structures, for example, information requests, or long turns.

The production of particular language forms is the condition which can develop language competence. It is well known that during communication, in order to be understood by his/her partner, learners test out hypotheses about target language rules and pay attention to meanings and to the form by which meanings are conveyed. This occurs clearly when an utterance (or a word in the utterance) is not understood by the interlocutor who signals non -comprehension by, for instance, requesting clarification, after which the primary speaker is forced to modify his/her preceeding output in order to make it comprehensible. This process applied to forms that characterize dominant behaviour in communication (e.g. asking for information, making long turns) might result in the learner's language development.

METHODOLOGY

In this section, research questions, data collection and analysis will be presented. The analytical framework will be discussed, relating the perspective adopted for this study to that of other research into dominance. The section will conclude with a discussion of the problems arising from data analysis in relation to each single dominance indicator (i.e. subsections 2.2.1, 2.2.2, 2.2.3).

Research questions and data collection

The study addresses issues related to language expertise (research question-RQ1) and content familiarity (RQ2) in Teletandem conversations. The research questions are:

RQ1: What is the role of the native speaker in conversations during exolingual communication for learning?

RQ2: What is the role of the L2 speaker when he/she has chosen the topic for conversation?

The data have been collected by video-recording via multimodal computer conversations practised by two female volunteer university students (informed consent has been obtained). One of them was an Italian native speaker (ITL1; age 29); the other was an English native speaker (ENGL1; age 22). The conversation was conducted via computer, using instant messaging and VoIP software (i.e. Skype). Their language proficiency in L2 ranged from upper-intermediate to advanced, as self-evaluated by the participants and confirmed in data. The data consists of three hours of recorded/transcribed computer-mediated conversations which constitute three different meetings, organized as follows:

- Meeting 1 (M1). During this meeting, during the first 30 minutes the language of conversation was Italian; in the second 30 minutes the language was English (M1ITENG). There was no previous topic choice, the conversation was free discussion for mutual introduction and for dealing with general subjects

- Meeting 2 (M2). During this meeting, the language of conversation was English (M2ENG). The topic was chosen by the Italian native speaker and agreed by the English native speaker partner via email. The topic was *travelling*;

- Meeting 3 (M3). During this meeting, the language of conversation was Italian (M3IT). The topic was selected by ENGL1 and agreed via email by ITL1. The topic was *rugby*, the sport practised by the English native speaker.

The analytical framework

The multidimensional analytical model adopted for the present study is based on previous research and aims to highlight the nature of Teletandem conversations. Hence, parameters for investigations will take into account the bi-focality of the communication process (i.e. focus on content and language of communication), emphasizing the role of interaction for language learning, and consequently the use of language forms as an opportunity for language practice and learning.

In previous studies, dominance in everyday conversation has been investigated in different contexts of use and has been measured in terms of the distribution of various communicative behaviours (e.g. fillers, turn length).

Much of this research consists of empirical investigations of communicative actions on the basis of gender factors. To cite just a few, Zimmerman and West (1975) and West and Zimmerman (1983) analysed the relationship between gender and language variation by looking at interruptions and overlaps. Fishman (1983: 405) examined "concrete conversational activity of couples in their homes from the perspective of the socially structured power relationship between males and females", by investigating the distribution of questions, statements, minimum responses, topic initiation. Gass and Varonis (1986), also aiming to highlight genre dominance in conversation in Japanese society, analysed the distribution of amount of talk, number of turns, questions and overlaps produced by male and female speakers when talking in ESL.

As regards native/non-native conversation, on which the present study focuses, Zuengler and Bent (1991) investigated the influence of content knowledge when participants had different expertise, by looking at the distribution of fillers, amount of talk, backchannels, interruptions, resisting interruptions and topic moves.

A fairly well-known attempt at defining the analytical framework of different social situations (e.g. ordinary conversations, radio call -in chat programmes, etc.) is the work by Linell and his associates (Linell and Gustavsson 1987; Linell et al. 1988; Linell 1990; Linell and Luckman 1991; Linell 2009) who propose a scheme of analysis based on the following dimensions of dominance: quantitative dominance, intended as the measure of words ut tered in a turn by each speaker and by the average turn length; topic (or semantic) dominance which is manifested by control of topics in the discussion, measurable for instance by the introduction of new content words, and interactional dominance. This last dimension deals with "patterns of asymmetry in terms of initiative-response (IR) structure" (Linell 1990: 158). Linell and his associates' model distinguishes 18 categories of turns, comprehending either an initiative (I) or a response (R) (Sinclair and Coulthard 1975), ordered on a six - point scale in relation to the strength each of them shows in structuring conversation. A strong move is an initiative such as a question which brings about new topics (Linell et al. 1988); in contrast, a weak move is a response which shows no tendency to develop the dialogue. The distinctive feature of the model proposed by Linell et al. (e.g. 1987, 1988) and Linell (1991, 2009) is the perspective of analysis which is not limited to local IR but attempts to capture interrelations between turns and macro-structure, i.e. topics and episodes, in order to highlight the co-construction dynamics of what he calls the "communicative project". This dialogical dimension of discourse supersedes the traditional Searlian speech act theory (Searle 1969), considered "monologist pragmatics". Linell et al.'s and Linell's interaction analysis is also a valuab le attempt to employ a quantitative analysis to capture differences among different social situations, ranging from symmetrical (e.g. peer to peer everyday conversations) to highly asymmetrical (e.g. court interviews) and to define differences between phases of the same social event.

Whereas the model proposed by Linell et al. and Linell aimed mostly at characterizing social situations, showing different interactional behaviours in symmetrical and asymmetrical contexts, for the purposes of the present stud y, it seems more appropriate to follow the analytical framework of Itakura (2001) which focuses on the description of a non-institutional context such as L1 and L2 conversations between Japanese male and female speakers, trying to capture differences in behaviour of each interlocutor. Like in Itakura (2001), the focus of the present study is just one social situation (which does not fall under the category of *asymmetrical*) and particularly the role assumed by each actor in relation to the conversation flow, including the role he/she plays in solving communication problems, which are particularly relevant in native/ non -native conversations. Instead of an ordinal scale ranging from strong to weak moves, the present analysis will be carried out by measuring behaviours pertaining to opposite extremities such as controlling and non-controlling moves. The former have an actual impact on the other speaker's contribution; In contrast, the latter do not determine modification in the discourse (e.g. a repair which is not followed by interlocutor's focus on form). Although this polar analytical measurement tends to bring about a less articulated description of the interaction structure, it nevertheless allows a comparison of different attitudes towards the conversation flow by two interlocutors who are sharing the same "communicative project" (see above).

The research design adopted is multidimensional and will measure conversational traits such as (see also Itakura 2001):
- sequential dominance, that is, the direction of interaction, resulting from the qualitative analysis and measurement of controlling topic moves (see also Fishman 1983; Linell 2009);
- participatory dominance, that is, the violation of the interlocutor's right to take part in the conversation, i.e. interruptions and overlap;
- the interaction space, that is, a quantitative measure of words and turns produced by each interlocutor.

In particular, for the purposes of this study, the average turn length was considered, since it also takes into account the distribution of turns among speakers, allowing a comparison of conversation structures during the three meetings.

For sequential and participatory dominance, data analysis highlighted qualitative themes which have then been quantified. Conversely, interaction dominance has been quantitatively measured. For sequential dominance the qualitative analysis consisted of identifying controlling moves and relating them as percentage to the total number of turns.

In order to compare data between meetings (in the first of which 30 min. were in Italian and 30 min. in English), both M2 and M3 have been divided into two events of 30 min. Thus, for the purposes of data analysis, six different events were considered (M1part1IT, M1part2ENG, M2part1ENG, M2part2ENG, M3part1IT, M3part2IT).

In the following subsections interactional traits considered for the purposes of this study will be described in more detail.

Sequential Dominance

The investigation of *sequential dominance* is based on the analysis of the relationship between moves in an exchange, the latter being a basic structure in which a topic develops. The analysis started from topic moves. A turn could contain one or more moves. Topic moves could be embedded into a response or follow a response. Therefore, a response plus a topic move (topic initiation or continuing move) was also possible. A response plus a topic move corresponds to two moves and two exchanges.

A topic move is considered controlling when it anticipates possible features of the following turn (Linell 2009: 179) and when it selects an appropriate response (Itakura 2001: 1865). Hence, the response which follows the initiation move must be a *complying action* which fulfils its illocutionary force. If an initiation move comes before a *non-complying initiation action* then it is considered *attempted control* (Itakura 2001: 1864).

In the analysis the bi-focal nature of Teletandem conversation was taken into account (see Section 1). Therefore together with initiations, having functions such as eliciting relevant information in relation to a topic, or introducing new material into the conversation (Tsui 1994) moves incorporated in metalingual sequences (e.g. negotiation of meaning) are also taken to constitute valid examples of *controlling moves*. For instance in example 1, the repetition request (*eh*) made by ENGL1, clearly linked to ITL1's strong initiative (*e:hm di piccola cilindrata tipo*), is considered a controlling move. Conversely, in Linell et al.'s (e.g. 1987, 1988) and Linell's (1991, 2009) model comprehension checks, requests for repetition, etc. are considered weak initiatives in relation to the following turn since they do not "introduce new material into the discourse" (Linell 2009: 179) and, furthermore, they do not provide the required response to the preceding turn. The before mentioned analytical perspective, if it can be appropriate for analysing and describing dominance in endolingual communication, does not seem to apply to exolingual communication in which the language competence gap between interlocutors makes metalingual exchanges an essential component of the communication process and, as regards Telatandem, of language development.

Ex.1- (M3_part1IT; 0:37:02.8- 0:37:35.1)

ENGL1:	wow è una passione molto differente ma mi piace a:hm e hai avuto il motorino vuol dire una motocicletta piccola sì
ITL1:	**e:hm di piccola cilindrata tipo**
ENGL1:	eh
ITL1:	piccola cilindrata
ENGL1:	mh
ITL1:	il motore è piccolo non so cilindrata va bene come
ENGL1:	eh sì e:hm è una parola tecnica no ((somebody is hitting on the key)) ma
ITL1:	che il motore è piccolo non ci vuole la patente come la vespa che l'hai vista in=
ENGL1:	=eh sì come una vespa no sì ah sì non è sì non è come qui negli stati uniti ci sono le harley davidsons sai ((laugh))[5]

Hence, indicators in the form of repetition requests (e.g. example 1 ENGL1: *eh*), are actually considered appropriate responses to an unclear utterance (see above), anticipating and projecting the metalingual focus of the subsequent contribution. For example, in example 1 ITL1 uses the expression *di piccola cilindrata tipo* which is probably unknown to ENGL1, thus this latter interlocutor replies by requesting a repetition and starts a new sequence whose focus is language. Thus, an utterance produced by the primary speaker, which is followed by indications of non-understanding, is a topic initiation move, the repetition request is both a response and a topic move with a metalingual focus that has consequences for the following turn.[6]

On the other hand, moves that have a focus on form but do not lead to a change in the behaviour of the next speaker are considered *non-controlling*. For example, in example 2 ENGL1 says *baking* thus recasting the incorrect English expression *cooking sweets*. The correct form by ENGL1 since it is not incorporated in ITL1's following turn – in fact the latter repeats *sweets* – is considered non-controlling, or specifically, *attempted control*.

Ex. 2 (M1_part2ENG; 0:54:03.0- 0:54:45.6)

ENGL1: I mean I've never really tried you know but I just don't have the patience I think I always like if I have to make food for myself I make like a salad or sandwich but I have never I never go fancy like I just don't I don't know but some day maybe [I'll take my time]

ITL1: [yes it is some] thing that since when I was really young I was always there you know watching my mother cooking and I was really curious then now that I live alone of course actually I'm not good in **cooking sweets**

ENGL1: ah ok **baking** [yeah]

ITL1: **[sweets]** I cannot do it really I don't know they don't work in my hands ((laugh))

Similarly, in example 3 ITL1 turn *no no* is coded as *non-controlling* since it has clear properties of response (i.e. pancakes is not the right word) but does not actually project any feature onto the following turn: *I mean I* said by ENGL1 which seems to be linked to the same speaker's preceding turn *e:hm I don't know pancake,* in both cases failing in the attempt to find, together with her partner, the right translation of *pan di spagna*. On the other hand, ITL1 shows her wish to avoid negotiation of meaning and continue the conversation by saying first *no no* and then *ok it doesn't matter,* then laughing at her partner's attempt to translate the word (i.e. *Spanish cake*), finally, by saying *anyway...*at the beginning of her long turn in which she avoids the use of the problematic word.

Ex. 3- (M1_part2ENG; 0:55:10.5- 0:55:48.4)

ITL1: yeah you know **I don't know in english how to say you know the cake in italian is pan di spagna** the soft cake that you have to fill with cream and so on to make

ENGL1: e:hm **I don't know pancake**

ITL1: no no

ENGL1: I mean I

ITL1: ok it doesn't matter

ENGL1: spanish cake

ITL1: **no no ((laughs))=**

ENGL1: =what about it=

ITL1: =anyway when I was trying to cook it it was a kind of stone because it was really crack ((gesture communicating something hard)) and they said wha-((laugh))

ENGL1: ((laughs))I think that not (XXX) happen

Furthermore, for their strictly interactional value, and for their shortage of initiative properties, also moves followed by listener responses (Clancy et al. 1996) such as backchannels (e.g. continuer, display of interest: ya ya ya, see example 9) and jointly constructed turns as forms of collaborative behaviour (example 4) and echo repetition (example 5) are coded as non-controlling. In example 4, ITL1 aims to complete her partner's preceding turn by saying *to miss me* which is an utterance that has no impact on the interlocutor's behaviour. Similarly, *al contrario* produced by ENGL1 does not anticipate any feature of the following turn.

Ex. 4 - (M1part2ENG; 0:41:56.7- 0:42:20)

ITL1: =yeah ((laughs)) but sometimes you know e:hm I think e:hm because I remember with my friend when she had to leave we were talking and she said but I will be sad as well and I told her no you won't because actually the people who will be sad is who remain at home ((laughs)) not the one who leaves ((laughs))
ENGL1: right because you feel like the emptiness whereas she's probably you know experiencing something new so **she doesn't have as much time to like you know**
ITL1: **to miss me ((laughter))**
ENGL1: ((laughter)) to (xx)
ITL1: yes but ok I I think that one day when my day will come and when I move I will see if it is the same or not ((laughs))
ENGL1: right

Ex. 5 (M3part2IT; 0:33:00-0:33:03)

ENGL1: sì bisogna avere un- una chitarra speciale no
ITL1: sì non tanto dover mettere le corde **al contrario**
ENGL1: **al contrario**[7]
ITL1: sì quindi ho provato a imparare a suonare la chitarra...

The application of a polar coding system that forced data interpretation according to a yes/no condition (i.e. a move could be counted as controlling or non-controlling) was problematic; limits in coding different turns were approached in a way that led to an underestimation of some characteristics of speech. There was some doubt, for instance, regarding the analysis of the proactive feature of closing turns of sequences such as a response in a greeting sequences, and forms of single or multiple acknowledgements of a preceding utterance (e.g. *right*, *ok*). Neither of these types of turns were shown to be particularly marked in defining the conditions for the next turn, hence they were classified as non-controlling action (see above), despite each of them actually leaving the interlocutor the opportunity to open a new discursive sequence.

In example 6, in the first greeting sequence the *hallo*, produced with a falling tone by ITL1, is a response to the primary locutor's initiative but it shows no real proactive features, setting primarily pragmatic conditions of relevance and leaving the interlocutor the possibility to open any type of sequence (see Linell 2009: 180). In fact, ENGL1 greets her interlocutor again. Conversely, *hallo* pronounced with a falling-rising tone, manifesting the speaker's surprise, would have had a stronger projection energy over the following action leading to an interpretation of this closing turn as a complying action (e.g. A: "Hallo"; B: "Hallo" -falling-rising tone-; A: "Long time no see").

Ex. 6 (0:00:33.8-0:00:41.1)

ENGL1: hallo

ITL1: **hallo** ((laugh))

ENGL1: hi

ITL1: hi Marta

Similarly, in sequences such as those in example 7, acknowledgements (single or multiple) are intended as an appropriate and relevant response to the preceding topic move but are not considered controlling in relation to the following turn since they only partially suggest what may follow.

Ex. 7 (M1_ENGL- 1.01.52.07-1.02.02.1)

ITL1: [uhm uhm] [[uhm]] =yes but languages are always useful also in the field you decide so it is perfect

ENGL1: **that's true**

ITL1: **ya**

ENGL1: **exactly**

ITL1: **it's so cool really**

Hence, although the analytical framework served the purposes of this study, it raised problems whose solutions have not proved entirely satisfactory.

Participatory dominance: overlaps and interruptions

"Interruption refers to simultaneous speech produced by a speaker who begins to speak in the middle of a current speaker's turn constructional component " (Itakura 2001: 1868). In contrast, "Overlap occurs when two speakers speak simultaneously at a turn transition relevance point where both speakers have the right to complete their respective utterances" (Itakura 2001: 1869). In the present study overlaps have been regarded as controlling when they lead to the primary speaker's withdrawal since, in this case, they violate his/her right to maintain and complete a turn. Therefore they function as interruptions. In example 8, there is an example of interruption leading to interlocutor withdrawal:

Ex. 8 (M1_part1IT- 0:13:18.6- 0:13:48.9)

ENGL1:: e:hm e che fai durante l'estate [dopo aver f-]

ITL1: [l'estate] finito tutto allora di solito torno a casa dalla mia famiglia che comunque taranto è proprio vicino al- è sul mare come città è carina di visitare sì sì e quindi di solito l'estate vado al mare non tanto perché come puoi vedere la pelle è troppo bianca mi scotto ((laugh)) il sole non lo sopporto più di tanto però vado al mare oppure quando ho potuto ho viaggiato8

Interaction space: quantitative dominance

Both spoken and written words are measured as components of interaction space. This dominance dimension was quite easy to consider since the transcription of Teletandem conversations annotated spoken words as well as chat texts. The average turn length was considered instead of the distribution of the number of words (like in Itakura 2001) since the former preserved the information about the distribution of turns, allowing observations to be made about the discourse variation in different meetings (see Section 3.1). [9]

RESULTS

In section 3, some general characteristics of the Teletandem exchanges between ITL1 and ENGL1 will be presented, focusing on the type of relationship that the experience allowed them to build. We will proceed to some considerations about communication strategies used by the partners (e.g. chat), after which data regarding every single conversational trait will be shown and discussed. The relationship among different analytical measures will be discussed and finally research questions will be answered.

General characteristics

In general, in most parts of the conversations subjects were engaged in talking. They appear to enjoy talking (e.g. they very often laugh) and they discuss common interests. The relationship grows during the three meetings so that during the third meeting they decide they will keep in touch even after the end of what they have called "the project", that is, data collection for this research. In contrast to what emerged in a study carried out with subjects with low - intermediate competence in L2 (Leone 2012), chat was rarely employed for communication. In fact, the need for using written texts seems to be more relevant when the language for the dialogue is not well known by one of the participants. In this situation, the graphic form of a word allows the low - competence non-native speaker" to look at the new word or utterance", keeping the small language sequence away from the voice and from" difficult pronunciation", sometimes hard to grasp (Leone 2009b).

Although speakers respect the "rule of talking in one language" (e.g. English for the second meeting), code-switching is often employed for facilitating communication (Anderson & Banelli 2005: 90-106; Leone 2012).

A shortage of metalingual talk shows "interlocutors' efforts" to avoid "troubles" (see example 4; Aston 1986). Although M2 and M3 develop around a topic, there are digressions from this main topic.

Sequential Dominance, Participatory Dominance and Interaction Space

As shown in Figure 1, in 5 events out of 6 the English native speaker produces more topic moves than her partner. Particularly, in M1, in the first 30 minutes, during which Italian is the vehicle language, the English native speaker produces more controlling topic moves than the Italian native speaker, whereas in the second event, during which English was the language for conversation, ITL1 makes re initiation moves. The gap between figures representing ENGL1's and her partner's behaviour in relation to this variable grows in the first event of the second meeting and in the third meeting.

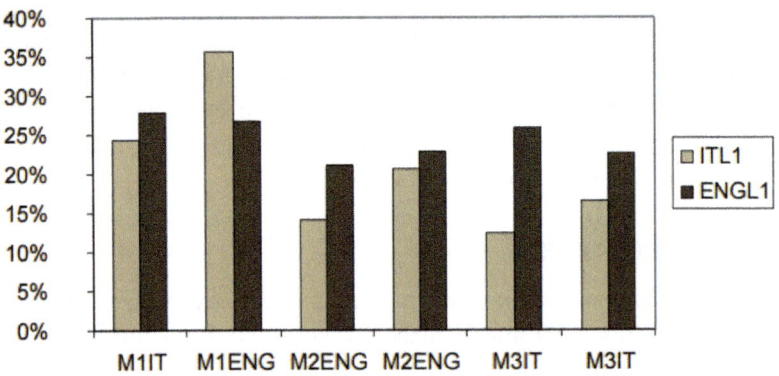

Figure 1: Percentage of controlling topic moves in relation to the total number of turns. Data are related to 3 Meetings lasting 1 hour each. Each meeting is divided into 2 events of 30 min. M1/2/3 indicate Meeting 1, 2 and 3. IT is the abbreviation for Italian, ENG for English.

Figure 2 and Tables 1–6 report data for interaction space. In particular, it represents the variation of the average turn length during the three meetings. As for measuring other dimensions, each meeting (1 hour) has been divided into 2 events of 30 min. The 6 tables show the number of words spoken and written in chat, the number of turns and the average turn length produced by each interlocutor during each meeting.

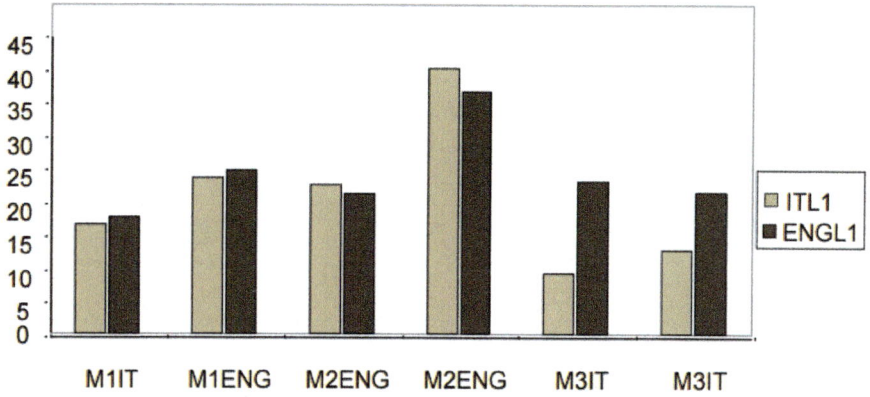

Figure 2: Average turn length (spoken and written words). Data are related to three meetings lasting 1 hour each. Each meeting is divided into 2 events of 30 min. M1/2/3 indicate Meeting 1, 2 and 3. IT is the abbreviation for Italian, ENG for English.

In M1 (Table 1 and 2) and in M2 (Table 3 and 4), there is not strong evidence of asymmetries between the average turn length produced by each interlocutor. Particularly, in M1 (Table 1 and 2, Figure 2), the ENGL1 talks longer. In M2 (Table 3 and 4, Figure 2), it is the ITL1 who "occupies a larger interaction space". On the other hand, asymmetries in turn length are very evident in M3 (Table 5 and 6, Figure 2), during which Italian is the vehicle language. The English native speaker talks longer in both events (M3part1IT and M3part2IT), and produces fewer turns than her interlocutor (114 in relation to 144 of her interlocutor); therefore the average turn length of her talk is higher than that of her partner.

Figures reported in Tables 1–6 show also that the second half of M2 (M2part2ENG; lasting 30 min., Table 4, Figure 2) has the greatest average turn length, having a number of words comparable to those of the other events but a number of turns inferior to others (less than 100). During this meeting English was employed for discussing travelling. After the first 30 min. of conversati on the two interlocutors became very involved in this topic, which allowed them to describe and discuss their personal experiences of visiting different countries and getting acquainted with people from different cultures.

Table 1: Number of words spoken and written in chat during Meeting 1, first 30 min. Vehicle language is Italian, free discussion (M1part1IT).

Speaker	Tokens	Turns	Average turn length
ITL1	2,212	130	17,02
ENGL1	2,345	130	18,04

Table 2: Number of words spoken and written in chat during Meeting 1, last 30 min. Vehicle language is Italian, free discussion (M1part2ENG).

Speaker	Tokens	Turns	Average turn length
ITL1	2,448	102	24
ENGL1	2,575	103	25

Table 3: Number of words spoken and written in chat during Meeting 2, first 30 min. Vehicle language is English, topic choice is "travelling" (M2part1ENG).

Speaker	Tokens	Turns	Average turn length
ITL1	2,532	111	22,81
ENGL1	2,484	115	21,6

Table 4: Number of words spoken and written in chat during Meeting 2, last 30 min. Vehicle language is English, topic choice is "travelling" (M2part2ENG).

Speaker	Tokens	Turns	Average turn length
ITL1	2913	72	40,46
ENGL1	2686	73	36,79

Table 5: Number of words spoken and written in chat during the Teletandem Meeting 3, first 30 min. Vehicle language is Italian, topic choice is "rugby" (M3part1IT).

Speaker	Tokens	Turns	Average turn length
ITL1	1,382	144	9,6
ENGL1	2,662	114	23,35

Table 6: Number of words spoken and written in chat during the Teletandem Meeting 3, last 30 min. Vehicle language is Italian, topic choice is "rugby" (M3part2IT).

Speaker	Tokens	Turns	Average turn length
ITL1	1,534	116	13,22
ENGL1	2,511	115	21,83

Violation of the interlocutor's rights to finish a discourse, by interrupting her talk, is the other measure considered for this study (participatory dominance). Data are reported in Table 7.

Table 7: Interruptions.

Speaker	Meeting 1	Meeting 2	Meeting 3
ITL1		3	3
ENGL1			2

As we can see, there are few interruptions during the course of the 3 meetings. In M1 there are none at all. This is probably because at the beginning of the experiment, the subjects are not acquainted with one another, and therefore turn-taking rules seem to be respected as form of politeness by each of them. In M2, ITL1 interrupts 3 times, and during M3 she is also responsible for 3 interruptions, her interlocutor 2.

As underlined by Itakura (2001: 1870), interruptions and overlaps as measures of participatory dominance are "likely to be a less significant indicator of conversational dominance than sequential dominance" in face-to-face communication, since they have a low frequency in data. Interruptions and overlaps become even less significant in computer-mediated communication since the use of technological apparatus further reduces the possibility of violating turn-taking rules.

Before answering the research questions, a discussion of the relationship between the different measures adopted for the analysis is inevitable. This implies highlighting their consistency which is verified when one speaker appears to be dominant according to two or more indicators. As already said, considering the low frequency of interruptions in our data, this indicator will not be considered; sequential and quantitative dominance will constitute our sole focus.

Consistency between Different Considered Measures

A comparison of data in Figures 1 and 2 show that in 3 events out of 6 there is consistency between percentage of topic moves and average turn length. This applies to the first event of M1 and during M3 when ENGL1 acts as dominant during a conversation in Italian. Conversely, during part 2 of M1, the Italian native speaker produces a noticeably higher number of topic moves (Figure 1) whereas the average turn length (Figure 2) is nearly equal to her interlocutor's. In M2, ENGL1 makes more topic moves but speaks less than her interlocutor.

Inconsistency between sequential and quantitative dominance has been observed in Gass and Varonis (1986), Linell et al. (1988) and partially in Itakura (2001). In this last study the author points out that "Inconsistency between sequential and quantitative dominance is observed when one speaker controls the development of the topic of conversation via short initiations that prospect longer responses" (Itakura 2001: 1872). This can happen in situations in which one of the speakers, recognizing the interlocutor as expert, makes many questions to which the other replies in long turns (Linell et al. 1988). This pattern is very typical of doctor-patient interaction and it is as well common in classrooms when the teacher tests student's knowledge by asking him/her questions. Example 9 from M2 is an example of this type of inconsistency: in this extract ITL1 produces a topic move (20 words) which is followed by a long response (149 words) after two turns: one displaying interest (*ya ya ya*, non-complying action, see Section 2.1.1), the other being unclear speech (ITL1: [(xxx)])

Ex. 9 (M2ENG: 12.40.8-14.08.5)

ITL1: yeah but actually I like this kind of let's say maybe exotic culture i don't know how to name there

ENGL1: yeah yeah yeah ITL1: [(xxx)]

ENGL1: **[well]** that's interesting 'cause I'm- I say - I think I would like too but and so now I've started only to pretty much like very european like developed like third world countries even you know I went to brazil and that was already that was a big big change for me like I- my travels have been you know portugal italy france spain you know the uk germany like I have done europe but I've not really gone outside those you know the european context even like when I was in south america there is one of my friend in argentina which it's so european and I liked it there because it was familiar to me like it was - it wasn't different but I've always said I'd love maybe go to egypt and india but I don't know if it would be a big shock like it's [it's]

Conversely, in M3 the relationship between sequential and quantitative dominance is consistent: ENGL1 produces long topic moves to which ITL1 makes short responses, the latter leaving the floor to her partner. An example is given in an exchange via chat at the beginning of Meeting 3 (example 10).

Ex. 10 (M3part1-00.00.00-00.00.54)

ENGL1: (chat: ciaooo il mio computer ha un problema con il suono aspetta un minuto)

ITL1: (chat: certo)[10]

Discussion

In the following subsections research questions regarding the impact of language and content expertise on the role assumed by each speaker in conversation will be answered.

Language competence and dominance

This analysis suggests no tendency for the native to be more active in conversations (RQ1). In fact, ITL1 does not produce either more topic moves or longer turns than her partner during the first event of M1 or in M3, whose language of conversation is Italian. Similarly, ENGL1 does not prove to be more active in relation to these two conversational behaviours either during the second event of M1 or in M2 in which the target language is English. These results suggest conclusions not exactly in line with what is stated in Kasper (2004), which analyzes sequences of "conversation for learning" (*Gesprächsrunde*) between a novice and a native speaker of German. In this study, Kasper observes that the German L1 speaker assumes the role of interaction manager who initiates sequences, asks questions, ratifies the answers, introduces and elaborates topics, and keeps the interaction going. German language expertise is invoked by the non-native speaker when communication is difficult. For instance by code-switching in her first language (English), she presents her problems in producing the utterance in the language of conversation (German) and indirectly asks the interlocutor for help. Metalingual exchanges, which occur together with ordinary conversation sequences – during which participants act as acquaintances – put the German language expert in the position of "interactional pivot" (Hauser 2003: 19; Kasper 2004), that is, s/he manages conversation. The difference in perspectives on data analysis between the present study and that of Kasper, along with the involvement here of more competent L2 speakers than those involved in Kasper's study, calls for caution in comparing the results of the two investigations. The microanalysis of metalingual sequences carried out by Kasper finds evidence of the active role of the native speaker in those specific events. Probably, a closer look at metalingual exchanges would highlight the role of dominance of the native speaker also in the Teletandem conversations analysed for the present study. As regards the participants' language competence, the relative ease with which ENGL1 and

ITL1 interact might have reduced the impact of language expertise on the overall conversation structure.

Content familiarity and dominance

Findings reveal participation patterns which only in M3 can be explained by the influence of content choice (RQ2). In fact, in the last meeting, in which Italian is the vehicle language and the chosen conversation topic is rugby, the non-native speaker exhibits dominant behaviour according to the considered indicators. Probably, the selected theme – ENGL1 is a relative expert in rugby not only because she loves it but also because she practises it – gave the English native speaker the opportunity for making long turns and for introducing new material in controlling topic moves. This condition, that is, the degree of expert knowledge in a content domain, seems to be close to that of the study by Zuengler and Bent (1991) in which content expertise and not familiarity was tested. Figures related to event 1 of M1 (Figure 1 and 2), where consistency between sequential and interaction dominance is shown and once again ENGL1 has a more active role, lead us to assume that the English native speaker probably has a personal orientation to the event as a controller of the conversation flow. The condition of content choice thus enhances the personal attitude that has emerged during free conversation. Conversely, in M2, which was in English, the Italian native speaker who chose the topic "travelling", produces (but not consistently) longer turns than her interlocutor but fewer topic moves (inconsistency between these two indicators is discussed above).

Thus showing ENGL1's orientation to get the L2 speaker to talk, giving her the opportunity to practice the target language.

CONCLUSION

This study analyses dominance in multimodal computer-mediated communication, in which two speakers of different L1 are involved and alternatively use their L2, the latter being the native language of the interlocutor. The research design aimed to shed light on those behaviours that might be salient for language learning. So patterns such as eliciting information, requests, forms of negotiation of meaning together with the possibility of elaborating a long discourse and the opportunity to finish a discourse, by not being interrupted, were considered relevant for this purpose.

Hence, the following conversational indicators were considered: sequential dominance, which consisted in identifying and counting topic moves; interaction dominance, that is, the average turn length and interruptions. For analysing topic moves a polar system, which distinguished controlling non - controlling acts, was applied. For measuring interaction dominance words said and written in chat were considered. The third indicator, interruptions, did not prove to be significant in the context under discussion due to their low frequency. It is probable that the use of the computer for communication reduces the possibility of violating turn-taking rules and creates the external condition for a "polite turn alternation".

The two different forms of expertise, language competence and content knowledge, considered for the present study, proved to have different impacts on the conversation structure. As regards language competence, data showed no tendency by the native speaker to control the conversation flow. In fact, neither ENGL1 nor ITL1 is dominant during events in which the language of conversation is English and Italian, respectively. As regards content domain familiarity, it seems to have an effect when the topic knowledge becomes expertise as it is in M3, when ENGL1 produces more topic moves and longer turns than her partner, confirming and enhancing an attitude she showed during the first event of M1 which was in her L2 (i.e. Italian). For other events interlocutors' participation seems to be balanced.

As far as the analytical framework is concerned, we can say that consistency between sequential dominance and average turn length demonstrates the participants' dominant and submissive behaviours (i.e. M3). Whereas, inconsistency becomes relevant for describing conversational structures when the gap between the two indicators in the same interlocutor is wide thus showing conversation patterns similar to those of an institutional asymmetrical contexts (e.g. teacher-student interaction in classroom).

The simplified framework adopted for describing sequential dominance, that is, a polar coding system, did not allow a consideration of different degrees of strength of topic moves, leading to an underestimation of the proactive feature of turns that concluded sequences such as unmarked last turn of greetings.

The small group of subjects and consequently the absence of statistical data suggest that caution is required in considering these findings, and generalizations should be avoided. Therefore the tendency shown in this study needs further investigation, particularly:

- all indicators must be further investigated with a larger group of subjects;
- a statistical analysis must be carried out (e.g. variance to define probability distribution, *t*-distribution for assessing the statistical significance of the difference between two means such as those of average turn length);
- metalingual exchanges require further investigation.

Qualitative and quantitative analysis of controlling moves (e.g. clarification request, confirmation check) which are part of negotiation of meaning processes will be considered separately from other indicators of sequential dominance to establish whether there is any consistency between the leader role of one speaker in topic development and in attempting to resolve communication trouble (or the speaker who leads the conversation flow in terms of topic development is the same who tries to resolve communication troubles).

REFERENCES

1. Anderson, L. & D. Banelli 2005. La commutazione di codice negli incontri Tandem. In G. Banti, A. Marra & E. Vineis (eds.), *Atti del 4° Congresso di Studi dell'Associazione Italiana di*
2. *Linguistica Applicata*. Perugia: Guerra Editore, 89–110.
3. Apfelbaum, B. 1993. *Erzählen im Tandem. Sprachlernaktivitäten und die Konstruktion eines Diskursmusters in der Fremdsprache (Zielsprachen: Französisch und Deutsch)*. Tübingen: Narr.
4. Aston, G. 1986. Trouble-shooting in interaction with learners: The more the merrier? *Applied Linguistics*, 7 (2), 128–143.
5. Bange, P. 1992. A propos de la communication et de l'apprendissage en L2, notamment dans le forme institutionnelles. *Aile*, 1, 53–55.
6. Brammerts, H. 2003. Autonomous language learning in tandem: The development of a concept. In T. Lewis & L. Walker (eds.), *Autonomous language learning in tandem*. Sheffield: Academy Electronic Publications, 27–36.
7. Clancy, P. M., S. A. Thompson, R. Suzuki & H. Tao 1996. The conversational use of reactive tokens in English, Japanese, and Mandarin. *Journal of Pragmatics*, 26, 355–387.
8. Fishman, P. M. 1983. Interaction: The work women do. In B. Thorne, C. Kramarae & N. Henly (eds.), *Language, gender and society*. Cambridge, MA: Newbury House, 89–101.

9. Gass, S. 1997. *Input, interaction and the second language learner.* Mahwah, NJ: Lawrence Erlbaum. Gass, S. & E. Varonis 1986. Sex differences in non-native speaker-non-native speaker interaction. *Studies in Second Language Acquisition*, 7, 37– 57.

10. Hakulinen, A. 2009. Conversation types. In S. D'hondt, J.- O. Östman & J. Verschueren (eds.),

11. *The pragmatics of interaction*. Amsterdam: John Benjamin, 55–65.

12. Hauser, E. 2003. "Corrective recasts" and other-correction of language form in interaction among native and nonnative speakers of English. Unpublished doctoral dissertation, University of Hawai'i. [Retrieved December 12, 2012]. Available at URL http://scholarspace.manoa.hawaii.edu/handle/10125/6893.

13. Itakura, H. 2001. Describing conversational dominance. *Journal of Pragmatics*, 33 (12), 1859-1880. Kasper, G. 2004. Participant orientations in German conversation-for-learning. *The Modern*

14. *Language Journal*, 88 (4), 551–567.

15. Leone, P. 2009a. Comunicazione mediata dal computer e apprendimento linguistico: gli incontri Teletandem. *Studi di Glottodidattica*, 3 (1), 90–106. [Retrieved December 12, 2012]. Available at URL http://ojs.cimedoc.uniba.it/index.php/glottodidattica/article/view/77/71.

16. Leone, P. 2009b. Processi negoziali nel corso di scambi comunicativi mediati dal computer. In C. Consani, C. Furiassi, F. Guazzelli & C. Perta (eds.), *Oralità/scrittura. In memoria di Giorgio*

17. *Raimondo Cardona, Atti del IX Congresso Internazionale dell'Associazione Italiana di Linguistica Applicata (AItLA)*. Perugia: Guerra Edizioni, 389–412.

18. Leone, P. 2012. È questo che volevi dire? Parlante nativo e non nativo nei dialoghi Teletandem. *Itals*, 10 (28), 79 – 103.

19. Linell, P. 1990. The power of dialogue dynamics. In I. Markovà & K. Foppa (eds.), *The dynamics of dialogue*. Hemel Hempstead: Harvester Wheatsheaf, 147–177.

20. Linell, P. 2009. *Rethinking language, mind, and world dialogically. Interactional and contextual theories of human sense-making.* Charlotte, NC: Information Age Publishing.

21. Linell, P. & L. Gustavsson 1987. *Initiativ och respons. Om dialogens dynamik, dominans och koherens.* Studies in Communication 15. Linköping: Department of Communication Studies.

22. Linell, P., L. Gustavsson & P. Juvonen 1988. Interactional dominance in

dyadic communication: A presentation of Initiative–Response Analysis. *Linguistics*, 26, 415–442.

23. Linell, P. & T. Luckmann 1991. Asymmetries in dialogue: Some conceptual preliminaries. In I. Markovà & K. Foppa (eds.), *Asymmetries in dialogue*. Hemel Hempstead: Harvester Wheatsheaf, 1–20.

24. Orletti, F. 2000. *La conversazione diseguale. Potere e interazione*. Roma: Carocci.

25. Philips, S. 1972. Participant structures and communicative competence: Warm Springs children in community and classroom. In C. Cazden, D. Hymes & V. John (eds.), *Functions of language in the classroom*. New York: Teachers College Press.

26. Philips, S. 1983. *The invisible culture: Communication in classroom and community on the Warm Springs Indian Reservation*. New York: Longman.

27. Rost-Roth, M. 1995. Deutsch als Fremdsprache und Verständigungsprobleme in der interkulturellen Kommunikation. In N. Dittmar & M. Rost-Roth (eds.), *Deutsch als Zweit-und Fremdsprache. Perspektiven und Methoden einer akademischen Disziplin*. Berlin: Peter Lang, 245–270.

28. Rost-Roth, M. 1999. Formulierungshilfen und Fehlerkorrekturen als Erwerbspotentiale. Freie Konversationen im Gruppenunterricht und Tandem-Interaktionen. *Deutsch als Fremdsprache*, 3 (36), 160–165.

29. Scott, M. 2008. *WordSmith Tools*. Version 5. Liverpool: Lexical Analysis Software.

30. Sinclair, J. & M. Coulthard 1975. *Towards an analysis of discourse: The English used by teachers and pupils*. Oxford: Oxford University Press.

31. Telles, J. A. (ed.) 2009. *Teletandem. Um contexto virtual, autônomo e colaborativo para aprendizagem de línguas estrangeiras no século XXI*. Campinas/SP: Pontes Editores.

32. Telles, J. & M. L. Vassallo 2006. Foreign language learning in-tandem: Teletandem as an alternative proposal. *CALLT, The ESPecialist*, 25 (2), 1–24.

33. Woods, D. & C. Fassnacht 2010. *Transana v2.42*. Madison, WI: The Board of Regents of the University of Wisconsin System.

34. Tsui, A. 1994. *English conversation*. Oxford: Oxford University Press..

35. Varonis, E. & S. Gass 1985. Non-native/non-native conversations: A model for negotiation of meaning. *Applied Linguistics*, 6 (1), 71–90.

36. West, C. & D. H. Zimmerman 1983. Small insults: A study of interruptions in cross-sex conversations between unacquainted persons. In B. Thorne, C. Kramarae & N. Henley (eds.), *Language, gender and society*. Cambridge, MA: Newbury House, 102–117.
37. Zhou, L., J. K. Burgoon, D. Zhang & J. F. Nunamaker 2004. Language dominance in interpersonal deception in computer-mediated communication. *Computers in Behaviour*, 20, 381–402.
38. Zimmerman, D. & C. West. 1975. Sex roles, interruptions and silences in conversations. In B. Thorne & N. Henley (eds.), *Language and sex: Difference and dominance*. Rowley, MA: Newbury House, 105–129.
39. Zuengler, J. & B. Bent 1991. Relative knowledge of content domains, an influence on native non-native conversations. *Applied Linguistics*, 12, 397–415.

Chapter 13

INTERLANGUAGE SPEECH RECOGNITION BY COMPUTER: IMPLICATIONS FOR SLA AND COMPUTATIONAL MACHINES

Larry Selinker and Rita Mascia

Centre for Interlanguage Studies, Birkbeck College, University of London

ABSTRACT

During the last decade, there has been a rapid growth in research into speech recognition by computer (SRC). Computerised voice recognition systems have been developed which are being used for a variety of applications. However there remain a whole range of issues which have to be elucidated and investigated before SRC can be broadly useful including for language learning purposes. It is well documented that speaker variability caused by accent is one of these issues and one of the major hurdles in accurate speech recognition. Foreign speaker recognition is particularly problematic to program for reasons that our work is beginning to suggest. In this paper we describe and compare the SRC of an interlanguage speaker of Italian/English versus a native speaker of English, both with repetitive strain disorder (RSD) and thus highly motivated, using the same software, DragonDictate, from Dragon Systems. Cognitive processes such as language transfer, fossilization and communication strategies are examined in light of the research. We illustrate the possibility of using SRC in second language research with particular emphasis on phonology. In this paper we not only explain our views of the potentials of this new technology in facilitating second language acquisition research but go to a more general applied linguistics issue where we briefly discuss some implications for the design of speech recognition systems for interlanguage speakers. This focus, we believe, can help make applied linguistics a main stream discipline, thereby increasing the job space for applied linguistics graduates.

INTRODUCTION

As far as we know, this is the first paper on the topic of interlanguage speech recognition by computer.

In this paper we explore the potential of one new class of technology in facilitating second language acquisition research: speech recognition by computer. There are a range of issues in second language research that we feel can be elucidated by this technology and we discuss these. Computerised voice recognition systems have been developed which are being used for a variety of applications. In second language acquisition terms, speaker variability caused by accent is one of the major hurdles in accurate speech recognition and will be referred to throughout this paper, passim. Non-native interlanguage speaker recognition is particularly problematic to program for reasons that our work is beginning to suggest; there are computer science questions concerning hardware and software requirements to cope with interlanguage speech recognition by computer which we will discuss elsewhere (Mascia & Selinker, in preparation). In this paper we focus on the role of automated speech recognition in second language acquisition research. Specifically, we describe and compare speech recognition by computer of an interlanguage speaker of Italian-English versus a native speaker of English, both with repetitive strain disorder who are thus both highly motivated. Both use the same software and hardware. Here, we illustrate the possibility of using speech recognition by computer in second language research with particular emphasis on phonology.

Our plan of the paper is as follows: we begin by discussing in an introductory manner three interlanguage cognitive processes in ways that fit most neatly into our empirical study; then we describe for the non-initiated, some principles underlying speech recognition technology. Next we present an empirical study which attempts to move speech recognition by computer into the interlanguage area and end the paper by discussing how this technology can be related to second language acquisition research and, importantly, possible implications for the design of speech recognition systems for interlanguage speakers.

THREE INTERLANGUAGE COGNITIVE PROCESSES

Language Transfer

Language transfer is one of the first and defining concepts of applied linguistics and second language acquisition. One only has to look at the early work of Weinreich (1953) and Lado (1957) to see it as a robust concept even in the 1950's. In fact, Rediscovering Interlanguage by Selinker in 1992 (referred to as RI in what follows) was in essence an attempt to show the historical foundation of that concept and others in interlanguage studies. To put things in perspective one of the earliest references discussed there is over 100 (!) years old (Whitney, 1881). To say that language transfer can be discussed in many ways is an understatement, to say the least. One popular definition of language transfer is from Random House Dictionary:

"Ling. the application of native language rules in attempted performance in a second language, in some cases resulting in deviations from target-language norms and in other cases facilitating second-language acquisition." (2009)

But this definition leaves out a host of effects that there is evidence in the literature for: transfer from a second to a third language called interlanguage transfer (see e.g. De Angelis, forthcoming), transfer back into the native language from an interlanguage, avoidance of a target language (TL) structure due to native language constraints and so on. (see Gass & Selinker, 1994, chapters 3 & 4; and forthcoming). Thus we think that a more useful way to conceive of language transfer is:

"Language transfer is best thought of as a cover term for a whole class of behaviors, processes and constraints, each of which has do with CLI (cross-linguistic influence), i.e. the influence and use of prior linguistic knowledge, usually but not exclusively native language (NL) knowledge." (Selinker, 1992: 208).

In that light, we think that for the purposes of this paper, we think it is useful to provide ten principles of language transfer that we think have justification from the research literature:

1. Transfer as a 'selection process' (Weinreich, 1953; chapters 2, 7 in RI).

2. Interlingual identifications as the basic learning strategy, where you 'make the same what cannot be the same' (ibid.)

"For example, /p/ in Russian (R/p/) is defined among others, by its' distinctive feature of non-palatality (in opposition to R /p'/, while the definition of English /p/ (E/p/) involves no such restriction. From the point of view of the languages, therefore, R/p/ and E/p/ cannot be 'the same." (Weinreich, 1953: 7)

In the next language, you look for what you have in your native language (Corder, 1983; chapter 6 in RI).

Perception and production have to be looked at differentially, at least in some transfer cases (Nemser, 1961; Briere, 1966; chapter 7 in RI).

'Blends' and 'autonomous material' are to be expected in interlanguage. (ibid).

Structural models, such as Lado (1957) emphasize 'holes' in the interlanguage, the learner using translation then as a learning strategy, seen clearly in interlanguage morphology (Harris, 1954).

'Transfer to somewhere' (Andersen, 1983, 1989; chapter 7 in RI) is often a necessary principle in language transfer (though 'transfer to nowhere' may also exist (Kellerman, 1996), especially with typologically distant L1's (Han, pc). An example would be Wode's (1976) claim that the earliest German-English negator in English is 'no' (i.e. not transfer), but that 'German post-verbal position to the negator *nicht* transfers to English only after the learner has developed a set of English auxiliaries' (cf. Andersen, 1989).

Andersen relates this principle to the 'one-to-many' principle in interlanguage, where the learner uses one interlanguage form for two or more language functions (cf. also, Rutherford, 1987)

Prediction of individual (on-line?) transfer effects may not be possible, so the principle of 'transferability', i.e. probability of transfer, was created by Weinreich (1954: 36) (which he attributes to Haugen) and recreated independently by Kellerman (1977) in the area of polysemous idioms. Cf. Kellerman's 'break' example where

"[...] learners tend to avoid one-to-one correspondence between L1 and L2, where meanings were perceived as far from prototypical, even though this led them unwittingly to gratuitous error."

Kellerman relates this principle to another principle he calls "psychotypology", viz: typological closeness.

Underlying linguistic principles may be transferred, e.g. apparently, the underlying phonological principle of 'tonality' in Thai is transferred to Thai-English and is one key reason why Thai speakers are often unintelligible in English (Rudaravanija, 1985; chapter 4 in RI).

To create equivalence in the next language, use key linguistic variables, especially structural and translation correspondences (ibid, all of the above). But, even if complex, language transfer cannot be seen as an isolated variable in determining the shape of interlanguage in second language acquisition. We must get beyond the tendency to describe isolated variables in isolated studies and make the difficult and serious attempt to interrelate important and crucial second language acquisition variables, no matter how hard the effort. Transfer has been seen to be a central factor in whether or not an item fossilizes in interlanguage and the relationship between the two has been termed the Multiple Effects Principle (Selinker & Lakshmanan, 1992), which we will return to at the end of this paper.

Fossilization

As with language transfer, there is a large literature which discusses fossilization and there are many and often contradictory points of view. Again, Random House Dictionary helps us begin by defining 'fossilize' in the following way:

"Ling. (of a linguistic form, feature, rule, etc) to become permanently established in the interlanguage of a second-language learner in a form that is deviant from the target-language norm and that continues to appear in performance regardless of further exposure to the target language." (755)

One complication is that over the past decades, as further delineated in Selinker & Han (in press), fossilization has been discussed within two distinct traditions: developmental and ultimate attainment (cf. Rutherford, 1984). The former tradition encompasses a wide range of perspectives, but often emphasizes the sociolinguistic (Preston, 1989; Tarone, 1994); the latter, interestingly, analyses the problem almost exclusively in terms of one or another form of universal grammar. In the developmental tradition, we find the nub of the fossilization question to be: How do we as observers know that interlanguage development has ceased? In the ultimate attainment tradition the question is put slightly differently: How do we as observers know that the attainment to date is in fact ultimate and that final steady state grammar, if such a thing exists, and this point is crucial to interlanguage speech recognition by computer, has been reached? When the focus is on near-natives or those who seem to know the language very very well (Coppieters, 1987, Birdsong, 1992, White and Genesee, 1996), answering this question is particularly crucial.

In retrospect, it is clear that the earliest definitions of fossilization delineated five basic properties: first, fossilization is equivalent to cessation of development; second, fossilizable features pertain to each and every aspect of interlanguage, including phonetic, phonological, morphological, syntactic, semantic, lexical, discoursal and pragmatic features; third, fossilizable features are persistent and resistant; fourth, fossilization hits both adult L2 learners and child L2 learners; fifth, fossilizable features usually manifest themselves as backslidings in performance, with re-emergence of forms being a key indicative marker, again an important point in interlanguage speech recognition by computer.

We need to relate fossilization to input, the most appropriate perspective for our study below. According to Gass and Selinker (1994), fossilization results when new (correct) input fails to have an impact on the learner's grammar, in other words when, the correct input is not apperceived or it is not comprehended. So what happens when the machine fails to perceive the interlanguage speaker's attempt to interact with it? Given that language transfer and fossilization appear to be linked, it is important to emphasize that all speech recognition programs, as far as we know, are intended for native speakers with their basic lexicon native speaker based. Thus, we must also look to other variables that have been shown to have an influence on the formation of interlanguage and here we turn to communication strategies.

Communication Strategies

A third set of cognitive processes are usually termed communication strategies (CS). As Kasper and Kellerman (1997) put it:

"Identification of CS depends to a great extent on what one considers a CS to be, and in this respect, it matters very much whether one conceives of CS as intraindividual or interindividual events." (8)

Again, as can be seen, there are many ways to approach this area as well. We have found the Kasper and Kellerman book to be particularly helpful in both giving us prime sources that are often not easily accessible but also in intelligently pulling the various issues together.

According to Faerch and Kasper (1983), cited as a central source in Kasper and Kellerman (1997) communication strategies are "potentially conscious plans for solving what to an individual presents itself as a problem in reaching a particular communicative goal". For example, interlanguage speakers trying to communicate with an interlocutor may use a communication strategy such as paraphrasing if they do not know or cannot access a particular lexical item. Kasper and Kellerman (1997) argue that this definition fits within what they call "the intraindividual view", a view widely held by early researchers in the field, which saw communication strategies as underlying processes occurring individual mind and importantly which did not have to engage the interlocutor for resolution.

The opposing view has been termed "the interindividual view" with Tarone (1983) as one of its main proponents, again cited as a key source by Kasper and Kellerman (1997, 3). Tarone (1983) sees communication strategies as used by both the interlanguage speaker and the interlocutor in attempts to "[...] bridge the gap between the linguistic knowledge of the second-language learner, and the linguistic knowledge of the target language interlocutor in real communication situations". Requests for clarification and comprehension checks are two examples of interactional communication strategies, which "operate on input which is too far ahead of the learner's current interlanguage competence and size it down to what the learner can manage" (Kasper & Kellerman, 1997, p.5). According to Larsen Freeman and Long (1991), again cited as a key source in Kasper and Kellerman (1997) "[...] all CS are helpful for acquisition because they enable learners to keep the conversation going and thereby provide more possibilities for input". We think this is not the whole story.

Kinahan and Selinker (1997) in an online paper, http://alt.venus.co.uk/VL/AppLingBBK/DB/kinahan/, argue that researchers may have overlooked the possibility that "communication strategies could be used as a learning tool to reveal the gaps between a learner's interlanguage and the target language". The conclusion from their data is that the particular communication strategies used by the learner studied during a taped conversation with a native speaker of the target language which are then analysed afterwards by both the learner and the native speaker, that this combination of procedures could help identify some of the gaps to the learner in that particular learner's interlanguage with relation to a particular target. This understanding, we believe, could give the learner the opportunity to receive "target-like input tailored specifically to that particular learner's needs" (Kinahan & Selinker, 1997). In that paper, it is argued that this type of joint analysis conducted by the learner with the native-speaker interlocutor is likely to reveal gaps in the learner's interlanguage which the learner may not specifically know about and data is presented there to argue for that claim. According to Perkins (1985 as cited Kaplan, 1997), "ability to find problems can be as important an ability as ability to solve problems" in second language learning. Kinahan and Selinker (1997) also argue that "it may be for some learners that the bringing to their consciousness of mistakes or errors could be a learning strategy in itself". However, in other cases learners may need to apply learning strategies in order to integrate into their interlanguage target-like grammatical structures or lexical items identified through the analysis of their use of communication strategies.

To continue the argument, Kinahan (1999) further hypothesises that target-like grammatical structures and lexical items brought to a learner's consciousness in this way are more likely to be noticed by the learner and integrated into their interlanguage system than target-like grammatical structures or lexical items corresponding to errors or mistakes the learner may have made during production but which caused little or no difficulties during communication (whether for the learner or the interlocutor). Thus communication strategies are well-integrated into the second language acquisition research literature and, it can be hypothesized that some sort of strategy use will occur when interaction with voice recognition software occurs. We have to ask what types of communication and thus communication strategies are involved between the human and the computational machine in this application.

One interesting possibility, which we believe we have evidence for, is that the human interlanguage user can find themselves treating the computer as another human interlocutor. In this case, the communication strategies used can become a set of intraindividual and interindividual strategies while the human interlanguage user is trying to dictate a text. It is our hypothesis that the only communication strategy likely to lead to the software 'understanding' a statement, is to ensure that in any interactions with the software, each and every word is pronounced exactly the same way each time in order to promote voice recognition. Communication strategies in real life are based around face-to-face communication. Thus, the reader should note that these strategies when applied to human-computer interaction may be counterproductive. Communication strategies will thus most likely be of no help at all to the interlanguage user.

Before we can describe our study so that it makes sense to those new to this area of technology, we present some background underlying speech recognition technology.

Background to speech recognition technology

During the last decade, there has been a rapid growth in research into speech recognition by computer. Although speech recognition systems have been developed in different application areas, there are still some key aspects that need researching before these applications can truly become effective. First of all, why has been so difficult to program speech recognition by computer? It has taken many decades, after numerous false starts, to produce software that is commercially viable and this has only happened in the past few years. A second, related question is how do language engineers tackle this difficulty? To tackle questions such as these, we need to have some basic understanding of how speech recognition programs work.

Current speech recognition programs operate by converting signals into a sequence of short spectrum representations which are then analysed to identify the phonemes of the corresponding words. In brief, the speech recognizer necessitates three elements in order to perform its task: an acoustic model, a language model and a pronunciation archive. The majority of current systems are based on Hidden Markov Models, acoustic statistical models of speech data used to represent these signals. They are called hidden because the sequential model is unknown and therefore 'hidden'. These statistical models are created by training an extensive corpora of samples. Based on the three previous elements, an algorithm is then created to perform the decoding of the speech units. Doing this type of search/decoding is computationally expensive and this we believe is part of the problem for the inadequacy of current system in recognizing foreign speakers accurately.

We will now briefly illustrate current research performance in removing some of the limits affecting speech recognition which we will describe below. The speech recognition problem is how to produce a machine readable transcription of spoken input in a world of great linguistic variation. In effect, the essence of speech is given by a combination of elements from different sources (syntax, phonology/phonetics, semantics, discourse analysis and the lexicon). The main challenge faced by programmers who design automated speech recognition is the variability of these sources in producing the spoken signal. We can summarise relevant variables according to:

- speaker variation: cultural-geographical, accent/dialect; gender; physiological, where the speaker can be sad, nervous or sick, for example.

- style variation: formal versus casual; reading versus conversing; clear versus unintelligible; fast versus slow speech and the accompanying reductions and deletions.

- environmental conditions: for example, voice carried through a telephone channel as opposed to face to face speech; background noise versus quiet conditions.

In order to cope with these array of variables and many more, speech recognition by computer has to limit them in some manageable way with the goal of current studies being in fact to remove ambiguity caused by these factors entirely, if at all possible! Current applications attempt to do this:

- by limiting vocabulary size: from simple applications like speech recognition for English Second Language having a very limited active vocabulary of about 600-1000 words to more sophisticated applications like DragonDictate and ViaVoice whose vocabulary ranges between 30,000 and 120,000+ words when customised by the user.

- by limiting mode of spoken input:

    a. discrete speech recognition, requiring a slight pause in between words which makes the dictation a bit artificial and less resembling natural speech, but requiring less co-articulation.

    b. continuous speech recognition, allowing text to be inputted at more or less natural speed. This latter is important as continuous speech recognition from unscripted sources has been particularly difficult to program.

- by limiting the loudness factor, resorting to the use of microphones and head mounted microphones

- by limiting the speaker variable:

    a. from speaker-dependent applications where the system needs training in order to recognise the characteristics of a particular speaker; to speaker-independent applications where the system can be used by anyone.

    b. customising the application according to regional accent and dialect, e.g. American English versus British English.

    c. fluent versus non fluent, e.g. software of English Second Language customised for different levels of learners

    d. native versus non-native, the variable which we attempt to describe in this paper.

The good news is that some of these limitations are being removed little by little. However, given the way speech recognition works, and considering that interlanguages have much variation, and in this sense are 'unstable', by definition, speech recognition of foreign speakers is still far from reaching the same level of accuracy than that of native speakers. In the section below we will describe our study, trying to highlight the problems experienced by our interlanguage subject and the way the use of this technology has helped us to refine our understanding of the user behavior. We will also relate the findings of our study to current concerns in second language acquisition research.

THE STUDY

Subjects

The two subjects we compared are both chronic RSD sufferers, strongly motivated to learn how to use the dictation software. The first user is a native speaker of Italian and Sardinian, 37 year old female, a very advanced interlanguage speaker of Italian-English, who has lived in an English-speaking countries for many years and who works and lives daily in English. The second user is a native speaker of standard American English, a 60 year old male. Both are well-versed in computers and both hope to replace the mouse and the keyboard by using as much speech recognition software as they possibly can.

Materials

Although continuous speech recognition is a recent technological innovation, for our particular purpose (an application to be used by RSD sufferers) we chose discrete speech recognition as the best solution because it allows the speaker to control the PC and the software programs by voice commands virtually 'hands-free'. After a review of both discrete and continuous speech recognition programs we selected DragonDictate Classic Edition, from Dragon Systems, Inc. (hereafter referred to as DD).

"DragonDictate represents pronunciations as hidden Markov models that are built from the speech of a reference speaker according to phonemic spellingsand (this allows DragonDictate) to adapt quickly to the user's own speech." (Mandel, 1992, 246).

The first element for creating a speech recognizer is what is technically called a 'vocabulary' (i.e. a list of words which have to be recognized). The vocabulary contains the most frequently used words and from this corpus a language model is assembled. In theory, if someone wanted to train a speech recognizer, they would have to pronounce each word until the whole vocabulary was complete. This method is obviously impractical for large size vocabularies and it is with this hurdle in mind that the model of DD was engineered.

"DragonDictate's [...] acoustic processing is based on a three-level analysis of each word: the phoneme, the phoneme in context, and the phonetic element. Theoretically a single model of each phoneme, together with rules for coarticulation and contextual allophony, would allow recognition of any word conforming to the phonology of the language. In actuality we need many models; some we extract from speech, and from these we generate others. For each language, the speech is that of a reference speaker; once the product is built, the models adapt to the user's speech in the process of being used." (Mandel, 1992, 238).

Mandel explains the three-level analysis in detail. He mentions that phonemes in English constitute a total of 24 consonant, 3 resonants, and 17 vowels and that for each vowel there are 78 phonemes (due to different stress levels). Although phonemes can also be marked for appearing in syllable final, Mandel explains that the cost of computing that feature is too high and it is thus disregarded. The second analysis is based on the phoneme in context (PICs) which is "[...] an augmented triphone, comprising:

- the phoneme before the one being modelled, as context
- the phoneme being modelled
- the phoneme after the one being modelled, as context

- the degree of prepausal lengthening of each phoneme due to its position in the word." (Mandel, 1992, 239).

It is at this point that the reference speaker records a subset of the vocabulary (what needs to be recorded are all the PICs, not all the words). The third element for the analysis is the phonetic element (PELs), a steady state which phones may share. For example, the /t/s of the triphones /eÅtÅ/, /ÅtÅ/ and /Åta/ have very similar onsets (for a more detailed phonetic description of the triphones, see Mandel, 1992, 239).

The importance of PELs derives from the fact that it is impractical to code all the PICs for the 25,000 words that DragonDictate allows. To obviate to this inconvenient, acoustically similar onsets are implemented using PELs. The exemplar of pronunciation is then regarded as a Markov model of an acoustic event[4]: a stochastic mechanism that in recurrent periods would originate acoustic events. More precisely Mandel talks of a hidden Markov model (HMM) because, as he puts it,

"We know the output of the model, but not the model itself (therefore 'hidden'), and the speech recognizer's task is to reconstruct it. Thus, from our language model together with the prior context, and our set of acoustic word models together with the acoustic data of the word just spoken, we have derived an ordered list of words that the speaker could have meant, arranged from most to least probable. Building on this ordered list, the DragonDictate interface lets the user select the correct word with minimum effort. In the best case, where it is at the head of the list, he or she needs only dictate the next word in the text to confirm it." (Mandel, 1992, 240).

The key feature of SRC is the process of adaptation. The first time people use the system, they have to create their own voice-file, which initially is based on the reference speaker's model. At each successive use of the program, DD adapts to the pronunciation of the user. Bamberg and Mandel (1991) carried out some tests to check the effects of adaptation of DD used by different users and in different conditions. Their tests showed that, initially, recognition performance is not very accurate when the user is of a different sex from that of the reference speaker used to model the recognizer. However, the recognition improves if the software is initially used by someone of the same sex as the user, confirming that adaptation does take place.

DragonDictate Classic Edition (DD), like the majority of the other speech recognition packages, features an enrolment session that lasts for a couple of minutes. The purpose of the enrolment is to create an individual user file which records the main characteristics of the user's voice. The enrolment prompts the speaker to indicate the type of their voice (high pitch or low pitch), test the microphone, and adjust the microphone volume if necessary. Although the enrolment session is sufficient to enable one to proceed to use the application, there is an optional tutorial which lasts approximately 20 minutes and it's called Quick Training. This training enables DD to recognise the users' particular speech pattern and adapt to their pronunciation. The Quick Training is made of 4 modules: Correction Words (up to 65 words), Common Commands (up to 110 words), Dictation Words (up to 230 words), and Additional Words (up to 365 words). In each module the words appear in a dialogue box and the user is supposed to pronounce them following the machine's instructions (see next picture below). If a pronunciation is not correctly recognised, the machine invites the user to repeat the word several times until it is recognized. It achieves this by showing some dots underneath the misrecognized word, which is highlighted until the pronunciation is satisfactory.

DD continuously adapts to the user's pronunciation. This is particularly important when using the system in Dictation Mode. Since many types of word pronunciation are accepted, it is important to correct misrecognized words as they take place, as the software can only correct the previous 16 words.

Accordingly, when dictating text, it is not advisable to leave misrecognized words until the end and then do a spell check (which would probably be the norm in a conventional use of a word-processing package). By doing so the program tends to make more errors in successive uses, because of the process of adaptation. Finally at the end of a particular task, the program confirms with the user if they want to save their user file, and if the speaker decides to save the file, the program enriches the user's speech archive.

Once the users have mastered the basic use of DD, there are a number of options which can be explored to improve the system's voice adaptation. For instance, in the feature Vocabulary Manager there is an archive of dictation words which can be re-trained to achieve better accuracy.

PROCEDURES

We carried out the following tasks:

1. Videorecording of training sessions

This task consisted of an enrolment session during which the users had to complete the Create New User Wizard (as detailed in the previous section), run the tutorial by repeating 15 basic command words, follow the demonstrations of WordPad use, Calculator use and again WordPad use. The entire task took approximately 20 minutes. The tutorial showed the speaker how to run those applications by using the control commands (which control the main drop-down menus) and the dictate commands.

2. Videorecording of training session and Dictation Task 1

For this task, the users had to complete four Quick Training Modules (as detailed above). The training lasted approximately 25 minutes in total and was followed by a dictation test. The test consisted of reading the summary of a book chapter, summarise it and dictate the gist of the synopsis using Microsoft WordPad. During the test the users made full use of correction commands such as Word History and Spell Mode.

3. Audiorecording of Dictation Task 2a

This task required the subjects to dictate three paragraphs from a different book chapter, but this time without correcting any unrecognised words, without using any formatting or any control commands, and without checking any spelling. The word-processing package used was Microsoft WordPad as before. The idea behind this test was to have an approximate indication of the degree of accuracy of word recognition for the two speakers. The text was compared to the text of the other user, and to the original text.

4. Audiorecording of Dictation Task 2b

This task was a replica of the previous one after about four months had elapsed between the two dictations. Prior to this, the two subjects used DD on average 15 hours per week, working in their own environment carrying out their normal type of work. The ultimate goal of this recording was to discover how quickly the system adapted to the two speakers' pronounciation and to compare the two texts in order to discover if there were any significant systematic differences between the two users.

DESIGN AND ADMINISTRATION

This study was conceived of as a comparative case study of two people, an interlanguage speaker and a native speaker, interacting in a certain way with a computer. The speech corpus was collected as spontaneous speech, although some of the tasks administered required samples of elicited speech and the sessions were recorded[7]. But in general, we followed as naturalistic an approach as possible. To get the feel of the aims of the program, i.e. the more the program was used, the better it was supposed to adapt to the user, as much like ordinary work conditions were maintained. The two subjects of the study then used the program on their own and in their own time. The only intervention was represented by technical assistants who limited their interventions to setting up the equipment and giving basic training instructions. The subjects therefore experienced very similar situations as having to deal with difficulties entirely on their own. During the administration of the first three tasks, the two subjects were unaware of each other's progress. In order to ensure correct operational measures, the validity of the study was constructed using videorecording, audiorecording and recorded interviews.

RESULTS

Native speaker speech recognition

Table 1 shows the statistics from the Quick Training Modules:

Table 1: Native speaker recognition accuracy in Quick Training Modules.

Quick Training Modules	words dictated	words misrecognized	recognition accuracy
correction commands	46	6	86.9%
common commands	124	14	94.7%
dictation words	94	12	87.2%
other common command words	35	0	100%
additional words	43	8	81.3%
total number of words	342	40	88.3%
total % of recognition accuracy			88.3%

The results from Dictation Task 1 are shown in Table 2:

Table 2: Native speaker recognition accuracy in Dictation Task 1.

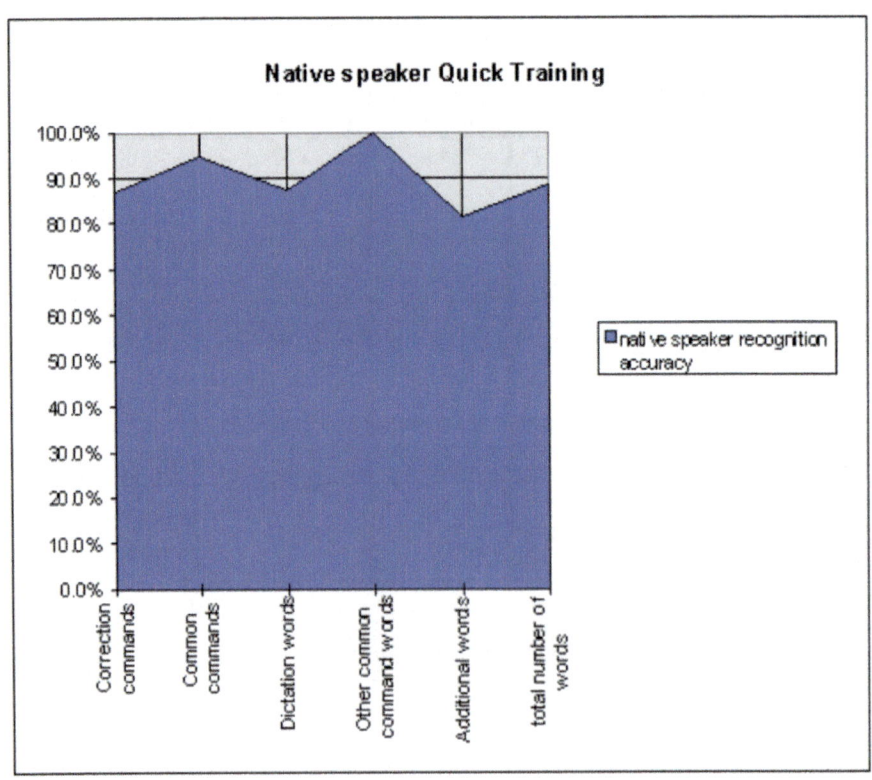

CHART NUMBER 1

	native speaker recognition accuracy
Correction commands	86.9%
Common commands	94.7%
Dictation words	87.2%
Other common commands	100.0%
Additional words	81.3%
total number of words	88.3%

Table 3: Native speaker recognition accuracy in Dictation Tasks 2a and 2b.

Dictation Task 1	words dictated	words recognized	recognition accuracy
command words	267	186	69.6%
command words + spelling words	295	214	72.5%
dictation words	256	71	27.70%
dictation words - spelling words	228	43	18.8%
command + dictation words	523	257	49.10%
total percentage of recognition accuracy			49.10%

INTERLANGUAGE SPEAKER SPEECH RECOGNITION

The results from the Quick Training Modules are shown in Table 4 below:

Table 4: Interlanguage speaker recognition accuracy in Quick Training Modules.

DICTATION TASK 2 a AND b	native speaker accuracy
dictation a	85.10%
dictation b	84.70%

Table 5 shows the results of Dictation Task 1 and Table 6 the results of Dictation tasks 2a and 2b.

Table 5: Interlanguage speaker recognition accuracy in Dictation Task 1.

Quick Training Modules	words dictated	words misrecognized	recognition percentage
correction commands	45	2	95.5%
common commands	122	14	88.5%
dictation words	134	12	91.0%
other common command words	24	6	75.0%
additional words	65	12	81.5%
total number of words	390	46	88.2%
total percentage of recognition accuracy			88.2%

Table 6: Interlanguage speaker recognition accuracy in Dictation Tasks 2a and 2b.

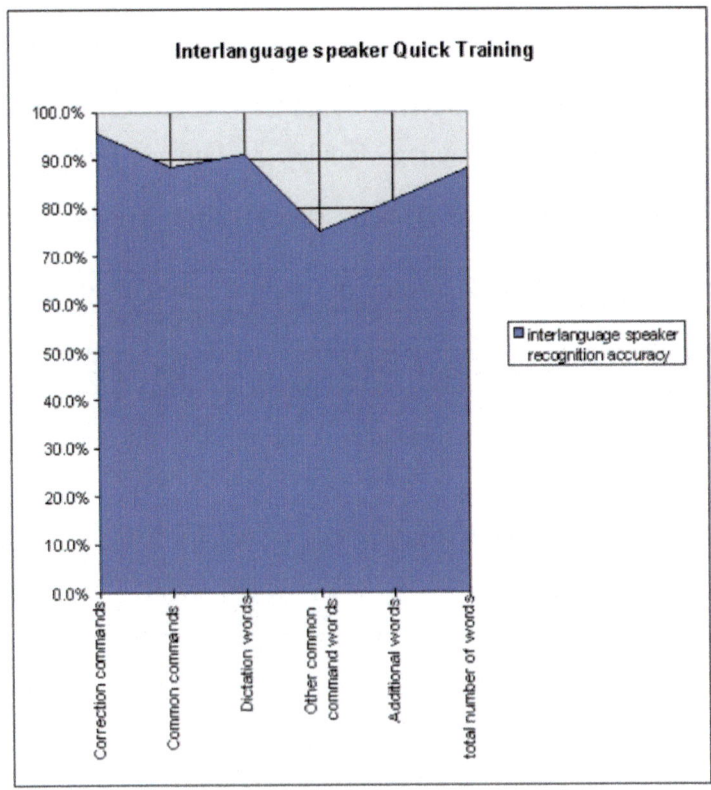

	interlanguage speaker recognition accuracy
Correction commands	95.5%
Common commands	88.5%
Dictation words	91.0%
Other common command words	75.0%
Additional words	81.5%
total number of words	88.2%

We now discuss the data, first focussing on a series of patterns we identified in this speaker's interlanguage (word numbers refer to the words listed in Appendix 2):

The first pattern: the interlanguage speaker sometimes had to 'guess' the target pronunciation. There were certain words which were unknown to the speaker for which the pronunciation was not obvious. This resulted in the interlanguage speaker relying on the Italian phonological system for filling in that gap (e.g. 1, the command word 'oops' which was pronounced as it had been an Italian word, or , 'begin document' /begin/ /dokument/ for the word 'begin' the user was unaware of the target language pronunciation for the vowel 'e' in the first syllable.

The second pattern: a wide-spread language transfer from the L1. For instance, the presence of cognates in the L1 resulted in transfer of phonological features (e.g. in #51, 'Diana' was pronounced once as /diana/ and once as /daiana/, the first word pronounced as if it was the Italian cognate word 'Diana'), including features such as stress (e.g. in 15, /ˈbravo/ /braˈvo/ where the user changed the syllable stress since the vowel sounds are the same as those in the Italian cognate word 'bravo'). A visual interference of the target word reminded the speaker of the L1 pronunciation (e.g. in 19, ˈequal signˈ/iˈkwol/ /saɪʲ/, the presence of /ʲ/ in 'sign' is another hypothesised instance of phonological transfer from the L1 where the two letters 'g' and 'n' when together are pronounced as above (/ʲ/).

The third pattern: several instances of apparently fossilized forms like the use of [d] instead of [ð] in 20 (greater than/greiter/ /den/) and the lack of aspiration in words containing [h] as in 26 (ˈhome keyˈ /oˈm/ /ki/. There were also some instances of backsliding to earlier interlanguage forms, for instance in 20, where the speaker backslided to earlier Italian/American English interlanguage forms where [r] would be pronounced at the end of a word.

The fourth pattern: a large amount phonological variation of a type often unexpected. Here we can only give a hint of this. One pattern obvious from the data is that the interlanguage seemed to alternate between production of target-like and non-target-like phonological features. An example of both target-like and non targetlike features is 4 (ˈDragonDictateˈ /dragondɪkteɪt/, the 'a' in 'Dragon' is pronounced as the Italian /a/ instead of the target English /æ/, while the 'a' in 'dictate' is pronounced as in target English [eI]). Other examples found were the variation of occurrence for schwa [□]which sometimes appeared especially in final position as in 5, /kompjuˈtə/ or 10, /kalkleɪtə/ , and sometimes was replaced by a final [r] as in 18, /oskar/. Likewise, we found free variation between the use of dark [ɫ] and clear [l] (e.g. 16, /deɫta/ and /delta/, and the use of [h], which sometimes was pronounced and sometimes was not (e.g. 26, home key /oˈm/ /ki/ /hoˈm/ /ki/).

The fifth pattern: the consistent use of various communication and learning strategies8 which characterised this speaker's interlanguage interaction with the machine and which resulted in different effects. For instance in 13 ('back space', /bak/ /speɪs/, /bak/ /speɪs/, /bek//speɪs/) the interlanguage user reported that she assumed that her pronunciation in the two first dictations was incorrect and tried to make it more target-like by changing the vowel sound in 'back' from /a/ to /e/. This looks like a type of hypothesis testing possibly due to the fact that the interlanguage speaker finds it difficult to distinguish between the different vowel sounds of the English phonological system9. Based on the same pattern, we also found instances of self-correction (e.g. in 21, 'alt key', /alt/ /ki//olt/ /ki/, where the interlanguage speaker assumed that the pronunciation was incorrect and as a strategy, she corrected herself). Hyper-correction was also reported (e.g. in 34, 'among' əmong/ and /əmon/, the first pronunciation had a [g] instead of [ŋ] and was not recognized, so in the second pronunciation the interlanguage speaker hypercorrected herself by eliminating the [g] all together). Overgeneralization took place in the form of the occurrence of phonological forms like in 16, 'delta' /delta//deɫta/ where in the second pronunciation of 'delta' there was an approximation of a velar /å/ and the interlanguage speaker overgeneralized the use of the dark [l] to this word, where there are only clear [l]s in Italian.

As a general observation, and not consistent enough to be categorised as patterns, the speaker tended to simplify the target language phonology (e.g. 24, 'enlarge 50%' /enlardʒ/ /fɪftɪ/ /per/ /sent/), lack discrimination between short and long vowels (e.g. 44, 'team' /tɪm/) and fail to produce diphthongs and triphthongs throughout.

The rate of accuracy for the native speaker was quite high compared to the interlanguage speaker as shown in Table 7 below. The interlanguage speaker showed a very low score on accuracy after the first and the second test (Dictation Tasks 2a and 2b, in Table 6 above), but there was a considerable improvement in performance. We tend to interpret this result as a consequence of the variability of the interlanguage system. Whilst the native speaker performance is relatively stable (hence the minimal variation after 4 months of use of the dictation software), the interlanguage speaker's performance is more subject to variation due to the instability of the interlanguage system. As a consequence of this variation, the accuracy of recognition tends to stay quite low on the whole, but improves considerably as a result of the interlanguage speaker's continuous learning.

The interlanguage speaker's metalinguistic awareness results in a pronunciation progressively closer to the target language as she interacts with the machine and becomes more careful especially in the pronunciation of those words which she perceives more difficult to articulate or those words for which she has had positive or negative feedback from native speakers. This might also explain why originally the results obtained for the first tasks (Quick Training Modules and Dictation Task 1) showed a better performance of the interlanguage speaker versus the native speaker. During the initial training, the interlanguage speaker was particularly conscious of her interlanguage phonology and therefore made the effort of pronouncing words carefully. However, during everyday use, she backslid to her normal pronunciation. This in turn resulted in the system adapting to her pronunciation in a much slower way than for the native speaker whose pronunciation did not change considerably from the original pronunciation of the training, except perhaps sometimes, due to performance effects such as casual articulation.

Table 7: Native vs. interlanguage speaker accuracy in Dictation Tasks 2a and 2b.

Dictation Task 1	words dictated	words recognized	recognition accuracy
command words	340	208	61.1%
command words + spelling words	394	262	66.4%
dictation words	206	109	52.9%
dictation words - spelling words	152	55	36.1%
command + dictation words	546	317	58.0%
total percentage of recognition accuracy			58%

Summarizing, the results of the two speakers' performances in the use of the speech recognition program were not significantly different during the accomplishment of the training and during the very first dictation (Dictation Task 1). In fact, at first, the results from the interlanguage speaker seemed to outrun those of the native speaker suggesting that there were no major differences. Subsequently, after the dictation of the first Trask's text (Dictation Task 2a), it became clear that there was a substantial contrast between the two, and that the adaptation for the interlanguage speaker was definitely slower, after four months, than the one for the native speaker. The accuracy of recognition seemed to particularly affect uncommon words (like 'glasnost' or 'rock'n'roll') and justifies the choice of using the Trask's chapter which included unusual words and many proper names. Finally the improved recognition of the interlanguage speaker could be a positive sign of the interlanguage system developing to incorporate more target language features, and this is an important aspect of language learning taking place. By contrast, the accuracy rate of the native speaker in the second dictation task (Dictation Task 2b) was more or less the same. The recognition percentage of the native speaker's dictation is high enough to justify the claim that the system adapts better, or perhaps faster, to the native speaker than to the interlanguage speaker, whose pronunciation is more unstable and requires more training.

CONCLUSIONS

In this paper we primarily explored the potential of one new class of technology – speech recognition by computer – in facilitating second language acquisition research. We would not be the first to claim the enormity of that potential, but what is new here is, as we said in the first paragraph of the paper is that as far as we know, this is the first paper on the topic of interlanguage speech recognition by computer, and, thus, importantly, there is no research literature to compare these exploratory results to. In the back of our minds, and we kept coming back to it in discussions with software people, was a secondary issue, a wider applied linguistics issue, the fit of speech recognition by computer, in principle, with interlanguage speakers, in bothe software and hardware terms, which we briefly discuss at the end of the paper.

What we hope is that we have shown some important detail leading to an extension of our usual research paradigms in SLA and interlanguage studies. We determined that there are a range of issues in second language research that can be elucidated by this technology and focussed on three central processes: language transfer, fossilization and communication strategies. We also referred in detail (passim) to the problem of speaker variability caused by accent, in both native and interlanguage speakers as being one of the major hurdles in accurate speech recognition. In the interlanguage area, as might be expected, variation is clearly greater than in the native speaker area. This is particularly important due to the fact – and its depth only became clear to us as a result of doing this research – that such recognition systems must have stability of pronunciation as input to the machine system. A consistent result for us in this case study is that the native speaker subject achieved this stabilization easier and faster than the interlanguage speaker, which has led us to the new concept of purposefully directed positive fossilization, where what we have here is a type of fossilization which could become a benefit, a topic which should be pursued in second language acquisition research.

It is generally accepted that language transfer is best thought of as a cover term for a whole class of behaviors, processes and constraints having to do with cross-linguistic influence (Selinker, 1992), in this case from several possible sources, the subject's native Sardinian, learned standard Italian and classroom French. In terms of the ten principles of language transfer listed above, in the one of the pronunciations produced, it is very clear that the principle 'transfer is a selection process' was shown here to be the case in that not all potential predictable instances of transfer occurred. The transfer principle of interlingual identifications where, the learner 'makes the same what cannot be the same' (see Weinreich, 1953), is also operative in our data in that equivalences were created across linguistic systems that were unexpected. Also, the transfer principle where 'blends and autonomous material' are to be expected in interlanguage, in the same manner held. Another thing that was clear is that the principle 'to create equivalence in the next language, use key linguistic variables' is operative in these data in that 'phonetic similarity' at times played a key role.

In the case of DD the interlanguage speaker is left with the option of testing new, and often untried, types of pronunciations until a satisfactory level is reached for the machine, if it is reached at all; as is shown in Appendix 2, in some cases, it is absolutely not reached at all. The implication of this testing, and we think it may be positive in terms of language learning, is that the interlanguage user may be forced to check her pronunciation against the phonological transcription of a dictionary or of a native speaker. This can become a successful strategy of 'communicating' with the computer if a pronunciation stability can be arrived at.

Also as a result of this work, we became aware that other ways to research second language acquisition begin to appear. Speech recognition by computer could be investigated as a device for investigating the improvement of pronunciation. What seems to be clear from our research is that the interlanguage user can become metalinguistically aware of a 'correct' pronunciation and, research could show if, in time, she be able to train the machine with a pronunciation very close to the target language, but care should be taken because backsliding can occur, as we have seen in our results. What is important is that in subsequent uses of the machine, the interlanguage speaker has to maintain the stability of that type of pronunciation and with the help of the native speaker/teacher check that she does indeed match the pronunciation originally recorded for the training.

We believe that the entire system could be made more suitable for pedagogical and research purposes if it were equipped with a speech synthesiser for then instances of misrecognition could be pointed out against a target language pronunciation model and then consulted by the learner at their request. These types of programs are already available[10] although their purposefulness often comes from feedback given on grammatical structure and not on phonology. One could research applications of this type which could be particularly useful for learning tonal languages like Chinese for instance. In this case the hypothesis would be that speech recognition by computer would enable the learner to check which tonally distinguished word-form has been recognized by the system.

One of the main theoretical implications of this study resides in the distinctive use of the recognition system by the interlanguage speaker. In this study, language transfer takes place extensively, but we think not necessarily in the same ways as it would occur in ordinary conversation. Language transfer, of some special, and perhaps, unknown kind, seems to be one of the major causes of poor machine recognition, though it appears to be mainly of the type that has been called 'negative transfer'. The reason for this is interesting: the interlanguage speaker, according to comments gained as retrospective data, consciously suppressed phonological transfer by trying to pronounce words in a target-like fashion, although in a normal conversation she would not have pronounced the same words that way. This is an example of a domain result in that we hypothesize that it would only occur in the software training domain.

But once the training task was over, transfer occurred mainly for those words which had cognates in the mother tongue. An implication of this phenomenon, which is peculiar to interlanguage speakers, is our conclusion that speech recognition by computer cannot function satisfactorily if the reference speaker model adopted is the same for native speakers and non-native speakers. If language transfer is a major interference to the speech recognition system, then we think that separate programs for interlanguage speakers may have to be developed which, among other things, will have to take into consideration issues like the presence of cognate words and their special linguistic and cognitive status. The serious computational problem is whether currently conceived hardware will suffice or whether new sorts and expensive sorts, of hardware will have to be envisioned. This is one place we feel sure that applied linguistics can help computer scientists and programmers understand issues of import to them.

One thing is clear to us from this research: dictation packages such as DD, in order to be successfully used by interlanguage speakers cannot afford to have a native English speaker as its reference model, the native speaker cannot have a priviledged place. Theoretically it would have to have an interlanguage speaker as the reference speaker, in this particular case, we think, an Italian speaker. Although objections can be made about the issue of which accent of Italian should be chosen for the modelling, the same can be said for the choice of the English accent (i.e. from which dialect of English should the reference speaker be chosen). In fact the choice of accent does not prevent the system from working fairly efficiently (albeit not wonderfully) for native speakers of

English and given that the model employed is a fuzzy model, that should allow interdialect variations.

In this scenario, the issue of fossilization takes on a new dimension. One effect of fossilization has to do with the user's need to interact efficiently with the machine and this appears to result in the interlanguage speaker actually becoming fossilized in the use of some forms for the purpose of being recognized. The interlanguage speaker commented that sometimes forms which she would not normally use, for instance /ð/, would appear in her interlanguage but as it was not recognized she pronounced it as she 'normally' would (i.e. /d/). Hence for instance the pronunciation of 'the' as [de] (as it was recorded initially) was becoming a candidate for fossilization because when the target language pronunciation [ðe] also appeared (as a result of linguistic variation), the machine would not recognize it, and the interlanguage speaker would revert to [de] in order to achieve better recognition. This is the case in which fossilization, in this context, can be seen as ‹positive› with regard to interacting with the computer.

The paradoxical aspect of the use of the speech recognition by computer is that it becomes an instrument for gaining greater linguistic awareness of target language pronunciations and noticing the gaps between interlanguage and target language, as discussed above. As a consequence apparently fossilized forms might become destabilized within the specific domain of human computer interaction. The interlanguage speaker might find herself constantly reminded of the interlanguage pronunciation and, unlike in normal human/ human communication where politeness plays a part in not pointing out a pronunciation deviant from the target language, the electronic medium which is oblivious of such pragmatic issues, draws attention to the error and functions as a very pedantic sort of teacher. The positive implication of this type of unsolicited feedback is that perhaps in the long term, this destabilization of apparently fossilized forms might extend to other domains outside the virtual environment.

As a consequence, there is a possibility that on the one hand, speech recognition by computer might reinforce interlanguage forms, stabilising or maybe even fossilizing interlanguage forms for reasons of efficiency of interaction with the adaptive recognition algorithm. On the other hand, speech recognition by computer might result in the interlanguage speaker becoming more aware of their interlanguage system, and as a positive consequence of that, the speaker might develop an interlanguage system closer to the target language. We need serious second language acquisition research of a new type related to our current technological age.

In this study we describe an aspect of human-computer interaction specifically comparing interlanguage speakers versus native speakers interacting with an electronic medium, in this case speech recognition by computer, to our knowledge a comparison not undertaken before and there is thus no literature available on it. This seems strange to us as there must be millions of non-native interlanguage users in a world where computers seem to have been built for California teen-agers.

The results here suggest that, although the ability of the machine to recognize interlanguage speakers, after 4 months was 65.6%, the degree of accuracy or the user friendliness of the program was illusory and far from being satisfactory. During the initial use of DD, for a successful recognition the speaker had to use as many command words (the majority of which were used for spelling and editing) as dictation words. This resulted in a tedious and frustrating experience. It could be argued that perhaps these disappointments are attributable to the design of the software and not, as suggested, by the non-nativeness of the user. However the results of the dictation tasks refute this conclusion given the considerable discrepancy in recognition between the two speakers (i.e. the native speaker recognition accuracy was 85% while the interlanguage speaker accuracy only 65 %, up from 49%).

This in turn provided a potential answer to considerations of comparative accuracy of interlanguage and native speakers: The accuracy rate was a great deal less than that for the native speaker (about 35% less after the first dictation task (Dictation task 2a), reduced to around 20% less at the end of the second task (Dictation task 2b)). A major result is that the adaptation for the interlanguage speaker was definitely slower (after four months) than the one for the native speaker and the accuracy of recognition seemed to particularly affect uncommon words. The improved recognition of the interlanguage speaker was interpreted as a positive sign of the phonological interlanguage system developing to incorporate more target language features, although apparently fossilized forms were found to co-exist with non-fossilized forms. Finally, the recognition percentage of the native speaker›s dictation was considered to be high enough to justify the claim that the system adapts better, or perhaps faster, to the native speaker than to the interlanguage speaker, whose pronunciation is more unstable and requires more training.

We also wanted to know if the use of this new technology affects the development of interlanguage systems: does it improve or impede them? According to retrospective comments by the interlanguage speaker, it often appeared that words initially not recognized, were recognized the second time because the speaker often remembered the pronunciation that she used for the training. In light of this situation, it appears that speech recognition by computer forces the speaker to pronounce words in a consistent way and if the pronunciation is target-like then, at least in this domain of computer mediated interaction, thanks to this new technology, the interlanguage phonology could be improved. We could argue here that this is a type of ‹forced stabilisation›. In this domain of speech recognition by computer, the interlanguage speaker›s phonological system might become stable. Whether this phenomenon would extend to other domains of interlanguage is a question that can be pursued for possible future research together with the question of whether the interlanguage would change as a result of the use of speech recognition by computer. This question requires a study which takes into consideration other domains of interlanguage (see e.g. Selinker & Douglas, 1989).

This research also provided we think some insights into the area of cognition in human-computer interaction. It appears that the interlanguage speaker treats the machine as an expert native speaker: if it does not recognise her, she thinks her pronunciation is wrong and she varies it. This phenomenon is deeply cognitive. Although at some level, the interlanguage speaker knows that the machine is ready to accept any articulation she gives it and it is ready to be trained to recognise that, she actually sits in front of the screen expecting the machine to respond best to RP English or standard American English. This causes her to doubt her own pronunciation because she is aware it is not RP or standard American English and that leaves her to having to ‹guess› the target pronunciation often relying on the L1 phonological system for filling in that gap.

Another aspect of this particular type of technology is the visual influence of the program which activates a different type of cognition. The interlanguage speaker reported in her retrospective comments that sometimes the visualisation of a certain word during the training would trigger certain pronunciations clearly influenced by transfer of phonological features from the L1 and she seemed to alternate between production of some target-like and non-target-like phonological forms.

Fossilization plays an important part as well since it becomes an instrument for achieving successful interaction by the interlanguage user with the machine, thus the new concept of ‹positive fossilization›. At the same time we can see that certain apparently already stabilised features of the interlanguage speaker (e.g. the lack of aspiration of word with [h] in initial position) will be difficult to eradicate. Yet there was evidence that in certain conditions fossilized forms were being destabilized (for instance the [r] at the end of words was progressively being substituted by a [□]] although the two forms both appeared in the system, showing a linguistic variability). However, given the essence of fossilization, the real test can only come from longitudinal studies on interlanguage SRC.

Finally, in terms of second language acquisition research, one of the results of the study, we should not forget is that the interlanguage speaker gained a better awareness of her phonological interlanguage system, as well as the gaps with the target language system, as a result of the use of the software and in some cases she was able to improve her pronunciation making it more target-like. The transfer effect of the user›s native language on the interlanguage, which often seemed to result in misrecognition by the computer, and inadequacy of the interlanguage communication strategies, especially where treating the machine as a human created problems, where communication strategies that worked with humans like repeated attempts at target pronunciation that worked with humans but not with computers. Given these factors, in virtue of the Multiple Effects Principle described above, it appeared that those words misrecognized more often as a result of transfer effect were the most likely candidates for fossilization. Thus, if the fossilization proved to be positive, as we think it did in some cases, though longitudinal studies would have to be carried out to be sure, the interlanguage speaker achieved a certain degree of stability in her interlanguage for reasons, perhaps, of efficiency with the computational machine.

Finally, we believe that it is incumbent upon applied linguists to become, where it is reasonable, part of the larger social and economic fabric, looking for ways to make applied linguistics a main stream discipline. This is not seen by us as an entirely altruistic activity since we feel that we should be consistently seeking ways to increase the job space for applied linguistics graduates. In pursuing the work of researching interlanguage speech recognition by computer, we have spoken to many software and hardware colleagues struggling to be the first to perfect SRC; many of these are indeed linguistically sophisticated and were easily able to integrate the interlanguage notion into their perspective. The topic of greatest interest was whether with more and more continuous recognition systems, to accommodate the sorts of interlanguage recognition problems we discovered here, would only new software solutions be adequate or would very expensive new sorts of hardware have to be developed. Not one of our computer informants was totally willing to bet on the only software option totally. Most of them could see a place, if they weren›t so busy surviving and creating product, for joint research ventures between interlanguage applied linguists and computer programmers and engineers. As was anticipated in the introduction, the task faced by computers in understanding human speech is extremely complex. A computer can recognize human speech by using model matching but it needs to overcome the problem of variability of different speakers, and that is the reason why programs like DragonDictate are speaker dependent. It is our conclusion that:

The speech recognition by computer solution of model matching works well for native speakers but less well for non-native speakers where interlanguage is often changing and where interlanguage speakers are often unsure of what the target should be.

It is an accepted fact by now that interlanguage speakers achieve variable success in second language acquisition and it is our conclusion that this results in speech models whose characteristics are not as fixed as native speakers› speech models. This has implications for speech recognition devices that applied linguists might wish to pay serious attention to for the reason listed above. Applied linguistics deserves to become a main stream discipline: after all, it is the only discipline that has the solution of practical language problems as one of its main foci. This is of concern also to other colleagues in applied linguistics who wish to work on language problems related to computer development, in general.

As we have seen above [ebov], the interlanguage speaker›s phonological variation seems to be one of the causes for the slower process of the software adaptation. An important factor for successful use of the software by non-native speakers is the relationship between the cognition of the interlanguage speaker and the social environment in which they interact. Note that in this case, the «normal» human social environment has been replaced by an artificial or virtual social environment, the electronic medium. In the speech recognition by computer systems we have seen, and of course one can never be totally up-to-date in these matters – the speaker only receives tacit feedback while using the system and the only explicit feedback she receives is negative in essence, because it appears only when there is word mis-recognition. This is opposed to «natural» human interlanguage communication, where human interlocutors are unlikely to interrupt a non-native speaker to correct their pronunciation (unless successful communication is at stake) and the native speaker›s body language or linguistic behaviour may well function as an indirect form of feedback to the interlanguage speaker. Interlanguage speakers seem to rely on very sophisticated pragmatic systems to meet their communicative needs. It is our view that such natural systems may not be very effective in the area of virtual life where the virtual medium uses brute language engineering whilst providing not always useful feedback to the user, which means to us that new sorts of communication strategies may have to be evolved by interlanguage speakers and by designers of speech recognition systems. If applied linguists work hard trying to make applied linguistics a main stream discipline in this way and begin to work with computer colleagues on these sorts of problems, we believe that there is a good chance that the job space for applied linguistics graduates may begin to approach the unfillable job space that now exists in Silicon Valley for computer people who may well need our skills, if we are inventive enough.

REFERENCES

1. Andersen, R.W. 1983. Transfer to somewhere. In S. Gass & L. Selinker (Eds.) Language Transfer in Language Learning. Rowley, MA: Newbury House.
2. Bamberg, & Mandel, M. 1991. Adaptable phoneme-based models for large-vocabulary speech recognition. Speech Communication, 10, 437–452.
3. Birdsong, D. 1992. Ultimate attainment in second language acquisition. Language, 68, 706–755.
4. Briere, E. 1968. A psycholinguistic study of phonological interference. The Hague: Mouton. Coppieters, R. 1987. Competence differences between native and near-native speakers.
5. Language, 63, 544–573.
6. Corder, S. 1983. A role for the mother tongue. In S. Gass & L. Selinker (Eds.), Language Transfer in Language Learning. Rowley, MA: Newbury House.
7. De Angelis, G. & Selinker, L. 2000. Interlanguage transfer and competing linguistic systems in the multilingual mind. In Jessner, U., Hufeisen, B. & Cenoz, J. (Eds.),
8. Cross-linguistic aspects of L3 acquisition. Clevedon: Multilingual Matters.
9. Eskinazi, M. 1999. Using automatic speech processing for foreign language pronunciation tutoring: some issues and a prototype. Language Learning and Technology, 2(2), 62–76.
10. Faerch, C. & Kasper, G. (Eds.) 1983a. Strategies in interlanguage communication. London: Longman
11. Faerch, C. & Kasper, G. 1983b. Plans & strategies in foreign language communication. In C. Faerch & G. Kasper (Eds.), Strategies in interlanguage communication (p20–60). London: Longman.
12. Gass, S. & Selinker, L. 1994. Second language acquisition: an introductory course. Hillsdale, NJ: Erlbaum.
13. Harris, Z. 1954. Transfer grammar. IJAL, 20, 259–70.

14. Kaplan, T. 1997. General learning strategies and the process of L2 acquisition: a critical overview. IRAL, 36(3), 233 – 246.
15. Kasper, G. & Kellerman, E. (Eds.) 1997. Communication Strategies: Psycholinguistic and Sociolinguistic Perspectives. Harlow, Essex: Longman.
16. Kellerman, E. 1995. Crosslinguistic Influence: Transfer to nowhere? Annual Review of Applied Linguistics, 15, 125–150.
17. Kellerman, E. 1977. Toward a characterization of the strategy of transfer in second language learning. Interlanguage Studies Bulletin 2, 58– 145.
18. Kinahan, C. 1999. Communication Strategies: How they may help the learner notice the gaps in their interlanguage. Paper presented at the 1999 Summer Institute Symposium, Manoa, Hawai'i.
19. Kinahan, C. & Selinker, L. 1997. Learning/Teaching Strategies pilot database. Webbed paper. http://alt.venus.co.uk/VL/AppLingBBK/VLDB.html
20. Lado, R. 1957. Linguistics across cultures. Ann Arbor: University of Michigan Press. Larsen-Freeman, D. & Long, M. 1991. An introduction to second language acquisition research. London: Longman.
21. Mandel, M. 1992. A commercial large-vocabulary discrete speech recognition system: DragonDictate. Language and Speech, 35, 237–246.
22. Mascia, R. & Selinker, L. in preparation. Speech recognition of interlanguage: is new hardware necessary?
23. Murray, D.E. 1995. Knowledge Machines: Language and information in a technological society. London: Longman.
24. Nemser, W. 1961. An experimental phonological study in the English of Hungarians. The Hague: Mouton.
25. Perkins, D.N. 1985. General cognitive skills: Why not? In S.F. Chipman, Segal & R. Glaser (Eds.), Thinking and Learning Skills, Vol. 2. Hillsdale, NJ: Erlbaum.
26. Preston, D. 1989. Sociolinguistics and Second Language Acquisition. Oxford: Basil Blackwell.
27. Radaravanija, 1966. An analysis of the elements in Thai that correspond to the basic intonation patterns of English. Unpublished Ph.D. dissertation. Columbia University.
28. Rutherford, W. 1984. Description and explanation in interlanguage syntax: state of the art. Language Learning 34, 127–55.

29. Rutherford, W. 1987. Second language grammar: learning and teaching. London: Longman. Selinker, L. 1972. Interlanguage. IRAL 10(3), 209–31.
30. Selinker, L. 1992. Rediscovering interlanguage. London: Longman.
31. Selinker, L. & Douglas, D. 1989. Research methodology in contextually-based second language research. Second language research, 5, 93–126.
32. Selinker, L. & Han, Z. in press. Fossilization: moving the concept into empirical longitudinal study.
33. Selinker, L. & Lakshmanan, U. 1992. Language Transfer and fossilization: The multiple effects principle. In S. Gass & L. Selinker (Eds.), Language Transfer in Language Learning. Rowley, MA: Newbury.
34. Tarone, E. 1983. Some thoughts on the notion of 'communication strategy'. In C. Faerch & G. Kasper (Eds.), Strategies in interlanguage communication (p61–74). London: Longman.
35. Tarone, E. 1993. On the variability of interlanguage systems. Applied Linguistics, 4, 143–63.
36. Trask, R.L. 1996. Historical Linguistics. London: Edward Arnold.
37. Weinreich, U. 1953. Linguistics across cultures. Linguistic Circle of NY (reprinted in paper by Mouton).
38. White, L. & Genesee, F. 1996. How native is near-native? The issue of ultimate attainment in second language acquisition. Second Language Research, 12, .
39. Whitney, W. D. 1881. On mixing in language. Transactions of the American Philological Association, 121, 1–26.
40. Wode, H. 1977. On the systematicity of L1 transfer in L2 acquisition. In C. Henning (Ed.), Proceedings of the Los Angeles Second Language Research Forum. Los Angeles: University of California.

CITATION

CHAPTER 1
Soliman, N. (2014) Using E-Learning to Develop EFL Students' Language Skills and Activate Their Independent Learning. Creative Education, 5, 752-757. doi: 10.4236/ce.2014.510088.

CHAPTER 2
Serge Gabarre, CécileGabarre, RosseniDin, ParilahShah, Aidah Abdul Karim, (2016) Addressing Foreign Language Learning Anxiety with Facebook. Creative Education, 07,93-104. doi:10.4236/ce.2016.71010

CHAPTER 3
Liu, S. & Liu, H. (2014). A Review of Models in Experimental Studies of Implicit Language Learning. Open Journal of Modern Linguistics, 4, 54-64. doi: 10.4236/ojml.2014.41006.

CHAPTER 4
Brooke, M. (2012). Why Asynchronous Computer-Mediated Communication (ACMC) Is a Powerful Tool for Language Learning. Open Journal of Modern Linguistics, 2, 125-129. doi: 10.4236/ojml.2012.23016.

CHAPTER 5
Kousuke Mouri and Hiroaki Ogata, Ubiquitous learning analytics in the real-world language learning, DOI 10.1186/s40561-015-0023-x.9

CHAPTER 6

Ilya V. Osipov, Alex A. Volinsky, Evgeny Nikulchev and Anna Y. Prasikova, Online elearning application for practicing foreign language skills with native speakers, DOI 10.1186/s40660-016-0009-1.

CHAPTER 7

Fu-Yun Yu, Yu-Ling Chang and Hui-Ling Wu, The effects of an online student question-generation strategy on elementary school student English learning, DOI 10.1186/s41039-015-0023-z.

CHAPTER 8

Veronica Popovici and Ramona Nicoleta Bunda (2010). Learning 2.0: Collaborative Technologies Reshaping Learning Pathways, Management and Services, Mamun Habib (Ed.), ISBN: 978-953-307-118-3, InTech, DOI: 10.5772/9951.

CHAPTER 9

Ana Cristina. Collaborative Language Learning in Teletandem: A Resource for Pre-Service Teacher Education. PROFILE Issues in Teachers' Professional Development, [S.l.], v. 13, n. 1, p. 139-156, jan. 2011. ISSN 2256-5760.

CHAPTER 11

Françoise Blin and Juha Jalkanen, Designing for Language Learning: Agency and languaging in hybrid environments, ISSN: 1457-9863

CHAPTER 12

Paola Leone, Content Domain and Language Competence in Computer-mediated Conversation for Learning, ISSN: 1457-9863

CHAPTER 13

Larry Selinker and Rita Mascia, Interlanguage speech recognition by computer: implications for SLA and computational machines, ISSN: 1457-9863

INDEX

A

artificial grammar learning (AGL) 31, 33

B

Body movements 227

C

Carry out 203, 209, 212
collaboration technologies 125
Common European Framework of Reference for Languages (CEFR) 100
Communication strategies (CS) 258
communicative language teaching 102, 119
Communicative Language Teaching' 48
Computer Supported Ubiquitous Learning (CSUL) 61, 62
Cultural historical activity theory (CHAT) 197, 199, 207

D

Design-based research (DBR) 202, 205

E

E-Learning 1, 2, 3, 5, 6, 7, 8, 9, 285
English as a second language (ESL) 170
English Foreign language\" (EFL) 1
English language learners (ELLs) 169
English language learning progressions (ELLP) 169
European Commission Directorate Education and Culture (DG EAC) 124

F

foreign language 11, 12, 13, 15, 17, 18, 22, 23, 24
frequently asked questions (FAQ) 130

G

geographic information system (GIS) 64
Goup dynamics 171
Grammatical usage 173

I

Intensive English programs (IEPs) 176
Internet 145

L

Language transfer 253, 255, 256, 257, 258, 271, 274, 276
Linguistic terms 200

M

methodologies 30
mobile assisted language learning (MALL) 22
Motivated Strategies for Learning Questionnaire (MSLQ) 112

O

online e-learning 89, 98
online learning system 99, 105, 122
Open university of the netherlands (OUNL) 202

P

Personal Digital Assistants (PDAs) 62
Primary motive 202
Psychological power 229

R

Repetitive strain disorder (RSD) 253

S

Second language acquisition (SLA) 170
Second Language Acquisition (SLA) 48
sequence learning (SL) 31, 33
social networking sites (SNS) 12
Speakers communicate 225
Speech recognition by computer (SRC) 253

T

Target language (TL) 255

U

Ubiquitous Learning Analytics (ULA) 61, 62
Ubiquitous Learning Graph (ULG) 61, 73
Ubiquitous Learning Log (ULL) 61, 65

V

Verbal communication 89
Virtual Learning Environment (VLE) 129

W

World Wide Web technology 123

Z

zone of proximal development (ZPD) 18